ADAMS

V.

TEXAS

ADAMS

V.

TEXAS

RANDALL DALE ADAMS

WILLIAM HOFFER

MARILYN MONA HOFFER

St. Martin's Press
New York

Design by Genet Abrahams

Library of Congress Cataloging-in-Publication Data

Adams, Randall.
    Adams v. Texas / Randall Adams, William Hoffer, and Marilyn Mona Hoffer.
        p.   cm.
    "A Thomas Dunne book."
    ISBN 0-312-05811-X
    1. Adams, Randall—Trials, litigation, etc.   2. Trials (Murder)—Texas—Dallas.   I. Hoffer, William.   II. Hoffer, Marilyn Mona.
III. title.   IV. Title: Adams v. Texas.
KF224.A36A36   1991
345.73'02523'097642812—dc20
[347.3052523097642812]
                                                                                90-27107
                                                                                CIP

FIRST EDITION JUNE 1991
10 9 8 7 6 5 4 3 2 1

This is a true story. The characters are authentic, the events real. Quotations have been recreated either from documented material or as accurately as long-term memory allows.

The names of a few characters have been changed for their protection, and for legal considerations. The pseudonums used for these characters are:

Charlie Washington
Roland King
Buster Watkins
Billy Fletcher
Jimmy Joe Smith
Happy Eddie Thompson
Skinny Gates
George Black
Mike Berry

In addition, the identity of the cellblock designated as "D-Line" has been altered.

This book is dedicated to
my mother Mildred and
the rest of my family for
their love, support, and
faith.

ACKNOWLEDGMENTS

Thanks to former Dallas attorney Dennis White, who believed in me from the start. I respect him for his honesty and good will. He paid a far higher price than necessary.

Thanks to former Dallas County assistant district attorneys Leslie McFarlane and John Cruezot, who could have gone along with others in their office, but were strong enough to stand up and say, "Hey, something's wrong here." Without their support, I might still be in prison.

Enormous thanks to Randy Schaffer, the best attorney in Texas.

Thanks to David Pasztor of the *Dallas Times-Herald* for approaching the story of my case from an unbiased viewpoint, and for being a friend as well as a reporter.

Thanks to Errol Morris, who brought national attention to my story via the film *The Thin Blue Line*. He was the Easter bunny who gathered the eggs of evidence into one basket so that we could present them to the court.

Thanks to Paul Mowry and Joey Silverman for their tireless work to organize and manage the "Free Randall Adams Campaign," a grass-roots effort that burgeoned beyond anyone's predictions. Thanks to the thousands of people who wrote to me and the millions who signed petitions in my behalf. They came from all across the country, but I must single out the people of Columbus, Ohio; my hometown of Grove City, Ohio; and the good and honorable citizens of Dallas, Texas, for demanding ultimate justice.

Thanks to Judge Larry Baraka of Dallas Criminal Court Number Two. It was refreshing to finally have an honest day in court.

Thanks to Michael Rosenthal of "PM Magazine," who hid me under an assumed name at Houston's Hyatt Regency Hotel the night following my release from prison. He was an enormous source of strength to my mother and the other members of my family.

Thanks to John Speight, a schoolteacher from West Nyack, New York, who took it upon himself to help my mother over some particularly difficult times, and who organized a fund-raiser for my benefit.

I thank the members of the jury who condemned me to death in 1977. Recently, several of them have commented to the press that, if they had been allowed to hear all of the pertinent evidence, they would have found me not guilty. I hold no malice in my heart for them; they were victims, too.

Officer Teresa Turko, likewise, was a victim of this entire episode. I trust that she can now put it behind her and continue her service. Indeed, I commend in general the officers of the Dallas police department for the honorable, decent, and difficult job that they perform. Every day they place their lives on "the thin blue line" and they are to be honored for their courage.

Thanks to Corrections Officer George Black and his wife Janet, for regarding me as a human being in an inhuman environment, and for risking their livelihood in the interests of justice.

Special thanks to George Waldron, warden of the Eastham unit of the Texas Department of Corrections. He listened to me when no one else would, and he was man enough to allow me to speak out when, very easily, he could have quieted me.

Thanks again to attorneys Randy Schaffer and Leslie McFarlane for their comments, corrections, additions, and insights regarding the manuscript, and for their overall encouragement.

Thanks to Tony Zanelotte of Fox Television, who encouraged me to tell my story and showed me how to do it.

Thanks to our agents, Henry Reisch, Michael Carlisle, and Mel Berger of the William Morris Agency, and to our editor, Thomas Dunne, for their professional advice and encouragement.

Thanks to Houston attorney Murray Fogler, who, without fee, helped me secure the rights to my own life story.

Finally, I wish to express my sympathy to the family of Officer Robert Wood. They were deprived of him in 1976, and then they were done further harm through systematic injustice over the years. I hope that now Officer Wood can be truly laid to rest. He is the one whom this story is really about.

PROLOGUE

Imagine you are dreaming:

You have been accused of murder. You have never seen or heard of the victim. You have no knowledge of where or when it occurred. All that you know is that the punishment is death in the electric chair.

Fingers point in your direction and the courtroom is filled with eyes that bore into you with hatred. State-appointed psychiatrists declare to the court that you are a vicious sociopath, beyond hope of redemption. You want to scream out, but your lawyer advises silence. You are tempted to lash out in righteous frustration, but handcuffs pin you. You think of running away, but shackles bind your ankles.

In your dream, you toss and turn but you do not awaken.

The words of the prosecutors echo in your mind as they describe what will happen to you: "they strap you down . . . your eyeballs explode . . . your fingernails and toenails pop off . . . you bleed from every orifice of your body."

The jury files into the room and twenty-four eyes stare through you. The bailiff reads the verdict:

Guilty!

Finally you awaken. You are drenched in perspiration, but you are filled with relief to realize that it was just a dream.

But for me, it was a real-life nightmare.

ADAMS V. TEXAS

PART ONE

1976 - 1980

HOUSE OF SORROW

1

THE CROSSROAD

AMID A CIRCULAR labyrinth of interchanges in Nashville, Tennessee, Interstate 65 crosses Interstates 40 and 24. As we approached this point on a Thursday in November 1976, two weeks before Thanksgiving, my brother Ray and I had to make a decision.

When we left home in Columbus, Ohio, our original plan was to drive due south to Nashville, and then turn southeast, through Chattanooga, Atlanta, Macon, and Savannah, and on to Florida. Taking turns at the wheel of Ray's seven-year-old blue Ford Galaxie, we had made good time to Louisville and beyond. Now, as we approached Nashville, Ray suggested a change in plans.

He spoke fondly of the time he had spent in southern California's semitropical climate, and suggested that I might find it more to my liking than Florida. The job market was good too, he said.

It sounded great, and so, in Nashville, I made a split-second decision. As we reached the crossroad Ray looked at me, and said, "Dale?" He used my middle name, for I had adopted its use during my time with the 82nd Airborne Division, when there were three other Randys in my unit.

I shrugged and replied, "Oh, okay."

We headed in the direction of Memphis, Little Rock, Dallas, and points west.

Hours later, somewhere between Little Rock and Texarkana, we stopped at a McDonald's. We ate in the car and, after we finished, I was plucking a few errant french fries from the front floorboard when I found a tape cassette under the seat, a Charlie Daniels Band album entitled *Fire on the Mountain*. Neither Ray nor I had bought it, so we figured that one of our friends must have left it behind.

With a shrug, I popped it into the tape deck and listened to words about a long-haired man enjoying a "toke." Ray glanced over and grinned, because the song sounded as if it had been written about me. My dark brown hair dangled down past my shoulders. And I did enjoy an occasional "toke" from the small supply of marijuana I had with me.

I was at that special stage of life when, I felt, I "almost" had things coming together. At the age of 27, I was beginning to think more seriously about the future. Maybe I would go back to school and begin to work toward a career in drafting.

The concept of stability was evermore appealing.

Life had not been easy for our family, ever since that day in July of 1960 when my Dad died suddenly. Technically, a heart attack killed him, but we all suspected that his death was a legacy from the coal mines of Welch, West Virginia, where he had labored for years before moving the family to Columbus. Whatever the cause, the effect was to leave my mother, Mildred Adams, with five children to raise. At eleven and a half, I was the youngest. Mom continued to work at her job as a cashier at Alber's grocery store, but she enrolled in evening courses and eventually earned a degree in practical nursing.

Serious readjustments were necessary and only now was I old enough to realize that their effects were lingering. As the eldest child, Ray knew that he had to, at the very least, begin to take care of himself. He joined the Army and became a Special Forces trooper. Something happened to Ray during his time in the service, but I did not know what. We talked easily on every subject but the army. One evening, a few years earlier, I had coaxed a story or two out of him. He broke down in tears that night, and I said to myself, If he needs to talk about it, I hope he'll come to me. But I'm never going to ask him about it again. Since his discharge Ray had been affected with a bit of wanderlust that was sometimes intriguing and sometimes disturbing. Still, he was a good man and, as the younger brother, I looked up to him.

Ron was the second oldest, and he too joined the service shortly after Dad's death. If anything, he came back even more restless than Ray. He was a carpet installer by trade, and had no difficulty finding employment. We heard from him every so often, whenever he called home to say that he had found work in some other city. Right then, he lived in Nashville and showed signs of establishing more-or-less permanent roots.

My sisters had reacted differently. Nancy married Jim Bapst, a trucker, and settled close to Mom. Mary and her husband Ken Burgess, a computer specialist, lived in Galion, Ohio, only a few hours' drive from Columbus. If Dad's death had spun Ray and Ron off into orbit, it also seemed to produce a gravitational pull that kept Nancy and Mary close, to one another, and to Mom.

I was tugged in both directions. After high school graduation in 1967, I studied mechanical drafting at Grove City Technical School. Then I spent the next two years working for a vending machine company. I had an honorable discharge from the U.S. Army, after serving three years active duty. Following that I had landed a job with the U.S. Postal Service and had every intention of establishing my life in Columbus.

My knees changed my mind. I was diagnosed with rheumatoid arthritis and, during my first winter back home, I missed more than a month of work. A doctor warned me that the condition would never improve and suggested that I try a warmer climate, at least for the winters.

And so I had found steady work in Jacksonville, Florida, and a steady friend in Kathy. We did not know whether we would remain in Jacksonville, but we were beginning to believe we would stay together. The normal family relationships that had eluded me in my teens now beckoned to me.

I returned to Ohio during the summer of 1976 to visit Mom and my sisters, and I picked up a good temporary job restoring wooden shipping pallets. It was honest labor and I liked the work, but as winter approached, my knees told me that it was time to move on. Ray, who was home for a visit, agreed to come with me to Florida.

Kathy waited in Jacksonville, tying up loose ends, before we moved farther south, probably somewhere along the Gulf Coast. I knew that she would squeal with delight when I called to tell her we were going to live in California instead.

It was dark by the time Ray and I reached Dallas. We were exhausted by now so we stopped for the night, booking a room in an inexpensive inn on Harry Hines Boulevard. Early Friday morning, we ate breakfast in a nearby diner. As Ray perused the front page of a local paper, I skimmed through the classifieds.

To my surprise, I immediately spotted an ad from an employer looking for someone who knew how to repair wooden shipping pallets. I showed it to Ray and he said, "Maybe you should check it out."

That very morning I drove to the Forest Hills Pallet Company located on the former site of Greater Southwest Airport, between Dallas and Forth Worth. I told the employer that I had been doing this kind of work in Columbus, and he hired me on the spot. I would start the next week. My pay would be enough to cover basic living expenses for both Ray and myself, if we watched our pennies. We rented a room at the Comfort Courts on Fort Worth Avenue, because it offered low weekly rates. Our room had a kitchenette, so we could cook our own food, subsisting on soup and sandwiches. Meanwhile, Ray would hunt for an ironworking job.

Once Ray was pulling in a paycheck, we could settle into an apartment and Kathy could join me. Our grand plan called for her to be there by Christmas, only six weeks away.

Dallas seemed to have welcomed us with open arms. Whether by happenstance or destiny, we had found our new home.

2

THE MURDER

Twenty-seven-year-old Robert Wood was a full-blooded Choctaw Indian, a compact 5'7", 132-pound, decorated war veteran who had served two hitches in Vietnam. In 1974, after he returned home, he joined the Dallas police department. He was a spit-and-polish devotee, described by George H. Reed, deputy chief at the Northwest substation where Wood was assigned, as "quiet, reserved," "dependable," and "very stable." He was a Sunday school teacher at a local Baptist church.

On November 13, 1976, Wood's buddy, Police Officer Alvin Moore, was shot to death while answering a domestic violence call in the housing projects of West Dallas. Moore and Wood had driven to work together that morning; now Moore was dead.

Following this tragedy, Wood's wife Toni bought him a bullet-proof vest, which she planned to surprise him with at Christmas.

But Christmas never arrived.

Shortly after midnight on Sunday, November 28, three days after Thanksgiving, Wood pulled his patrol car up to the drive-thru window of a Burger King at the intersection of North Hampton Road and Vicker Street in West Dallas, only eight blocks away from where Moore was slain fifteen days earlier. At his side was the partner he had worked with since the previous January, twenty-four-year-old Police Officer Teresa Turko. They were less than an hour into their eight-hour shift. Wood asked for a cup of coffee, but, despite the uncharacteristically chilly twenty-nine degree temperature, Turko ordered a milkshake.

Before their order was ready, the two officers noticed a car pass by at an excessive rate of speed. Wood pulled the cruiser into the eastbound lane of Vicker Street and pursued for several blocks. After he halted the car, Turko approached the driver and wrote a speeding ticket. As she did so, Wood took his assigned post at the right rear fender of the speeder's car, the point from which he could offer optimum assistance, in the unlikely event it became necessary. This was proper police procedure.

The officers returned to the Burger King and found their order waiting. After picking it up, they spotted another car, traveling southbound on North Hampton, with only its parking lights on. Wood handed his coffee cup to Turko, pulled in behind the car and activated his bubble-top light.

Neither Wood nor Turko bothered with the prescribed procedure of calling in the car's license plate number for a routine check. Wood grabbed his flashlight, but he left his ticket book in the squad car, for he simply planned to caution the driver to turn on his headlights and pay more attention to what he was doing. A .357 Magnum revolver remained buttoned into the holster at his side.

As Officer Wood emerged into the night air and approached the car in front of him, the driver rolled down his window, pointed a .22 caliber High Standard revolver and squeezed the trigger.

One hollow-point bullet passed completely through the middle joint of Wood's left pinkie and shattered the flashlight he was holding. A second bullet found the right chest, just above the nipple, pierced the right lung, and lodged in the soft tissue in his back. Wood staggered, turning instinctively away from the source of the pain, twisting from left to right. As he began to fall, a third bullet crashed into him from the back, on the right side, just below the shoulder, passed through the upper lobe of the right lung, stopping near the fifth rib. A fourth bullet entered lower through the back, penetrated the right lung, grazed the liver, and came to rest in the sternum. A fifth bullet caught Wood in the back of the head, on the right side, slightly above the ears; it split into two fragments, one portion remaining in the brain and the other exiting through the scalp. A sixth bullet entered his right coat sleeve near the shoulder seam of his jacket and exited out the back without striking him. Wood's body landed face down on the pavement as his attacker sped off, spinning the wheels of his car in the gravel of the shoulder.

It happened so quickly that the car was pulling away before Turko could react. Instinctively, she threw her milkshake container off into the grass and grabbed for her gun. She fired several shots, and then ran to the police radio. At 12:39 A.M. she called in an emergency message: "Five-fourteen. My partner's just been shot. Suspect's going westbound, uh . . . southbound on Hampton."

In the confusion of the moment, Turko was unable to give the police dispatcher her exact location. The dispatcher told responding officers to drive down North Hampton Avenue until they found the scene of the shooting.

Turko ran to her partner. She turned him over and saw blood covering his face, emanating from his mouth and nose. A motorist stopped to help and together they managed to roll the stricken officer onto his back, dragging him about six feet away from where he fell.

Three police cruisers arrived at the scene almost simultaneously. The first backup team, consisting of Officers Fred Hall and A.D. White, arrived two minutes and seven seconds after Turko reported the shooting. Three seconds later, Officers R.W. Benson and D.J. Bonicard arrived and were immediately joined by Officers D.W. Chapman and J.E. Little. Turko told them that she thought the shooter's vehicle was a blue Vega with only one person in it.

Seeing the amount of blood present at the scene, the backup teams decided not to wait for an ambulance. Fifty-nine seconds after their arrival, they placed Officer Wood in the rear seat of a cruiser. Little drove and Chapman rode in the back with Wood as they sped toward Parkland Memorial Hospital. The victim moved his lips as if to speak, but no sound came out.

Within minutes, Wood was rushed into the same emergency room where President John F. Kennedy had died thirteen years earlier. Doctors Ed Schwartz and Charles Howard began emergency treatment.

Meanwhile, Benson began to question Turko and was soon joined by Officer Paul Hammond. They broadcast a description of the suspect's vehicle and added, "The one occupant, don't know whether he's black or white."

Detectives from the Dallas police department's Crimes Against Persons Bureau arrived at the scene of the shooting and took charge. They attempted to elicit additional information from Turko to aid in a search for the shooter. About all she could tell them was that he was wearing a coat with a furry upturned collar. She did not know the license plate number of the assailant's car, but she believed that it was a blue Chevrolet Vega with Texas plates, and she thought that the first two letters of the plates were "HC," which would indicate a Dallas County registration.

Physical Evidence Section investigators began a crime scene search. They collected Officer Wood's flashlight with the bullet hole in it and blood samples from the pavement in front of the parked police vehicle. They snapped photos of the scene, took measurements—the length of the tire tracks left on the pavement from the accelerating car, the distance of the bloodstains from the shoulder of the road, the location of the milkshake container that Turko had thrown (it was more than ten feet away from the police cruiser, on a direct line from the passenger side door)—and searched for spent shells, slugs, and broken glass.

At Parkland Memorial Hospital, forty minutes after the shooting, at 1:10 A.M., Dr. Ed Schwartz pronounced Officer Robert Wood dead. Officers were immediately sent to Wood's home and his wife,

11

Toni, was escorted to the hospital where a chaplain informed her of her husband's death.

Turko was given a light sedative to help her get through the night.

The following day investigators photographed aerial views of the crime scene from a helicopter. Others removed a slab of concrete from the roadway containing tire traces from the suspect's car.

Following standard procedure, Turko dictated a letter to Police Chief D.A. Byrd. In that letter she reported that the windows of the suspect's vehicle were "very dirty." She heard Wood say something, and then heard three shots. She responded by firing five shots at the car as it sped away.

Searching for a killer of unknown race, age, height, and weight, police followed up on a barrage of tips. The Department of Public Safety in Austin provided a list of nearly three hundred Vegas in the Dallas area, and fifty investigators hit the streets Monday morning to track the leads. Schepps Dairy, Inc., and the Dallas Police Association (DPA) each posted a $5,000 reward for information leading to the arrest and indictment of the killer. In announcing his group's reward, Lieutenant Charles Burnley, president of the DPA, commented, "This is the first time that a police officer has been murdered and the suspect was not caught that same day, in my memory."

Records dating back to 1951 confirmed the comment. In the twelve police slayings since that time, every case was solved almost immediately; nine of the killers were arrested and three were themselves killed.

Wood's murder proved to be the exception. Investigators, many of them working double shifts, paid particular attention to a report concerning a man who was said to have driven his blue Vega into a garage on Singleton Boulevard, where he sought to have it cut up and destroyed because it had bullet holes in it.

At noon on the day of Officer Wood's funeral, police arrested this individual on suspicion of murder. He was a rather light-skinned black man with a large Afro haircut. Even as he was being interrogated, Police Chief Byrd, presenting a funeral oration in front of eight hundred mourners at Cooper-Sorrells Funeral Home in Bonham, Texas, announced that Wood's killer was under arrest and, he said, "everything pointed to this individual."

However, when Detective Tom Sewell examined the man's car, he found it to be in immaculate condition; there were no bullet holes. Sewell checked with the garage owner, who denied the report that the man had sought to have his car destroyed. The suspect's alibi checked out, and he passed a polygraph test. He was released, and the investigation continued.

For a time, anyone driving a blue Vega in Dallas was subject to being stopped on the spot and questioned about his or her whereabouts on the night of the murder. An anonymous donor doubled the reward fund to $20,000.

The investigation was hampered by discrepancies that arose in the reports of eyewitnesses. The closest known witness was Turko, but the information she provided in her initial written statement of November 28 seemed scant. She was the first woman police officer in Dallas to be on the scene when another officer was murdered, and this fact elicited some chauvinistic grumbling about the abilities of a woman officer. There was some question as to whether she had taken up her proper post. This was based in part upon the fact that her discarded milkshake was found adjacent to the police cruiser, rather than farther forward, although she could well have thrown it behind her.

For ten days after the murder, Turko was held out of her normal duty rotation. She was subjected to an investigation, concerning her position at the moment of the shooting, conducted by Officer Dale Holt of the Internal Affairs Division; and Captain Milligan, Lieutenant Southall, and Sergeant Gus Rose of the Crimes Against Persons Bureau. Rose, the bureau's chief detective, was a legendary figure. He was one of the last detectives to interview Lee Harvey Oswald after the Kennedy assassination. In the intervening years he had developed a statewide reputation as an expert and merciless interrogator.

Deputy Chief George H. Reed supervised this probe and Police Chief Byrd himself attended at least one of Turko's interrogation sessions.

On December 4, Dallas newspapers reported that a new witness had come forward, someone who had been riding past the scene at

13

the time of the murder. This new unnamed witness described the suspect as a young adult male with a medium-length Afro haircut; he was either of Latin American descent or was a light-skinned black. One investigator declared to the press, "I told you Monday that we would get him, that we've never failed to get our man in a cop killing. I was beginning to have my doubts yesterday, but now I know we'll get him."

This same day, Turko submitted voluntarily to a polygraph test to convince her colleagues that she was telling the truth, as best as she could remember it. A local newspaper disclosed that she had failed. Charmayne Marsh of the *Dallas Morning News* reported Turko's explanation. The police officer noted that she had been interrogated for three hours prior to the test and had eaten nothing since the previous day. Turko said she had been going through "hell."

On December 5, Marsh reported: "Miss Turko underwent hypnosis in an effort to recall more details of the shooting but police said the session failed to turn up any more facts of value." Under hypnosis, Turko was able to recall a license plate number, but when police checked it out, they found that the car belonged to an elderly couple with no involvement in the crime. (Turko later stated that although she met with a hypnotist, she was never successfully hypnotized.)

Four days later Turko signed a second written statement, which supposedly clarified the first, but stressed that she could "barely see" inside the car.

On December 15, the *Dallas Times-Herald* reported that a second witness contradicted some of the details in Officer Turko's version of the murder, claiming that she had remained seated in the police cruiser and had not fired any shots at the fleeing vehicle.

Unnamed sources reported to the newspaper that the police now tended to believe Turko's account, since the unidentified witness was "a much greater distance" from the crime than they had originally believed. Furthermore, ballistics tests confirmed that five bullets had been fired from Turko's six-shot police revolver.

On December 13, Deputy Chief Reed informed Turko that she had been cleared to return to duty.

Nearly two more weeks passed—a month since the murder—and

the police seemed no closer to solving the crime. Wood's death was now the longest unsolved cop killing in Dallas County history. The press grumbled over the delay in tracking down the man who had slaughtered, for no apparent reason, an innocent policeman.

It was somewhat galling to the Dallas police department that the first real break in the case came from the tiny town of Vidor, in southeast Texas, eight miles east of Beaumont, and about three hundred miles away from where Officer Robert Wood was murdered.

3

THE ARREST

I GLANCED UP from my work to see a dark, solid-color, official-looking car approaching the trailer that served as the boss's office at the Forest Hills Pallet Company. The two men inside the car were dressed in dark business suits, both wore serious expressions under their gray Stetsons. Around me, I noticed several of my Hispanic coworkers melt quietly into the background. I wondered if these men were immigration officers.

It was midmorning on Tuesday, December 21, four days after my twenty-eighth birthday and four days before Christmas, 1976.

The two visitors, whoever they were, obviously had business with the boss. Just as obviously, it was of no concern to me, so I turned my attention back to my labor. This was piecework; the more pallets I repaired, the more money I earned.

I was bending to my task when the boss yelled over, "Hey, Adams, come here a minute." Looking up, I saw him beckoning to me.

I dropped my hammer and walked over, eyeing the two grim-faced men. I weighed 185 pounds and was in good physical shape, but both of these men looked powerful enough to be persuasive.

"This is Adams," my boss said.

The two men flipped open their wallets, revealing badges that identified them as Detective J.W. Johnson and Investigator Luther of the Dallas police department. Johnson did the talking, and as he spoke, he looked directly into my eyes with a wary expression, almost as if he were afraid of me. "Mr. Adams," he asked, "did you used to live in a motel down on Fort Worth Avenue?"

"Yes."

"May I ask how long it's been since you lived there?"

"We moved out a week or so ago."

The two officers shared a brief glance. Then one of them said, "We were wondering if you would mind coming downtown with us?"

"What for?"

"Well, we have a witness downtown who says you were involved in a breaking and entering in Houston."

I told them I'd never been to Houston, but they still wanted me to come with them. "When did this breaking and entering supposedly take place?" I asked.

"Well, if you'll come downtown we'll discuss all that."

I looked to my boss for assistance and said, "If you'll tell me what day this was supposed to have happened, this man right here can vouch for me. I work six days a week. Never missed a day. So, you know, unless this thing happened on a Sunday, this man is gonna tell you that I didn't do it."

My boss nodded his agreement.

Johnson pulled a photograph from his jacket pocket and, as I leaned forward to view it, Luther sidled out of my field of vision.

I recognized the face in the photo immediately. It was a picture of a kid who had helped me out weeks before when I had run out of gas. I tried to remember his name—Davis . . . McDavis . . . or something like that. "Yeah," I replied. "I met him about a month ago . . . Why?"

My words stopped when I felt the cold hard barrel of Luther's gun pressed against the back of my head. "Don't move!" Johnson commanded. Quickly he drew his own revolver and pointed it at my chest. "We're taking you downtown. Put your hands behind your back."

The handcuffs were in place before I could sort out what was happening. My arms pinned effectively, I was very suddenly off-balance and vulnerable.

Confusion registered on my boss's face also. "Hey, what is this?" he asked. "Have you got an arrest warrant for this man?"

Johnson kept his gun leveled at my chest, and he kept his eyes locked upon mine. I noticed that he did not appear to be afraid of me any longer. Out of the side of his mouth he offered my boss a piece of advice: "The best thing you can do is get your ass in your trailer and don't get involved in something you don't need to be involved in. Mr. Adams is coming with us." No one else showed any signs of helping me.

The detectives prodded me toward their car. I stumbled, worried that I might pitch facedown onto the ground with no way to break my fall. I muttered over my shoulder to my boss, "Hey, if I'm not back here in a couple of hours, tell Rick to tell my brother what happened." Rick Darty was my friend at work, now sharing an apartment with Ray and me.

The two officers pushed me into the backseat of their car, and hopped into the front. The hard metal of the cuffs bit into the skin of my wrists. Already my arms, held fast from the back, were beginning to cramp.

Within minutes the car was moving along a freeway at a very high rate of speed. I surveyed the interior; there were no handles to open the doors or roll down the windows.

In the front seat, the two officers busied themselves with radio communications. Their words filtered back to me: "We've got Adams. We're bringing him in." I sat in silence as visions of Dallas— the suburbs, the outlying commercial areas, shopping malls, and restaurants—flew past my eyes. Ahead lay the urban skyline. How long is it going to take me to straighten this out? I wondered. I told these men I had never been to Houston.

It took only twenty minutes to get to our destination, the Dallas

Government Center complex. This was "downtown." The car pulled into an underground parking lot and jerked to a halt. Johnson asked, "Do you want to cover your head? There's a lot of press around here."

"No," I said.

Johnson jumped out, opened the back door, and pulled me from the seat. Flanking me, the two officers marched me through an underground corridor. Flashbulbs popped from every direction as reporters jockeyed for position. The sound of my name echoed through the hallway, "Mr. Adams, Mr. Adams . . . is it true?" I could make no sense of their questions, and kept my eyes focused straight ahead.

My shoulder-length hair, disheveled and windblown, flew into my eyes, and I had no way to brush it free.

Once inside the building, the detectives released me from the handcuffs and allowed me a moment to massage my wrists. Then, at 12:15 P.M., still flanked by the two officers, I stood in a small room, in front of Justice of the Peace Robert R. Cole, who intoned, "State your name, please."

"Randall Dale Adams."

"Do you know what you're being brought before me for?"

"I've been told something about a breaking and entering in Houston."

As Cole read from a paper he held in front of him, only a few of the words crept through to my consciousness: "Randall Dale Adams . . . arraigned . . . killing of a police officer in the performance of his duty . . ."

I felt as though the wind had been knocked out of me. From somewhere off in the distance, it seemed, I heard the official voice declare that this was a capital offense.

Do something, I commanded myself. Say something.

"Do you have an attorney?" Cole asked.

"No."

"Have you been allowed a phone call?"

"No."

"Well, you'll be allowed to take care of that upstairs." Justice Cole set bond at $100,000, which was, of course, a joke.

We left the arraignment room and stepped outside to a hallway jammed with blue-jacketed officers and men in business suits. Around me, everyone was talking. I glanced about and saw eyes, filled with menace, boring through me. The oxygen seemed to have been drawn out of the air so that there was none left to inhale.

The officers took me "upstairs," to a rectangular room with dingy white walls. An aging metal table sat in the center, stretching nearly the full width of the room. Two folding chairs were on either side. Directly above, a single bare light bulb dangled from the ceiling. There was an ashtray on the table, but nothing else.

I sat on one side of the table and lit a Marlboro. Get your head together, I commanded myself. We, the Dallas police and I, have a problem here.

A couple of times during the past hour or so I had heard the mumbo-jumbo explanation of my rights. Had Johnson recited the litany while we were still at the job site? I couldn't quite remember. Magistrate Cole had certainly reminded me of my rights in the arraignment room. Beyond that, I had watched enough police shows on television to know that I had a right to a phone call and an attorney.

None of that seemed important at the moment. What mattered was that I finally had a chance to sit down and reason with these men.

The two detectives appeared to relax a bit. They asked me to tell them everything I knew about the boy in the photograph.

There wasn't much to tell, I said. This kid Davis, or whatever his name was, had helped me out when I ran out of gas about a month ago. His first name was Mack, or something like that. What, exactly did they want to know?

Everything, they replied. They wanted a blow-by-blow description of my activities on that day, Saturday, November 27, 1976, two days after Thanksgiving. Just start at the beginning, they said, and tell us everything.

"It was a month ago," I complained.

"Try," Johnson said.

"Okay." I explained that I had thought I was going to work that day. Apparently, my boss was unable to get enough workers on this holiday weekend and had decided to close the shop, but I was not notified. So I left my brother Ray asleep at the motel and drove his car to work, arriving before 8:00 A.M. To my surprise, no one else had shown up, not even the boss. I reasoned that everyone was starting slowly today.

To pass some time, I slipped over to a nearby 7-11, grabbed a cup of coffee, and spent about a half hour talking with the young woman cashier. Then I returned to the job site, saw that it was still deserted, and concluded that there must have been a change in plans. I headed back toward the motel.

Ray and I were running low on cash, so when I reached the motel I decided to pawn my portable eight-track stereo and three tapes. I changed out of my work shirt and into a T-shirt and a light jacket, grabbed the stereo equipment and drove to a pawn shop that I knew of on Highway 183. The owner and I haggled over money, and he did not offer enough, so I left.

I was on my way back to the motel when I noticed that the needle of the gas gauge was hovering on empty and I searched for a service station that might be open on this lazy Saturday morning. Within minutes the engine sputtered and died. I steered the car over to the shoulder and let it coast to a stop.

I opened the trunk, hoping that Ray had a gas can stashed there, but the only container I found was an empty plastic milk jug. I grabbed that and trudged forward on foot.

About a quarter of a mile ahead I found an open Sinclair station, but the attendant told me that it was illegal to dispense gasoline into a plastic container, and no, he did not have a can that he could loan or sell me. All he could offer was the information that there was another gas station four or five blocks down the street, but he did not know if it was open.

As I stood in front of the station with the empty milk jug in my hand, wondering what to do, a blue Mercury Comet pulled up. A young man—I figured him to be about eighteen or nineteen—was driving.

"What time was it?" Officer Johnson asked.

I shrugged.

"About?"

"Maybe nine-thirty," I said.

Johnson took note of this and instructed, "Go on."

I related how the driver leaned over, rolled down the passenger window, and asked, "Is that your car back there?"

I told him it was and that I had run out of gas. "They won't let me use this," I said, hoisting the plastic jug.

He said he would help. I hopped into his car and he drove the few blocks to the next station, where they did allow me to pump a bit of gas into the jug. Then the stranger drove me back to my car.

We introduced ourselves. I told him I was Dale Adams and I think he said he was Mack Davis. He was from Houston and had come to Dallas looking for work. He said he was an electrician's helper and, indeed, the floor of the passenger's seat was littered with tools. The backseat was filled with clothes. It reminded me of the way our car had looked a few weeks earlier when Ray and I had pulled into town.

We poured a jugful of gas into Ray's Ford and then the kid followed me back to the gas station, where I filled the tank.

That might have been the end of the encounter, but I wanted to thank him for his help. He was new in town, just like me, and he was looking for a job. I told him that I was going to visit some pawn shops out near where I worked and if he wanted, he could come along. "We could run back out to my job site," I said. "If my boss has shown up, I can introduce you. He can probably use you." He liked the idea. "But first," I added, "I need to swing by my place." I wanted to get Ray's car back to him.

We drove in a two-car caravan back to the motel. Ray was up and about, and he mumbled a greeting to my new acquaintance. Then we drove off in the kid's car. I directed him to a pawn shop on Harry Hines Boulevard, and as I prepared to get out of the car, he pulled a pistol from underneath the driver's seat and asked if I would pawn it.

"No," I said, and inside I shuddered a bit. These Texans, in the few weeks I had known them, all seemed to be gun crazy. I hated guns. It was still like the old west in some ways.

I pawned my stereo and tapes for ten dollars, and then I directed the kid toward the freeway ramp, but he pulled the car into the parking lot of a convenience store instead. I agreed with him that a cold beer sounded great.

He remained in the car as I bought two quarts of beer. The moment I hopped back into the passenger's seat, he stepped heavily on the gas pedal, spewing a cloud of gravel and dust in our wake. I shot him a quizzical look. "Oops, excuse me," he apologized.

He had never been to Dallas before, and he found the maze of freeways confusing. He made several wrong turns before we finally arrived at the job site.

The site still appeared to be deserted, but I went over to my boss's trailer and knocked on the door on the chance that he might be inside. There was no answer. When I walked back toward the car I found the kid sitting on the hood, drinking his beer, and twirling the pistol around his finger.

"Are there any tin cans around here?" he asked. He wanted some target practice.

"I don't think it's too cool to be doing that out here," I told him. "This is private property. Why don't you just put that thing in the trunk?"

He started to protest, but finally shrugged and did as I asked. It was then that I noticed that he also had a rifle in the backseat, enclosed in a leather case and stashed underneath some clothing. I asked him to put that in the trunk too.

He headed back toward the driver's seat, but I suggested, "Hey, look, why don't you just let me drive?" Unfamiliar with the roadways, he agreed.

Johnson stopped my narrative and asked, "You were driving the other guy's car?"

"Yes."

"Go on."

As we drove off, the kid asked if I would pawn some of his electrician's tools and I agreed to do it for him on the way back to the motel. In Grand Prairie, we found a pawnbroker who was interested, but he said that it was just after noon and a city ordinance would not allow him to pawn any items after that time. He offered to buy the tools outright, and Davis agreed.

The afternoon still loomed in front of us, appearing from this range to be the midpoint of a long lonely holiday weekend. Davis was on his own in the city and it was obvious that he wanted some company. I would just as soon have spent the afternoon watching a football game on the motel TV, but I felt obliged to him for helping me out.

We worked our way back to the motel slowly, stopping at a place called the Bronco Bowl. Davis said he would rent us a pool table, but he got into an argument when the proprietor asked for identification. Rather than show any ID, he said he had changed his mind.

By now it was about 3:00 P.M., and I decided that I had repaid the obligation to my Good Samaritan. I was ready to go about my own quiet business. I told him this, and again mentioned that he was welcome to come out to the job site on Monday.

"Well, look," he said. "I need to buy a radio. Is there a mall around here?"

I told him that the Irving Mall was located almost right across from where we were, just a short distance from Highway 183.

The mall was jammed on this Saturday afternoon, the second day of the Christmas shopping season. We joined in amid the slow-moving procession of shoppers. Before I realized what was happening, Davis sidled up behind a shapely young woman and patted her on the backside. She turned in anger, but he was already lost in the crowd.

When I caught up with him I growled, "You're gonna get yourself into trouble."

He laughed off my concern and scooted ahead, down the central corridor of the mall, and I followed.

When I again caught up with him I said, "Look, we came here to buy a radio. Now let's get it and get out of here."

"Aw, the hell with it," he said.

We returned to the car and, by now, early winter darkness was beginning to descend upon us. The boy's obvious case of loneliness returned. He said, "Hey, look, I have no place to go, nothing to do. Would you go to a drive-in movie if I pay for it? I'll buy us a six-pack."

I was not interested in spending any more time with this kid, but he flashed a broad grin and shrugged his shoulders. Finally I said, "Well, why not."

Across the street from the mall, we picked up a bucket of fast-food chicken. Then we headed for Highway 183.

"You still driving?" Johnson asked.

"Yes."

My eyes scanned the road, searching for a drive-in theater. Just as I turned onto the highway, I heard a sharp "popping" sound. I jerked my head to the right to see that my companion had fired a gunshot at the Yield sign on the freeway ramp.

"What the hell are you doin'?" I demanded.

"Oh, just target practice," he said.

"Well, put that thing up." He placed the gun on the seat between us. I grabbed it and shoved it under the seat. "What the hell did you get that out of the trunk for?" I asked, but he just shrugged off the question.

Anxious now to get through this day and away from my puzzling companion, I pulled the car into the first theater I found, the 183 Drive-In. Only after we were inside did I realize that the movies were "grade B" productions, soft-core skin flicks. The first movie was already underway.

I endured it as best I could, and forced myself to sit through the first half of the second movie, *The Swinging Cheerleaders*. I whiled away the time with another beer.

While Davis was off at the refreshment stand, buying some popcorn, I decided it was time to call it a night. Shortly after he returned, I said, "Look, man, I'm really tired. I'm ready to head back home." He protested, but I was insistent. "You can come back here if you want to," I told him, "but I am really beat."

Johnson leaned forward and asked, "What time did you leave the drive-in?"

"Must have been about nine-thirty," I replied.

"Huh. And who was driving?"

"I was still driving."

Johnson said, "Go on."

On the ride back to the motel, Davis asked me a question I had already anticipated: could he stay the night in our room. He would be happy to sleep on the floor. I told him that the place was much too small for three people.

I pulled his car to a stop in front of a small convenience store adjacent to the motel. Once again he asked if he could spend the night in our room. Once again I turned him down, but I told him if he showed up early Monday morning, he could follow me to the job site. "See you Monday," I said.

I went into the store and bought cigarettes. When I came out, I saw that his car was still there, but I did not want any further conversation. I turned my back and walked to my room.

Ray mumbled a word of greeting, but turned back to his sleep. The room was dark, except for the soft glow of the TV screen. I ate a bowl of vegetable soup that Ray had made, finished the beer I had been drinking, and watched the last few minutes of the "Carol Burnett Show" and the first few minutes of the ten o'clock news. Then I turned off the set and went to sleep.

That was the last time I ever saw this guy, I told the officers, and the last time I ever thought about him until they showed me his photograph this morning.

Johnson said quietly, "Now, tell us what we know to be the truth."

They had me go over the story again. Then again. And again.

There was no clock in the room and I wore no watch, but my dwindling supply of cigarettes told me that many hours had passed. Still the questions continued:

"Let's go over it again . . . one more time Adams."

I related the story three or four more times before Johnson said, "Well, the kid seems to recall that you two got high that afternoon. Do you smoke marijuana Mr. Adams?"

The comment startled me. I had almost forgotten that we shared a couple of joints. Sheepishly I admitted, "Yeah."

The officers grinned at one another. Johnson said, "Let's go through this story one more time and see if we can't get to the truth of the matter."

They offered no food and no water and no opportunity to rest. Several times I asked if I could call my brother so that he would know where I was. Each time I was told, "You can make a phone call in a few minutes."

It must have been late in the afternoon when Johnson mumbled that he had some last minute Christmas shopping to do. He left and a uniformed police officer took his place in the small room, standing sentry. Luther continued to question me.

Some time later Johnson returned in fresh clothes, full of renewed energy. Luther took a break, but the barrage of questions continued. "Let's go back over November 27th," Johnson said.

"Man, I've been doing that all night."

"Well, who gives a shit? You do it with me too."

My mind grew fuzzy. I was hungry. I was thirsty. I wanted to call Ray. I wanted sleep. But, most of all I wanted these men to leave me alone.

Johnson attacked my story from all angles, asking me to repeat details, jumping around in the time frame of events. Often I replied, "How many times do I have to tell you? What's the purpose?"

Johnson responded, "Just answer the question, Mr. Adams."

I lost track of how many times I repeated my story before the Dallas police escalated their attack. Johnson suddenly stopped grilling me. He rose, beckoned to the cop standing at the door, and they left the room.

It was the first time I had been alone since this ordeal began. I was exhausted, both mentally and physically. I knew that I had to keep my senses on full alert, but all I could do was repeat to myself: you're in deep shit.

Moments later another man entered and identified himself as Sergeant Gus Rose, chief detective of the Crimes Against Persons Bureau. He stood about six feet tall and appeared to be in his early forties, with just a hint of gray at his temples. Beneath his dark pin-striped suit was an athletic muscular body. All business, he tossed a single typewritten page onto the table and said, "You just sign your fucking name to this piece of paper here."

"I won't sign anything without reading it."

"Oh, you can read it, if that's what you want to do."

I scanned the lines of type. It was an aborted version of the story I had been telling, and I realized immediately that the time frame in this statement was different from what I had been saying. I told the detectives that I first encountered the kid at the gas station around ten in the morning; this paper said it was after noon. I said we were at the pawn shop around noon; they said 2:30 P.M. I said we left the movie shortly after 9:00 P.M.; this said midnight.

"What is this?" I asked.

"It's a confession," Rose announced.

I placed the typed sheet of paper carefully back down on the table and said simply, "I can't sign this."

Rose stalked out of the room, slamming the door behind him.

He returned a few minutes later. This time he held a gun in his hand, and he tossed it onto the table in front of me, commanding, "Look at that."

I stared at it.

"You ever seen that before?"

"Well, I don't know . . ."

"I told you to look at it," he growled.

"I am looking at it."

"Pick the son of a bitch up and look at it!"

Did he want my fingerprints on it? Did he want me to appear armed, so that he could shoot me in "self-defense?" I replied as calmly as I could, "No sir, I will not touch that thing."

Our eyes met and locked for many moments. I could feel the arteries in my temples pulsating. I dared not move a muscle. With deliberate movements, Rose pulled his service revolver from its shoulder holster, pointed it at my forehead, and cocked it. "I ought to blow your shit away," he said.

All I could see was the barrel of his gun aimed between my eyes. Keep your voice polite, I commanded myself. Keep your hands steady. I gulped and admitted, "You probably could, and get away with it."

He held his service revolver steady for several tense moments. Then, finally, he shoved it back into its holster and stormed out of the room.

Johnson and Luther returned to continue the interrogation, as if nothing had happened. Johnson produced a sheet of paper and sketched a map that included Highway 183, Inwood Avenue, Fort Worth Avenue, the job site, the motel, and the drive-in theater. "You leave the theater, you're coming down 183, and you get off on the Inwood exit," he said, pointing to the map. "There's a red light there, do you remember that red light?"

"Yeah."

"What happened there?"

"What do you mean what happened there?"

"Do you remember the red light there?"

"Of course. I travel that road twice a day."

"Well, do you remember what you and the kid were doing? What were you talking about then?"

"Probably about him coming out to the job site on Monday."

"What else?"

"Hell, I don't know. It's been a month ago!"

"So you don't remember what you talked about?"

I shook my head in reply.

The questions continued in a never-ending circle until I decided that if I did not give these men some kind of statement, this could go on forever. I told them that if they would allow me to dictate a statement in my own words, I would sign it.

They brought in a clerk-typist, Carla Crenshaw, and once more we went over the story. When Crenshaw left to transcribe my statement, the mood grew more relaxed. Johnson brought me a cup of coffee and tossed a package of cheese crackers onto the table, but I had no appetite.

Soon we began reviewing the typed statement, line by line. The detectives were not happy with it. Their biggest problem continued to be time. They pounded away at me, insisting that I adjust the timing of the entire day by two or three hours, but I held firm. Finally, we agreed to a compromise; we would simply leave out the times altogether. They crossed out any mention of time. Then we hassled over a few other details.

Twenty minutes later, Crenshaw furnished us with a clean copy. I read it carefully. It was a straightforward account of the events of the somewhat boring day, ending with our actions after leaving the drive-in.

> We headed toward Dallas on Highway 183. When
> I reached the Inwood Road exit I took it and then
> made a right turn on Inwood and continued on south.
> I do not remember anything after I took a right on

Inwood until I was turning left on Fort Worth Avenue.

I still did not understand why this intersection was so important to the officers, but I no longer cared. My weary mind decided that this was a fairly accurate account. It did not make any reference to time, nor did it carry my story to the end of the day, when I returned to the motel to catch the last few minutes of the "Carol Burnett Show." But these details no longer seemed important.

I signed the paper and Crenshaw witnessed my signature. A sense of finality flooded the small room.

I was fingerprinted and photographed. An officer handcuffed me once again, but this time my hands were in front of me. He clamped cuffs around my ankles and strapped a leather belt about my waist. Then he threaded a length of chain to connect both the wrist and ankle cuffs to the leather belt. Shuffling slowly, I was led through dingy halls and into a waiting car for the short four-block drive to the old city jail.

My new home was a six-by-ten foot cubicle fashioned of concrete block on three sides, with iron bars enclosing the front. A metal structure, a combination sink and toilet, was mounted on the back wall. It smelled rancid. The unflushable toilet was filled to the brim with urine and feces, and a previous occupant had left a pile of excrement in one corner. A complaint to the guard brought only a shrug and the comment, "It's not my job." The trusty who swept the corridors cussed me out when I asked him to clean it up.

Aging coats of institutional paint in chipped layers of white, green, and yellow surrounded the graffiti that decorated the walls, proclaiming the same variety of messages that you would see on the walls of a barroom bathroom. Most appropriate was the proclamation scrawled by a former occupant, left here to taunt anyone, such as myself, who might run afoul of the criminal justice system in Dallas. It read simply:

FUCK YOU

Some hours later, after a few hours of fitful sleep, I was chained once more and taken back to the government center, where Detective Johnson asked if I would consent to stand in a lineup. Maybe I shouldn't do this, I said to myself, but I agreed anyway.

Soon I was ushered into a room with eight other men, all of them handcuffed, and instructed to stand in line with them. I studied the others. I had no idea where any of them came from, but I could see that few of them resembled me even superficially. Only one other man had long hair.

We stood on a platform, in front of a wall with black lines painted onto it, delineating our heights. Bright lights bore into my eyes so that I could see nothing in front of me. I felt like a specimen on a microscope slide, or an animal in a zoo.

One by one we were called to step forward, told to turn to the right, then to the left. Routine questions were asked, so that our voices would be heard. The process took less than half an hour.

Shortly afterward, Detective Johnson informed me, with a note of finality in his voice, "Well, Adams, you've been identified."

"What do you mean?" I asked. "Who picked me out?"

Johnson wouldn't say, but when I thought about it I realized that it must have been Mack Davis.

On the following day, I consented to take a lie detector test, hoping to convince these steel-jawed men that I was telling the truth. As I was ushered through the underground corridor of the government center—the same place where press photographers had first snapped my picture—a detective commented in an intimidating manner, "Hey, Adams, you ever seen this hallway before?" I did not respond. He explained that this was a famous location, the spot where, thirteen years earlier, Jack Ruby had executed President Kennedy's accused assassin, Lee Harvey Oswald. The detective said, "Yeah, we left the blood on the wall for a few days."

Somewhere inside the building, I was introduced to a stocky balding man dressed in a rumpled gray suit. "This is a polygraph machine," he said. "Do you know how it works?" He told me that he would ask a series of questions from a list he had in front of him. Once the machine was attached, I was to answer only Yes or No to his questions.

"Is your name Randall Dale Adams?" he began.

"Yes."

"Have you ever been in trouble with the police before?"

"No."

"Have you ever been locked up before?"

"No."

"Did you, in fact, on November 27th of this year, meet a young man who helped you get gas?"

"Yes."

"Did you go to the Bronco Bowl?"

"Yes."

"Did you kill a police officer?"

"No."

When he was finished, I waited in the hallway with a cigarette and a cup of coffee. Already I was becoming adept at smoking while handcuffed. Fifteen minutes passed before the polygraph operator came out and announced that the results were "inconclusive." He asked me to repeat the test.

The results of the second test were also deemed "inconclusive." But the man predicted, "The third time's a charm, Mr. Adams."

Again we went through the list of questions. Again I answered "yes" or "no." Again I was sent out into the hall to wait.

This time only five minutes passed before the polygraph operator rushed into the hall and declared that I had failed.

Two detectives were assigned to escort me back to jail. We stopped at the weapons room, where one of them picked up his gun and then announced, "I'm going to get the car."

The other detective attended to paperwork for a few moments before he looked up and appeared surprised that I was still with him. "Go out and meet him in the car," he said.

"No, sir. I'm not going anywhere without an escort."

"Get your ass out there to the car!"

I stood my ground and waited until he had finished the paperwork.

. . .

Wearing a bright orange jumpsuit that identified me as a dangerous prisoner, my hands cuffed in front of me, I sat on a bench in the medical department, waiting for a doctor to give me what I figured would be a perfunctory, obligatory physical, when a man dressed in a black suit walked in. His outfit was embellished by cowboy boots and a cream-colored Stetson.

The prisoner sitting next to me called out, "Chaplain!" They fell into a brief discussion about the previous Sunday's service.

When they had finished their conversation, I said, "Excuse me, sir . . ."

"Yeah," he responded.

"Are you the chaplain for the jail?"

"Yes."

I told him that I had been confined here for several days and had not been allowed any reading material. I was desperate to find some way to pass the time and I had always been a voracious reader. "Is there any way possible that I could get some religious tracts or a Bible, perhaps?" I asked.

He pulled a small notebook from his breast pocket and asked me what cell I was in.

I told him.

As he jotted down my cell number, he told me he would get me some books written by a certain Chaplain Ray. "What's your name?" he asked.

"Randall Adams."

His pen stopped in mid-stroke. "You the cop killer?"

The words made me freeze for an instant. I wanted to lash out at the man, but I spoke softly and politely, so as not to alert the watching guards.

"Well, that's what I'm in here for," I admitted.

"Do you really think a Bible would help you?"

I said bitterly, "No, sir, I really don't think it would. In fact, forget it."

The preacher repented and said softly, "Hey, wait a minute, I'll make sure you get a Bible."

"No, thank you. If that's your religion, I don't want any part of it. Don't send me any books. If you do, I'll throw them down the hallway."

. . .

One day all activity ceased abruptly, and I was alone in a cell with only my thoughts for companionship, isolated in my concrete and iron cubicle.

Since my arrest, I had not seen a newspaper, nor watched the news on TV, nor heard a radio. I had no idea where Ray was, or whether anyone else in my family had learned of my predicament; the phone call that the justice of the peace and the detectives had promised still had not materialized.

My mind kept returning to Columbus, Ohio, and I prayed that there was some way I could get out of this scrape without ever having to let Mom know about it. She had endured enough pain in her life and I did not want to add to it. She suffered from high blood pressure, and I feared for her health if she should learn that I had been arrested for killing a Dallas police officer.

Sometime during this quiet, dismal morning, I found myself lying upon my bunk, musing, trying to figure out what day it was. Suddenly I sat bolt upright and mumbled aloud, "Merry Christmas, Randall."

4

THE VISITORS

HAVING WEATHERED THE incredible pain of widow-
hood, having raised her children, Mom had every reason to believe
that her troubles were over. The evening after Christmas she stood
in the kitchen of her home in Grove City, Ohio, adjacent to the
south side of Columbus, washing the supper dishes. Her spirits were
as clouded as the soapy water. Normally a cheerful optimistic person, she was perturbed by what she could only describe as a "heavy"
feeling. Something was not as it should be, but she could not seem
to identify it.

The sharp ring of the telephone interrupted her thoughts. "Hello,"
she said.

The man on the other end of the line identified himself as Rick
Darty, a friend of her sons Randy and Ray. He was calling from

Dallas. Rick got right to the point. "Randy is in trouble," he said.

Mom's body began to quiver. "What kind of trouble?" she asked.

"He's accused of killing a police officer here in Dallas," Rick said, "and I want to give you the name and telephone number of an attorney."

Mom's knees gave way under her and she slid to the floor, still clutching the telephone. Around her, it seemed as if the house were shaking upon its foundations. It was a supreme test of will to force herself to continue to function. Her hand trembled so severely that she could barely write down the information that this stranger provided. She had heard the words, but she could not comprehend them. "Why didn't Ray call me?" she asked.

"I don't know where he is," Rick said.

"Is Randy all right? Is he hurt?"

"No, ma'm, I don't think so." It was obvious that Rick had very little information.

Call the girls, I've got to call the girls, Mom said to herself. She thanked Rick for calling, hung up the phone and moved into action, dialing the number of my sister Nancy.

"I need you," she said simply. "Randy is in trouble."

Nancy heard the tremor in Mom's voice and replied without hesitation, "I'll be right there." She, her husband Jim, and their two young sons lived only ten minutes away.

Mom made the same call to my sister Mary in Galion, Ohio, who said she was on her way. Then she called my brother Ron in Nashville. He said that he, too, was coming and that everyone should stay put until he arrived.

While she waited, Mom called the number that Rick had given her. The attorney's name was Dennis White. Although it was late, he was in his office.

"Mrs. Adams," he said, "it doesn't look good. Randall has been accused of killing a police officer here in Dallas and you need to get here. He's been in jail almost a week already."

Nancy and Jim arrived within minutes, and Nancy's first concern was for Mom's health. They had seen one another just yesterday—Christmas—but today Mom's silver hair appeared several shades lighter and her skin was ashen. "She's in shock," Nancy whispered to Jim. Aloud, she said, "Mom, what's going on? What's wrong with Randy?"

"There's some mistake," Mom said, "some terrible mistake."

By the time Mary arrived from Galion, Mom and Nancy realized that it would have been easier to just meet Ron in Nashville and continue south from there, but it was too late to change plans. Ron was in his van screaming headlong toward Columbus, and they had no choice but to wait.

Nancy's husband Jim felt helpless. Searching for something to do, he drove to a newsstand at James Road and Main Street, which he knew featured an array of out-of-town newspapers. He bought a copy of the *Dallas Morning News* and did a double take when he saw me on the front page. The photo was of me being taken "downtown." I had been laboring outside for hours, my hands were cuffed behind me, and my long hair was unkempt and frazzled. In my eyes was an expression that could either be total confusion or madness.

Above my photo, a headline screamed: Cop Killer Confesses.

Confesses? Jim was perplexed. Like the rest of my family, he was conditioned to believe what the authorities declared, and what the newspapers reported. But he had known me for years. Long before he married my sister, he had coached me on a football team. I was the one who cried if a puppy was injured. The contention that I had murdered a cop was, to him, ludicrous. He simply did not know what to make of all this.

He returned to Mom's house. Wordlessly he handed over the newspaper. Mom was too upset to read the story, but the picture of her youngest son and the headline burned into her memory.

She folded the newspaper and hid it under some clothes in a bureau drawer. I don't want anybody to see this, she said to herself. Ever.

Ron's van was designed for hauling carpet, not people, but it was the only family vehicle that could hold everyone. Twenty-four hours after Mom received the phone call that turned her world upside down, Mom, Ron, Nancy, Mary, and Ken crawled into the van and headed south. Jim remained behind to watch the kids.

"Somebody out there wants to talk to you," a guard said.

What did they want from me now? I rolled out of my bunk, threw on some clothes and stood submissively, waiting for handcuffs to appear.

"No cuffs," the guard mumbled.

He led me down the corridor to a room, ushered me inside, and locked the door behind me. It was a small chamber furnished only with a chair and a desk. Bars reached from the ceiling to the desktop, separating the room into two compartments.

The man who sat on the other side was a stranger. In a soft-spoken voice, he identified himself as Dennis L. White, an attorney. He explained that my friend Rick had contacted him. He had tried to visit me sooner, but it had taken him several days to locate me within the maze of the Dallas jail system. Officials had kept him on a merry-go-round, spinning between the old Dallas jail and the government center. "Where have you been?" he asked.

"Right here," I said. But I had no idea where "here" was.

He told me that I was on the eighth floor of the government center. Then we got down to business. He said that he was primarily a civil lawyer and had handled only a few criminal cases, but he was willing to represent me, if I so desired.

"You're the only person talking with me at this point," I said. "I'm not going to object to that."

His smile was kind, but the words were necessarily cold as he spelled out the formalities of the complaint against me, to make sure I understood. I was charged with the murder of Police Officer Robert Wood, and it was a capital offense, meaning that the state of Texas, if it was able to bring the full weight of the law down upon me, could send me to the electric chair.

With a lump in my throat, I assured him that I understood all of this.

He went over the details of the case against me. At this point, he had only sketchy information, but he assured me that, prior to trial, the prosecution would have to disclose the particulars. Well before the trial, the district attorney's office would be required to supply us with a list of all witnesses who might testify during the presentation of the case. This was a common requirement issued in a spirit of fair play, and based on the contention that the defendant has a right to know the identity of his accusers. We would have time to check them out, to delve into their backgrounds, to ferret out their motives. Furthermore, once a witness testified, the state would have to supply us with copies of any previous written statements that witness had given to the authorities. We would have a chance to study those statements prior to cross-examination, so that we could discover any inconsistencies. What's more, White said, the district attorney would be under a broad and well-recognized obligation to turn over to us any exculpatory material that might prove my innocence.

Nevertheless, at the moment, we were operating in the dark. About all we knew was that my arrest was based on accusations made by the young man I remembered as Mack Davis, whose real name, White had learned, was David Harris. Finding out more about this kid was our major task.

White asked me several questions, taking notes as I answered. He wanted to know the time of my arrest, details of the interrogation, the lineup, the lie detector test. Grim-faced, he announced that I was front-page news in the local papers. He saw the shock in my eyes and explained further. The Dallas press was reporting statements made by police officers, declaring that pawn shop tickets had linked me to "several robberies and a burglary." Detectives, according to the newspapers, claimed that I had a "bad memory" concerning the events of that night, and that I had "blacked out." But the bottom line, they said, was that I had signed a "confession."

He was clearly concerned about the issue of trial-by-newspaper. Before I appeared in the lineup, he said, the papers had printed my photograph on their front pages. Subsequently, I was identified in the lineup, not only by David Harris, but by some other mysterious witness. It was all incredibly confusing. How can this be real? I asked myself.

White reassured me, "I believe nothing of what I've heard or read."

. . .

The family drove nonstop from Columbus, pausing only for food, facilities and gasoline, or to change drivers. There was no heat in the back of the van, and the windchill factor, as they sped through Joplin, Missouri, was murderous.

They were exhausted as they approached Dallas. Mom pulled a scrap of paper from her purse containing Dennis White's address and phone number. She clutched it fiercely.

Ahead, the lights of the sprawling city seemed to encompass the universe. Mom, Nancy, Ron, Mary, and Ken were confused and anxious strangers in an unknown land.

The van moved headlong into a vicious winter thunderstorm. Daggers of lightning shot about and deafening peals of thunder assaulted their ears.

Mom muttered to no one, and to everyone, "This is like driving into hell."

They linked up with Ray and discovered why he had not been the first to call with the news. The Dallas police had picked him up the same day I was arrested. They held him for seven or eight hours, questioning him, demanding that he tell them what he knew about the murder of Officer Wood, threatening to charge him as an accessory. Finally, they let him go, but Ray had changed within the space of days. Somewhat morose to begin with, he now appeared to be caught in a web of intrigue and fear that left him baffled. In the army, he could shoot back. Here, he did not know what to do. For days he had been virtually unable to act. Nancy and Mary pressed him for details concerning his interrogation, but he would not, or could not, respond. It was strange, unaccountably eerie.

With a shudder, Nancy realized instinctively that they all had changed. Just like that, through circumstances they had not created, their lives had been altered forever. What was to come of it? she wondered.

They met with Dennis White. He was a quiet man who impressed them with his intelligence and his sense of honesty. I was in serious trouble, he admitted, but if my family believed in me, their honest faith was a great asset. They would work together to see that the truth of the matter came out.

This was an acceptable strategy. Somehow, my family had pooled its limited resources and scraped together a fund of ten thousand dollars for my defense. White accepted this as a retainer, although Mom suspected that it would take far more money than this to defend a capital case.

My mother stood across from me, peering through a tiny screened window in the jail visiting room. Tears flowed freely from her eyes. To speak to me, she had to lean way down and put her mouth up close to a tiny grate; she choked on every word. Her complexion was ghostly, her hands shook, her voice quivered. Like Nancy, I thought that her graying hair seemed to have turned several shades whiter. She looked, suddenly, much older than her fifty-three years.

It was good to see her; at the same time it was wrenching.

"I'm praying for you, Randy," she cried. "I'm going to have the whole church pray for you."

5

THE TARGET

ON THE FINAL day of 1976, a grand jury, described officially as "good and lawful men of the County of Dallas," returned a true bill of indictment, formally charging me with the murder of Officer Robert Wood.

The second or third time I met with White, he told me about the other attorneys who would be involved in the trial. He was currently tied up in the litigation of a large estate case, so he had retained a cocounsel, Edith James, who would concentrate on research, the writing of court briefs, and jury selection. She was a jovial heavyset woman, he said, with a decided bent toward feistiness.

White said he was personally acquainted with the man assigned to try my case, the Honorable Donald Metcalfe, judge of Criminal District Court Number Two.

We faced formidable opponents in the district attorney's office. Ever since 1950, law enforcement in Dallas County had been the bailiwick of Henry Wade, the elected criminal district attorney, a silver-haired man with heavy jowls and a ruddy complexion. Wade first came to national prominence by prosecuting Jack Ruby for the murder of Lee Harvey Oswald, and again in 1973 as the titular defendant in *Roe v. Wade,* the landmark abortion case. He courted the voters of Dallas County with seasoned precision and knew his constituency as "good ol' boys" who expected the police and the district attorney's office to keep law and order. He did such a good job, by Texas standards, that few ever bothered to oppose him for reelection.

It was said that Wade judged his prosecutors solely upon their won-lost records, never questioning their methods. As a result the atmosphere in the district attorney's office was fiercely competitive. It was a contest to see who could win not only the most cases, but the harshest sentences as well.

The prosecutor in my case was First Assistant District Attorney Douglas D. "Mad Dog" Mulder. White knew him well, for they had graduated in the same law school class, from Southern Methodist University in 1964. Mulder had joined the district attorney's office right out of law school, just as it had achieved national prominence owing to the Jack Ruby case. Before he was thirty years old he had worked his way up to the post of first assistant, and it was an open secret that Mulder hoped to succeed Wade when the old man retired. White paused in his narrative, cleared his throat, and told me that in his dozen years on the job, Mulder had never lost a case. Never.

White warned me that during a murder trial, I might be forced to sit and listen to the prosecution and its witnesses say all manner of negative things about me. It was part of the process, and I had to submit to it. Even though I might want to explode, he cautioned, I had to restrain my emotions. A judge and a jury, seeing a murder defendant react with hostility, may draw their own serious conclusions, even if they are not warranted by the evidence. On that same theme, he suggested that I get a haircut from the jail barber.

"Are you willing to testify, if need be?" he asked.

"Of course," I replied.

White explained that we would make that decision during the trial itself. It depended on how strong the prosecution's case was. It was always a risk to put a murder defendant on the stand and expose him to cross-examination.

It was all right, I repeated. I was eager to tell my side of the story.

Again White paused. Then he said, "Look, I've got to ask something here. This is between you and me and whatever you tell me goes no further. I am going to ask you now, if Mulder offers you a life sentence to plead guilty, to keep from getting a death sentence, will you go for that?"

Without hesitation I said, "No."

On the long solemn drive back home to Columbus, Mom made a decision. I was front-page news in Dallas, but the Columbus media had not picked up on the story, or had simply ignored it. She knew that she would have difficulty explaining the sketchy details of my plight to friends and acquaintances and she decided, at least for the time being, to keep the news quiet.

The moment she returned home, she took the copy of the *Dallas Morning News* from its hiding place in her dresser drawer and burned it.

There were a few people in whom she would confide. At work, she told her supervisor that she would need some extended leave from time to time, and she told her why. Her boss was empathetic and agreed to keep the secret.

She tried to see the governor of Ohio, and was routed to his assistant, Robin Rachford. He offered advice: This is going to be a long hard pull. You have told me that your husband is dead. Randall has brothers and sisters and they may work for him for a while, but they have their own families to look after, so it is really going to be up to you to handle things. You had better get your nerves under control, or, he said, referring to a local mental hospital, "we're going to have you out here on the hill someplace."

Mom had been an active member of the Southwest Freewill Baptist Church for many years, and at Sunday service she stood up and declared, "I need prayer, and I've got a son who needs prayer. I just got back from Dallas, Texas, where my son has been accused of killing a police officer. I know a lot of you people don't know Randy, but Randy did not do this. The people who know Randy will tell you, my son did not do this terrible thing."

The jail menu could bring about death by slow starvation. Breakfast was coffee, served lukewarm in a styrofoam cup, and a small stale pastry that they called a bearclaw. Lunch was two bologna sandwiches and a cup of tea or a hot plate with a slab of chicken or turkey loaf, a hunk of potatoes, and a hint of a vegetable. Dinner was leftovers from lunch.

With no TV, radio, or newspapers, I searched for ways to remain occupied, to drown the encompassing feelings of helplessness and claustrophobia. I began to keep a journal, and tried my hand at pencil drawings, but most of the time, I merely paced the small cell.

With a start, one day I realized that, less than a month after my arrest, I was already learning how to do time.

My amenities were cigarettes and coffee. Both of these were too costly to buy from the commissary man who made his rounds on an unscheduled basis; it was much cheaper to buy tobacco and papers from him, and roll my own. I bought a submersible heating coil, called a "stinger," from the commissary vendor, so that I could make instant coffee. The family gave me a welcome gift, a subscription to *Time*.

The guards bristled at even these simple pleasures. They searched my cell on the average of once a day, yanking me into the hall to watch helplessly as they pored over my meager belongings, often spilling my tobacco and coffee onto the dingy floor. They continued to check on me almost hourly, shining a bright flashlight beam into my eyes at all hours of the day and night, depriving me of any chance for normal sleep.

The worst part was the isolation. I had almost no contact with the outside world, no way to know whether anyone was doing anything to help.

• • •

It was difficult to pick up the details, but I slowly became aware that something of deep importance was happening in Utah. From fragments of conversation, and my *Time* magazine, I learned that a death row inmate named Gary Gilmore, tired of fighting for his life, had instructed his attorney to abandon his appeals, clearing the way for the first execution in the United States since 1967. Gilmore was a firm believer in reincarnation, and reasoned that death was the most expedient way to get out of prison.

He simply wanted to commit suicide, I concluded, and the state of Utah complied with his wishes on the morning of January 17, 1977. Guards strapped him into a chair and then the warden asked if Gilmore had anything to say.

"Let's do it," Gilmore replied.

The state medical examiner pinned a target on Gilmore's black T-shirt, right over the heart. A priest placed his hands on Gilmore's right shoulder and intoned the last rites. Gilmore's final words were "*Dominus vobiscum*" ("The Lord be with you").

The priest stepped safely aside, and the warden glanced toward a curtain, twenty-six feet away from Gilmore. There were five slots in the curtain and the barrels of five .30-30 deer rifles poked through, aiming at the target on Gilmore's chest. Four of the rifles were loaded with steel-jacketed shells and one was loaded with a blank; no one knew which was which.

The warden signaled with his hand and four bullets tore into their target.

Prisoners in nearby cell blocks, hearing the sound, screamed obscenities, as did their brother inmates in jails and prisons throughout America.

My issue of *Time* noted: "For 358 other inmates on death rows in 20 states, the big question now is: Who will be next?" The magazine guessed that it would be someone in Georgia, Florida, or Texas.

6

THE WITNESS

DENNIS WHITE FILED a standard pretrial application for a writ of habeas corpus, demanding that the state provide evidence in support of its charge, or set me free. On the afternoon of Friday, January 21, 1977, Judge Donald J. Metcalfe convened a hearing to consider the motion.

First Assistant District Attorney Mulder was there to prosecute the case. It was the first time that I, knowingly, had seen him, but I received the impression that he already knew me well. He was confident in his case, and reasoned that he only had to call a single witness, a sixteen-year-old boy from Vidor, Texas.

We already knew the broad outlines of what David Ray Harris would say. After his initial statement, Dallas police department Deputy Chief J.D. Bryant had told the press, "Credence was given to the boy's story because he so vividly described the scene on North Hampton where the shooting occurred and he must have been at the scene or somebody else gave him a very vivid description of it." When Detectives Gus Rose and Clyde Haygood brought him to Dallas, he guided them to the location where Officer Wood had been killed, and then showed them the route back to the Comfort Courts, where Ray and I had been staying. From this, the deputy chief had concluded "he had to have firsthand knowledge of the scene."

Harris took the stand and, in a smooth low-pitched drawl, admitted to the judge that he had stolen the car he was driving when he arrived in Dallas that Saturday after Thanksgiving. He identified me as the man he had helped out after my car ran out of gas. He described the aimless day we spent together, and he said that it was about midnight when we left the drive-in theater. I was driving. A short time later, he said, we were stopped by a patrol car.

Mulder asked, "What happened next?"

"The police officer got out of the car and Dale got my pistol out from underneath the seat," Harris testified.

I tried to level a stare at him, but he would not meet my gaze.

"All right," Mulder continued. "You say the police officer got out of the car. Did you have occasion to say anything to Dale?"

"Whenever he went for the gun, I just asked him what he was going to do and he just told me to get down so I got down farther and about that time I guess the police officer walked up and he started shooting him."

I felt the reaction in my gut. I wanted to stand up and shout, "Hey, wait a minute!" But I remembered White's warning and I labored to keep still. I felt my hands quivering and I wondered if my face was red. Again I tried to catch Harris's gaze, but my accuser would not look me in the eye.

"Do you know how many times he shot him?" Mulder asked.

"Five or six."

Harris glanced up and, despite his reluctance, our eyes met for an instant. He eased back in the witness chair, so that the edge of the judge's bench blocked our line of vision.

"What happened after he shot five or six times?"

"He took off."

Following the murder, Harris said, I told him "not to worry about it, forget I ever saw it."

On cross-examination, Dennis White began the major task of our defense. Between now and the trial, we had to learn everything we could about this witness, to identify his reasons for pegging me as the murderer of Officer Wood, to attack the credibility that his baby-faced expression would naturally present to a jury. White took Harris through the story again, fishing for detail. He elicited the facts that Harris had not only stolen the car from his neighbor in Vidor, Calvin Cunningham, but that he had also burglarized the Cunningham house and stolen a jar containing some forty dollars worth of dimes. He forced Harris to admit that he was carrying a 12-gauge shotgun and a .22 caliber pistol, both of which he stole from his father.

White concentrated on Harris's timing of the events of the day. This was critical at each step, for my version of the story ended with my arrival back at the Comfort Courts in time to catch the last few minutes of the "Carol Burnett Show," which ended at 10:00 P.M. Harris's version kept me out on the streets until 1:00 A.M., a half hour after Officer Wood was killed. Whenever White asked Harris to pinpoint the time when something occurred, the witness recalled it happening two or three hours later than what I had told the police.

In an effort to find out more about this boy, White asked, "Had you been arrested prior to November 27th?"

Mulder objected to the question, and the judge sustained the objection, preventing Harris from answering.

In response, White argued, "Judge, I believe we have a right, since this witness's testimony is critical to the state's case, to go into anything that might reflect upon his credibility as a witness." In fact, he said, the state should be required to supply him with the arrest records of any and all witnesses in the case.

The judge said he would deal with that issue later but, as of the moment, White could ask no questions about Harris's criminal record.

This debate seemed very strange to me. My concept of a courtroom was that it was, perhaps, the one place in the world where simple truth was the paramount goal. Why couldn't White ask David Harris anything he wanted to ask him? My life was at stake here, so how could the judge put arbitrary limits on my defense?

Harris was excused, and I had a few moments at the defense table to ask White about this. He told me not to worry, that the procedures of the court were set up so as to manage everything in an orderly efficient fashion. If truth is what we were after, he assured me that we would have ample opportunity to seek it.

After the hearing, White's cocounsel, Edith James, made a quick trip to Vidor and discovered that Harris did, indeed, have a juvenile record stretching back to 1975, including arrests for burglaries and car theft. Furthermore, there was evidence that when he broke into his neighbor's home on November 26, he began a crime spree that extended beyond his trip to Dallas, at least through December 5.

White filed a motion for continuance, so that he and James could do some additional legwork in Vidor. To justify this delay, White had to appear in another hearing before Judge Metcalfe, wherein he detailed the dates of his upcoming trip.

I wrote to Mom:

> I hope Mr. White finds out a few things on his trip. I'm sure it will help if he does. I would like to get out of here by March if possible. I am very optimistic about this kid. I would like to know what the state offered him, by way of keeping him out of this. Mr. White says they had to have made some sort of deal with him for him to still be free after all he's done.
>
> Well, he is crazy, so I bet Mr. White finds out a lot.

Vidor is a provincial community that does not always take kindly to strangers; it is the state headquarters of the Ku Klux Klan. It was late at night when White, along with his wife and Edith James, arrived and checked into a motel. In the morning, James was up early, and left her room in search of her associates. She was surprised when a stranger called out to her from a parked car, "If you're looking for the lawyer, he's in *that* room."

As the attorneys made their way around town they discovered that someone from Dallas had been there the day before. White reported later that several people in Vidor had been warned that "an eastern liberal-educated lawyer" was on his way down to try to scare up evidence to stain the reputation of a local boy.

Despite the fact that they found themselves outmaneuvered, White and James managed to locate witnesses who could help paint the picture of Harris as a troubled young man who had already left an array of crimes in his wake. In fact, White came back armed with a request for Judge Metcalfe to issue subpoenas to thirty-five witnesses from Vidor who would attest to the defects in Harris's character.

They were able to piece together a comprehensive profile of the young man:

On the surface, he was polite and soft-spoken, a likable boy. But something lay beneath the surface, some impulse that periodically brought him afoul of the law. Perhaps it stemmed from the trauma of his childhood; when he was three years old, his four-year-old brother had drowned in a neighborhood pool. That tragedy, of course, had changed the family forever, and for many years, David's parents had reasoned that it was the worst pain they would ever have to endure.

But as he grew into his teens, David began to exhibit serious antisocial behavior. On July 27, 1976, he was placed on probation for a series of offenses committed in and around Vidor, including breaking and entering and the theft of his mother's car. He was legally adjudged to be a juvenile delinquent. In addition to the normal terms of probation, Juvenile Court Judge Grover Halliburton had formally instructed, "You must attend Sunday school and church each and every Sunday."

Harris was aware that if he got into further trouble his probation would be revoked and he would be committed to a juvenile facility, but this did not deter him.

On Friday, November 26, 1976, the day after Thanksgiving, he decided to run away from home. About 3:00 P.M., he broke into the Cunningham home, at 450 West Davis Street, by prying the

51

door open with a screwdriver, and perhaps also using an axe (photographs showed the door full of holes). Once inside, he swiped the jar full of dimes and a spare set of keys to the Cunninghams' blue 1972 Mercury Comet, which was not at the house at the time.

Harris spent the next hour or two drinking beer with his friends, then he returned to his own home and stuffed a pair of pants, a couple of shirts, some underwear and socks, and a can of shaving lotion into an overnight bag. He took his father's 12-gauge shotgun and .22 caliber pearl-handled pistol, and a box containing about fifty rounds of ammunition for the pistol. He hid these supplies in a ditch about a block away from the house.

About 11:00 P.M. he returned to the Cunningham home. By now the Mercury Comet was parked in the driveway, and the house was dark and quiet. He tried to push the car out into the street, but could not budge it. Undaunted, Harris started the car and pulled away to the spot down the road where he had left the cache of supplies. He put his clothes and the shotgun in the backseat and stashed the pistol underneath the front seat. He noticed that Mr. Cunningham's electrician's tools were on the floor of the passenger's side of the front seat.

Then he headed the car through Beaumont and Galveston and on into Houston, arriving about 2:00 A.M. Sometime later, he decided to drive north on I-45 toward Dallas.

During the ensuing day and night in Dallas, David Harris encountered me, and he also encountered Officer Robert Wood. Whatever happened in Dallas—and whatever role Harris played in the events—caused him to hightail it back home to Vidor.

By Sunday night, twenty-two hours after the murder of Officer Wood, Harris had sought refuge at his friend Hootie Nelson's house. He was watching the "Channel 6 News" with Nelson and Nelson's friend Lynn Brown, when the station broadcast a report on the cop killing in Dallas. Harris boasted that it was he who had killed the "pig."

Nelson did not believe the story, and challenged Harris to swear upon it.

Harris said, "I swear, man, really I killed him."

Nelson and Brown were still skeptical, so Harris took them outside to examine the Comet for any signs of gunshot damage. When they could not find any bullet holes from the gun fired by Officer Turko, Harris opened the trunk and exhibited the .22 caliber pistol. He repeated, "I killed the pig in Dallas."

Harris was riding with Nelson and Brown a few days later when he asked them to drop him off at a house trailer. After they drove, he burglarized the trailer.

Several more days passed. Then one evening, Dennis Johnson and Randy Hayes encountered Harris at Bill's Gas Station in Vidor. Their friend told them that he was alone and needed a place to stay because Hootie Nelson had kicked him out. Johnson offered him shelter, and Harris hopped into the car.

During the ensuing conversation, Harris boasted that he had killed a policeman in Dallas.

Later that evening Harris took a .22 caliber rifle into O'Banion's Convenience Store. He forced clerk Judy Moore to lay down on the floor at rifle point as he cleaned out the cash register.

To Vidor Police Officer Sam Kittrell, the local crimes fit the pattern of troubled young David Harris. The boy was already wanted for suspicion of burglary and car theft at the Cunningham home, and now Kittrell sought to question him regarding the latest felonies.

Harris, perhaps operating on the theory that it would be better to go in than to be brought in, turned himself over to Kittrell on December 5. He signed a statement confessing to both crimes. He implicated his friends as accomplices, even though he was the only one who entered the house trailer and the convenience store. Throughout his interrogation, he told Kittrell nothing about his trip to Dallas.

Nevertheless, the Vidor police believed there was more to Harris's story. After stealing Cunningham's car, the boy said, he had driven it to Galveston and back. But that was only about a two hundred-mile round-trip, and Cunningham reported that more than one thousand miles had been added to the odometer.

Two weeks passed. As the Vidor police investigated Harris's activities, they learned that the boy had boasted of killing a policeman in Dallas. Acting on a tip, police searched the wetlands behind Hootie Nelson's house. Kittrell watched as Nelson's father reached into the water and pulled out a 9-shot, .22 caliber pistol. It was covered with oil and encased in a sock. Ballistics tests in Dallas identified it as the weapon that had killed Officer Wood.

On Monday, December 20, Officer Sam Pickens picked up Harris for questioning. Lieutenant Robert E. Smith and Captain J.L. Reynolds interviewed him concerning the murder of Officer Wood, and Harris realized that he was not only the prime suspect in the cop killing, he was the only suspect.

After several hours of questioning, Harris asked, "Well, what if I knew who did it, but I was there and just knew who did it?"

An officer replied that the consequences, to Harris, would depend upon the extent of his cooperation in apprehending and convicting the murderer.

Hearing this, Harris admitted that he had bragged about killing a cop, but now he said that he had been lying, merely trying to make himself look tough in the eyes of his friends. He said that he was there at the time, in the blue Mercury Comet that Officer Wood stopped. He said that it was, indeed, the .22 caliber pistol he had stolen from his parents that killed the policeman. But he insisted that he was not the killer.

Who was it then, who had squeezed the trigger six times at nearly point-blank range?

Harris said that the killer was a long-haired hitchhiker whom he knew only by the name of Dale, whom he had picked up earlier in the day.

Police in Dallas checked with local pawn shops until they found a receipt for November 27 in the name of Randall Dale Adams, whose address was listed as the Comfort Courts Motel. They questioned the motel manager, who did not know the address of the apartment where Ray and I had moved, but who did remember where I worked.

Dallas County authorities made no secret of the fact that they believed Harris's story. On February 22, District Attorney Henry Wade filed a formal notice in Criminal District Court Number Two in the case of *Dallas County v. Randall Dale Adams*:

> NOW COMES the Criminal District Attorney of
> Dallas County, Texas, and represents to the Court
> that the Defendant herein is indicted for a capital
> felony offense, to wit: Capital Murder, and hereby
> makes it known to the Court in this written instru-
> ment and in open court that the State will seek the
> Death Penalty.

The words were cold, formal, legalistic. But their intent was all too clear. Dallas County was going to attempt to execute me on the basis of an accusation by a sixteen-year-old thief.

White met with me in the attorneys' room on the eighth floor of the government center and discussed basic strategy. The case boiled down to Harris's word against mine and our task was to show the jury that the boy was a budding sociopath, and that he had much to gain by implicating me as the killer of Officer Wood. His crimes prior to his trip to Dallas were serious enough so that authorities in Vidor were considering revoking his probation, which would send him to a juvenile facility for a period of a year or so. But the real problems Harris faced were the pending charges of burglary and armed robbery, crimes he committed after returning to Vidor. For these offenses, he could be tried as an adult and sentenced to a maximum term of life in prison.

White assured me that by the time our parade of witnesses had taken the stand, no jury in the world would believe this troubled kid.

He applied the standard lawyer's yardstick to the case. Who had the means, the motive, and the opportunity to kill Officer Wood? The means was the gun that Harris stole from his parents. Harris had a motive. When Officer Wood stopped the car on North Hampton Avenue, Harris knew that it was a stolen vehicle, undoubtedly listed as so in the state computer system. On the other hand, I had no idea the car was stolen. Harris certainly had the opportunity, for by his own admission he was at the scene of the crime. Was I there?

Did I have the opportunity? Only if you accepted Harris's version of the story.

Considering it all, White declared, "They don't have a case."

Increasingly I wondered, if the state does not have a case, why am I stuck in a cell on the eighth floor of the government center?

The agony of simple solitude was often excruciating. Loneliness encompassed me and was, at times, physically suffocating. I had no one to talk to, nothing to do, and there seemed to be not a single action I could take to improve my lot. As each day inched by, I felt myself slipping deeper into lethargy. A few months earlier I was the picture of health, working a good hard job. But by late March my weight had dropped from 185 pounds to about 140 pounds and I had lost a considerable amount of hair.

Other than my attorney, I could only see visitors once every two weeks. Ray came faithfully, but the time was fleeting, and the conversation strained.

Beyond that, there were occasional opportunities to telephone my family at home in Columbus. We never discussed specifics about the case, for we could not know who might be listening or what use they might make of any information. Instead, we played a game with one another. I assured Mom that I was being treated well, and she assured me that everyone at home was all right. But I could hear the tension in her voice. I knew, too, that my family had to be strapped financially. They had scraped together what they could to pay Dennis White, and they were also saving for another trip to Dallas. They all wanted to be present for the trial.

The cell next to mine was occupied by a young prisoner, whose family brought him a small portable TV set. The sound of its muted tones was tantalizing, especially when the news was on. I had the feeling that everyone else in Dallas knew more about my case than I did, and I craved information. Somewhere out there were a dozen men and women who would soon be given the responsibility to decide whether I should walk back out into the free world or walk into the execution chamber in Huntsville. What was the local media telling them about me?

I discovered that a bolt was missing from a seam in the metal-plated wall between our cells. If I stood at just the right angle, I could watch TV through this bolt hole. I called out to my neighbor, asking him to turn up the volume, and he obliged.

That same day I wrote a letter to Mom, and mentioned this encouraging development. About six hours after I handed this letter to a guard, in a sealed envelope, a construction crew arrived and shored up my cell walls, making sure that they covered up the bolt hole.

Once again, I had nothing to do but think, and this drove me deeper toward despair. I was twenty-eight years old, just on the brink, I had thought, of getting my life together. Suddenly it was all turned upside down.

Over and over I relived the past few months in my mind, most especially the events of November 27. Why had I not dumped David Harris early in the day? Why had I let him suck me into this mess? It was so easy, in hindsight, to decide what I should have done. But hindsight and regrets could not get me out of this cell.

I berated myself: Hey, you used to think you had some control over your life, and look where you are now.

I wrote to Kathy in Jacksonville and told her not to come to visit me in Dallas. It was better for her to forget about me. I wondered what the future held for her.

Mulder filed a motion to quash the subpoenas of the thirty-five witnesses from Vidor, and Judge Metcalfe called a hearing in March to decide the issue.

Dennis White and Edith James were forced to take the witness stand to justify each and every one of the thirty-five subpoenas. White grumbled that this was going to expose our entire case to the prosecution, but he had no choice. In the end, Judge Metcalfe quashed nineteen of our thirty-five subpoenas. All of the forbidden witnesses were faculty members of the Vidor Independent School District who would have much to say about the character of the prosecution's star witness.

But this was not the most critical setback. At this same hearing,

Mulder argued that evidence regarding Harris's criminal record should be barred from the trial. He said that it consisted of "extraneous offenses" that did not pertain to the case at hand.

In large part, Judge Metcalfe agreed, but he decided to reserve judgment on the specifics. During the trial, he ruled any testimony regarding Harris's criminal background would have to be presented outside the presence of the jury first. Then he would decide whether or not it was permissible for the jury to hear it. He indicated that he would allow the jury to hear evidence showing that the teenager had been convicted of serious crimes prior to the date in question, but he would not allow White to tell the jury about the pending charges of burglary and armed robbery because they were not yet disposed of by the courts.

White was visibly shaken by this decision, for it cut out the heart of our defensive strategy. He had to convince the jury that Harris had strong motivation to testify against me—as strong as the threat of a possible life sentence for his crimes in Vidor. What's more, he needed to show that Harris had implicated his friends in the house trailer burglary, just as he had implicated me in Officer Wood's murder. Without the chance to portray to the jury the true character of the prosecution's star witness, we were in serious trouble.

My attorney's anxiety was infectious. It heightened the awesome realization that had begun to form in my mind during the habeas corpus hearing in January. Despite White's counsel, this did not appear to be an unbiased search for truth. It was more of a public relations spectacle that boiled down to this:

Dallas authorities had to blame one of two people for this crime. One was David Harris, a fresh-faced boy with a familiar Texas twang who, although he had gotten himself into some trouble along the way, had a glib tongue and, on the surface, a likable personality. The other was me, an outsider, a blue-collar worker new to Texas who presented them with the image of a long-haired pot-smoking "hippie."

Another factor was the Texas political climate, which seemed to believe that the public cried out for harsh justice, demanding that someone should die in retaliation for Officer Wood's death. Because of his youth, David Harris could not be executed for murdering a police officer. On the other hand, a twenty-eight-year-old whom the judge himself described as a "drifter" was a prime candidate for the electric chair.

In sum, the district attorney's office had been forced into a decision. Should it try David Harris for the murder of Officer Wood, or should it try me? If the prosecution blamed me, it had a witness who said he was sitting in the passenger's seat at the time. If it chose Harris, it had no witness.

Back home in Columbus, whenever the ache grew too painful, Mom grabbed a supply of gospel music tapes, slid behind the wheel of her car, plugged in the tapes, and drove out into the country, with no particular destination. When she found herself satisfyingly lost, she pulled the car over and sat for a time, praying.

"Lord," she said aloud, "You know Randy didn't do this. I know Randy didn't do this. Please bring him home. And please, Lord, while he's there, keep Your arm around him."

7

THE JURY

THE TRIAL BEGAN on March 28, 1977, with the tedious process of selecting jurors from a pool assembled, ostensibly, via a random sampling of the computerized records of Dallas County's 654,000 registered voters.

Each side, of course, hoped to impanel a jury that was, at the very least, impartial, and there were three ways to weed out jurors who might be biased. First, Judge Metcalfe could excuse any juror "for cause" if he was convinced that bias existed within that juror's heart. In addition, both the prosecution and the defense were granted fifteen arbitrary strikes. During the course of jury selection, each side could excuse as many as fifteen jurors without stating any reason. Whenever possible, we preferred to have the judge strike a juror "for cause," so that we could hoard our arbitrary strikes.

Dennis White was concerned that the state had an unfair advantage in this process, and Judge Metcalfe listened carefully as my attorney made a curious request, based upon a rumor. It was the stuff of local legend that the district attorney's office kept careful records, on index cards, of citizens who had previously served as jurors. In serious cases, it was said, prosecutors checked prospective jurors against these files, to determine whether or not they had convicted someone of a similar offense in the past. If it was true, Mulder could use these files in an attempt to load the jury with men and women who had previously voted for the death penalty. White said that, if the rumored files existed, the defense should have equal access to them.

Mulder argued against the motion, noting that he did not bother to use the files.

Judge Metcalfe said to White, "I don't know of any authority that says you are entitled to those cards, it is certainly a work product of the state and as such is not subject to discovery under the code of criminal procedure." He denied the request.

Sitting alongside White at the defense table, I realized that both Mulder and Judge Metcalfe had tacitly acknowledged that the rumored files did, indeed, exist.

Sporting a fresh haircut obtained from the jail barber and wearing a clean pressed suit, courtesy of my family, I once more fought to keep my mouth shut as the attorneys questioned prospective jurors. I found it difficult to keep my hands from shaking. The response was, perhaps, due to my poor diet and lack of sleep, combined with almost unbearable tension.

"What do you think of the death sentence?" was, perhaps, the most common question put to the prospective jurors, and the answer was critical. Ever since the U.S. Supreme Court struck down all existing death penalty statutes, state legislatures and their courts had struggled to create laws and procedures for capital crimes that would receive the approval of the nation's highest court. The process was still in its nit-picking phase. Except for Gilmore, who wanted to die, the Court had not yet allowed a single execution in this new era. Death penalty advocates moaned that the "liberals" on the Court would not allow anyone to be executed; the Court responded that its paramount concern was fairness.

Jury selection in capital cases throughout the U.S. was codified by a 1968 Supreme Court decision known as *Witherspoon v. Illinois,* referred to in lawyer's shorthand simply as *Witherspoon.* Here, the Court spelled out the proper procedure for jury selection in a capital case. In the past, states had allowed judges to disqualify prospective jurors because they opposed the death penalty, but the *Witherspoon* decision said that this was unfair. A jury of one's peers must necessarily reflect contemporary community standards, and the modern community was in the midst of a great debate over the wisdom of the death penalty. If a jury comprised solely death penalty supporters, it did not reflect the full balance of contemporary views. *Witherspoon* allowed a judge to disqualify a potential juror who said, unequivocally, that he or she could *never* vote for the death penalty, but the court could not exclude a death penalty opponent who proclaimed that he or she could follow the dictates of law regardless of personal views.

Courts throughout the land now followed the lead of *Witherspoon,* but in Texas and some other states, additional rules were implemented. In Texas, a capital trial is conducted in two distinct phases. The first is the guilt-or-innocence phase. If the defendant is found guilty, the trial enters its penalty phase, wherein the prosecution argues for the death penalty and the defense seeks life imprisonment.

Texas was concerned that a juror, knowing that the second phase of the trial would require a life-or-death decision, might allow his or her judgment to be affected during the first phase. Thus, under the provisions of Texas Penal Code 12.31(b), "A prospective juror shall be disqualified from serving as a juror unless he states under oath that the mandatory penalty of death or imprisonment for life will not affect his deliberations on any issue of fact."

This statute had never been approved or disapproved by the U.S. Supreme Court, but there were many attorneys in Texas who believed that it violated the strict jury selection procedures dictated by *Witherspoon.* Some prosecutors, therefore, decided not to rely upon it, while others, notably the hard-line law-and-order district attorneys in Dallas County, were determined to bring the full weight of state law to bear upon the defendant.

This is what Mulder and his assistants, Winfield Scott and Stephen Tokely, were getting at when they asked a prospective juror's opinion of the death penalty. If the answer was hesitant, the district attorneys were happy to explain what happens when someone is electrocuted: his eyeballs explode, his fingernails and toenails pop off, he bleeds from every orifice of his body.

The graphic description was repeated many times. Afterward, if the listener shuddered and expressed doubt that he or she could take the required oath, Judge Metcalfe would promptly excuse the juror "for cause," thus saving one of the state's arbitrary strikes.

Mrs. Francis Mahon said she had always been a believer in capital punishment, but she was unsure that she could swear that the issue would not affect her deliberations. "I just don't know," she said. "I really do not know whether it would affect me or not when it comes right down to it."

Judge Metcalfe asked her, "What you're saying, you cannot give us your assurance that you would not be influenced by the punishment in answering the questions on fact issues?"

She replied, "Well, I'm saying I could be influenced and I think most anyone could be."

Judge Metcalfe excused her for cause.

The process dragged on slowly.

Prospective juror Forrest Jenson declared, "Well, I think I believe in letting the punishment fit the crime. I've never had to decide whether or not somebody lived or died and I don't know if I could do it or not. . . . I'm just human like everybody else. . . . I don't believe anybody could [not be affected] because you might as well get a computer to sit on the jury."

Judge Metcalfe excused him for cause.

Mrs. Nelda Coyle favored the death penalty in some circumstances, and said she would vote for it if the facts of the case called for it. Would the overriding issue of life or death affect her deliberations in the initial phase. "I cannot tell you because I do not know," she admitted.

Judge Metcalfe, noting that the court was "in a situation where you are not able to give the assurance that the law requires," excused her for cause.

And so it went. These were jurors that we may very well have wanted, for they seemed to bring a reasonable human orientation to the task. But the judge excused them all.

During the process of jury selection, White informed me that he had filed a motion for a psychiatric examination of David Harris. Mulder had consented on the condition that I also submit to the procedure.

This was good news, for I was confident of my own sanity, and quite willing to have a professional compare me with Harris. In fact, two psychiatrists interviewed me.

The first man came early in April. He met me in a small visiting room on the eighth floor of the government center and introduced himself as Dr. James Grigson. He reminded me of an ostrich, tall and skinny. He placed a pencil and a few sheets of paper in front of me, asked me to look at some drawings, and copy them onto the paper.

They were simple line drawings of basic shapes: a square, a circle, and a few more intricate designs. "You want me to draw them exactly as they are?" I asked.

"Just copy them any way you like," Dr. Grigson said. "I'm going to get a cup of coffee. I'll be back in a few minutes."

Left alone, I dutifully copied the drawings, wondering what in the world this activity could disclose about my mental condition.

I was finished by the time Dr. Grigson returned. He glanced at the drawings, gathered them up and said, "Okay, I've got a couple of questions for you. Just answer them as best you can. What does 'a rolling stone gathers no moss' mean to you?"

"Are you kidding?" I asked, still wondering what these parlor games had to do with my mental stability.

"No, I'd really like to know."

I told him that it meant that it was difficult for people to get close to or cling to a person who doesn't stay in one place for any length of time.

He made some notes, then asked, "Okay, how about 'a bird in the hand is worth two in the bush?' "

I replied that it would be silly to let go of something you have for only a chance of getting something else. "If you can get something else, fine," I said, "but don't give up what you have in order to get it."

Dr. Grigson made a few additional notes and left.

After ten days in court, we had managed to select only five jurors, and we all knew that we were in for an extended process. Once, during a break in the proceedings, I found myself in the holding cell behind the courtroom, housed alongside a defendant in another capital case. He told me that his trial was beginning its jury selection phase that very day.

Late that afternoon, I was again waiting in the holding cell, prior to being returned to the eighth floor, when I had a chance to speak with the man again. To my surprise, I realized that he had already been convicted. In this one swift day his jury was selected, the prosecution presented its case, the defense countered, the attorneys argued, the judge issued instructions, the jury deliberated, and found him guilty!

This knowledge bolstered my confidence in White and James. It appeared that it was going to take them nearly a full month just to impanel a jury to hear my case. Obviously they were working hard for me.

Mrs. Lloyd White was not happy about being a prospective juror in a capital case. She told the court, "I think I believe in capital punishment but I don't want to have anything to do with it, is that clear?"

Indeed, it was. The prosecution wanted her off of the jury, and we wanted her on. Edith James probed, and got her to admit that, if she was impaneled on the jury, she would attempt to perform her duty honestly, despite her personal feelings. But Judge Metcalfe questioned her again, and when she admitted, "I couldn't lay my feelings aside," he excused her for cause.

Prospective juror Curtis Williams vacillated as to whether or not he could vote for the death penalty. At one point he declared, "I just couldn't." Later, he softened that position, saying, "I don't think I could." Still later he allowed, "I think I could."

Somewhat frustrated, the judge posed the question in the exact language of Section 12.31(b): "Would you be affected in your deliberations by the punishment of death or life imprisonment?"

"That's right."

Judge Metcalfe excused him for cause.

As soon as I was brought into court one morning, I told Dennis White that I had a few questions for him. He demurred. He had to rush off to another courtroom for a hearing in the civil case he was handling. He told me that Edith James would remain to represent me in the continuing jury selection process, and we would have a chance to speak later in the afternoon. He hustled out through the swinging doors at the back of the courtroom, and I turned my attention to James.

Suddenly we heard two quick sharp popping sounds—unmistakable gunshots—come from the hallway. Before I could react, I felt the pawlike hands of a bailiff grab the back of my shirt collar. He jerked me up from my chair, dragged me to the back of the courtroom, threw me into the prisoners' hallway, and slammed the door shut.

I remained there for about fifteen minutes without any word, frantic with concern over White, whom I considered my friend as well as my attorney.

Finally, the bailiff returned and told me that a man had been shot in the hallway. It was not Mr. White. Apparently the victim was a defendant in another trial who, unbeknownst to the bailiff assigned to him, and been granted bail. When the court officer saw the defendant walking down the hallway, he thought the man was attempting to escape. He shouted at him to stop and heard the response: "Fuck you!" Without further debate, the bailiff drew his gun and shot the man in the legs, twice.

The incident took place in a hallway crowded with prospective jurors waiting to be called in my case. Each of them received a lesson in the way they did things in Dallas County.

The second psychiatrist came to visit me on April 15. The date was fixed in my mind because I was filling out my income taxes at the time, reasoning that I would get a refund of more than $250. I was busy with this task when a guard appeared and announced, "You have a visitor."

"Who is it?"

"Some damn doctor wants to talk to you."

On the way to the visiting room, we happened to walk past the medical department, which had a huge clock on the wall. I glanced at it and noted the time. It was about 2:00 P.M.

We met in the same room where I had scrawled my drawings for Dr. Grigson. I was already seated when a fastidiously dressed man entered and introduced himself as Dr. John Holbrook. He set a cup of coffee and a pack of cigarettes on the table.

For about an hour, he asked me what seemed to be typical psychiatric questions, probing for information on my relationship with my family. The conversation seemed of little consequence.

He left briefly and then returned. "Well, Mr. Adams," he said, "that's just about it. I really have only one more question to ask you."

"What's that?"

"About how long have we been in here?"

What a strange question? I thought. Where did that come from? "In this room?" I asked. He nodded and I responded, "I don't know. An hour and a half, two hours, maybe."

"Would you believe we've been in here three hours?"

"No."

"Would you believe we've been in here four hours?"

"No."

He then declared that we had been in the room for three hours, but I still did not believe him.

The same guard took me back to my cell. On the way, I asked him, "How long was I in there?"

"About an hour and a half," he answered, and as we passed the medical department, I checked the clock on the wall and confirmed that the visit with Dr. Holbrook had lasted approximately one hour and forty-five minutes. I could only conclude that the psychiatrist must be a bit eccentric.

I wrote to Mom to finalize her plans for coming down for the testimony phase of the trial. I reported that I had just received a visit from a second "quack," and added:

> Mr. White is confident in defending me, and I am ready to take it to court. I pray that I get a fair trial, and the state doesn't pull any illegal things, but I don't put anything past them.

At first, Penny McDonald stated that she could not vote for the death penalty in this type of case, but upon further questioning by the prosecution she said, "I think I would have to know more of the circumstances. . . . I can't say I'm flat against capital punishment until I have heard the facts of the case."

Judge Metcalfe asked, "Well, are you saying that even though you're against it, since it is a law, that you could serve on a jury and vote for it if the facts were proper?"

"Yes, I could," she replied.

Assistant District Attorney Scott asked, "Would the mandatory sentence of death or life affect your deliberation on the issue of guilt or innocence?"

"Not the guilt or innocence. If the man is guilty, he's guilty, and the next step is the next step."

Scott pressed. Would her personal views affect her decision if and when she was involved in the penalty phase?

"Might," she admitted. "I don't know. Like I said before, I would have to hear all of the circumstances and all of the facts. I think anyone . . . would inject their own feelings."

Scott asked, "Would you set aside your conscience?"

She declared. "If I was on a jury, I don't know how I could do anything else."

She seemed like a fair-minded person, but perhaps she was too honest to be on this jury. The oath required by Texas law was the sticking point.

"I can't take that oath and be honest about it," Ms. McDonald declared. "I can't take an oath and tell y'all that I'm going to knock out the whole fact that the death penalty is involved in it, because I don't know when I get there. I don't know about the facts or anything. The facts may prove that I could do it, and I would do it and vote for the death penalty."

James advised, "To keep an open mind, that's all we are really asking you to do."

"You're asking me to take an oath," Ms. McDonald clarified, "and I can't take an oath."

Thus, under the provisions of Section 12.31(b), Judge Metcalfe excused her for cause.

Interspersed with the jury selection procedure, Judge Metcalfe made decisions on a number of defense motions. Most of them were routine, and these seemed to clarify White's previous explanation to me. There were, indeed, rules at work here designed to ferret out the truth. For example, the judge instructed Mulder that the state would be required to provide the defense with a list of any and all witnesses that it might call during the initial presentation of its case. That way, we could not be caught off guard.

The judge also notified Mulder that, immediately after a witness testified, if that witness had given any previous written statement to the authorities, the state was required to supply a copy of such a statement to the defense before cross-examination began. Judge Metcalfe granted White's routine motion and Mulder promised, "I will have that."

As to White's previous request for copies of the criminal arrest records of witnesses, the judge declared, "I will grant that motion only as to the witnesses the state intends to call in the case in chief, since as a practical matter very often they don't know who they will call in rebuttal." He added a second consideration, repeating that White could present evidence concerning David Harris's criminal record prior to the murder, but he would not be allowed to tell the jury about the pending charges of burglary and armed robbery.

White then raised the issue of what was known as the *Brady* motion, which required that the prosecution turn over to the defense any information helpful to our case.

To settle the matter, Metcalfe asked Mulder, "Have you got anything at all in your file or do you have access or have you had access to anything that you know of that would go to show the innocence of this defendant?"

Mulder replied, "No, I have nothing."

Another thorny question dealt with my wardrobe. Mom had shipped me a new suit to wear for the trial. It fit well, but White did not like the light shade of gray. He suggested that a conventional dark suit with a white shirt would be the most appropriate outfit to counteract the image that the prosecution wanted to portray. Hearing this, Mom gathered every available suit and sport jacket from the closets of my brothers and brothers-in-law and brought them with her when she returned to Dallas for the trial. Some of them hung a bit awkwardly on my thinning frame, but they were usable; and I could mix and match the jackets and slacks so that, even if the trial was an extended one, I could wear a different outfit every day. In fact, I had so many sets of clothes to wear that the state complained that it did not have enough storage room to accommodate me.

Dennis White presented a formal argument to Judge Metcalfe on this issue. He pointed out that newspapers had characterized me as a "transient hitchhiker," and we wanted to counteract the image.

Is this theater or law? I wondered.

The judge ruled in our favor, requiring the bailiffs to set aside a special dressing room for me. It was a small but encouraging victory.

White had one final complaint. Mulder had still not complied with his part of the bargain to have Harris examined by a psychiatrist. The first assistant district attorney promised to have Dr. Grigson examine the boy on the afternoon of April 26.

One day prior to that, after four weeks of tedium, Judge Metcalfe impaneled a dozen men and women to sit in judgment on me. They were identified for the record as Mrs. Willie Milholland, Mr. Mankin, Mrs. Fain, Paul Matlock, Mrs. Pritchett, Mrs. Burgess, Mr. Scublin, Mrs. Lucien, Doris Hooper, Elliott Raney, Lester Hutchins, and Giles Fizzell.

Most of them were well past middle age and lived in the more affluent Dallas suburbs.

In theory, they were my peers.

8

THE PROSECUTION

THE COURTROOM WAS a sea of blue uniforms on April 26; it seemed as if every off-duty officer in Dallas County was there to make sure that justice was done. My brother Ron, my sister Mary, and my brother-in-law Ken sat near the defense table on the left side of the room; Mary had worked in a law office for several years, and she busied herself taking notes in shorthand. Mom, Ray, and Nancy had to remain in the witness room or the hallway, for they were scheduled as character witnesses and, like all witnesses, were not supposed to listen to the testimony of others. Many more of my family and friends were here in spirit, for Mom made sure that a prayer circle was under way back in Columbus.

Out in the hallway, Mom allowed herself the luxury of a day-dream. As soon as this jury found me innocent, everyone would apologize and tell her that they had made a dreadful mistake. They would say, "Oh, we are so sorry that we put you people through this. . . ."

Inside the courtroom, the realities were different. Henry Wade himself, flanked by two sheriff's deputies, sat directly behind me. He was the personification of law and order in Dallas County and his grim expression as he stared at the back of my head sent a clear message to everyone. At the very last moment, before the judge's entrance, Officer Wood's twenty one year old widow Toni, dressed in black, was escorted into the courtroom by a police captain in full dress uniform. She occupied a prominent spot on the prosecution side of the courtroom, drew a pure white handkerchief from her pocketbook, and dabbed at her eyes.

The bailiff called us to our feet and Judge Metcalfe entered. Nothing felt real.

The jurors were isolated in a small room off to one side, behind a paper-thin door that did little to prevent them from hearing what was going on in court. Furthermore, reporters were present in abundance when Mulder, arguing a procedural point with White, got off the initial salvo. He nearly shouted out the statement, "It was my idea and my thought that we had this man polygraphed. He failed miserably. He had his independent polygrapher to come up to the jail and polygraph him and he again failed. . . . I had David Harris and he passed it."

White objected, but, of course, the damage was done. In the first place, I wondered if Mulder had misstated the facts. In my recollection, one man had given me a lie detector test. Second, the laws of Texas declared that polygraph evidence was too unreliable to be admissible in court. Nevertheless, the notion was now safely lodged within the memories of the jurors that I had failed two lie detector tests.

In restoring order, the judge admonished both attorneys not to refer to polygraph tests in the presence of the jury.

Mulder agreed, and demurred, "I brought that up to show the court my good faith and we were just interested in getting to the bottom of this matter."

Finally, the jurors entered, and for the remainder of the trial, the widow never took her eyes off of them.

Mulder opened the state's case by calling Police Officer Teresa Turko to the witness stand. She, too, was attired in full uniform. She testified that, as Officer Wood approached the driver's window of the car that night, she positioned herself at the correct backup position, at the right rear. She described the shooting briefly, then Mulder asked, "And how many people did you see in the blue compact?"

"I only saw one and that was the driver," Turko answered. This seemed favorable to me, for Harris claimed we were both in the car.

"Did you see him full face?"

"No, sir, I did not." From her perspective, she said, she could only see the back of the driver's head and his jacket. But she could discern that he was a white man.

"Would you describe his hair for us, please?" Mulder asked.

"It was dark brown and it was more fuller than mine, it was kind of bushy and stuck out of the sides and came down at least to his collar."

Mulder directed Turko to step down from the witness stand and approach the defense table. He asked if my hair was like that of the man who shot Officer Wood.

"It's different," Turko said. "It's a lot shorter and it's more close to the head."

"How about the color, is the color right?"

"The color is the same."

Sending Turko back to the witness stand, Mulder now instructed that David Harris be brought into the courtroom. A few moments passed before the chief witness entered. Mulder took one glance at the boy's Levi jeans and open-necked western shirt and petitioned Judge Metcalfe for a recess, which the judge granted without discussion.

When court reconvened, Harris reappeared in a three-piece suit that looked as if it had just come off the rack at Sears. His hair was freshly trimmed.

Mulder instructed Harris not to say anything. He asked the teenager to stand in front of Turko, turn to the side, and then away. Then he sent Harris out of the room.

"Did you get a good look?" Mulder asked.

"Yes, sir," Turko answered.

"Okay. And will you tell the jury whether or not his hair color and the style of his hair is consistent and compatible with the bushy-haired driver of the compact vehicle or whether his hair style and hair color is different, which is it?"

"It is different, most different . . . his hair is a lot lighter, it's more blonde than dark brown . . . and it's a lot shorter and very close-cut to the head."

Mulder noted that Turko had submitted two written reports to the Crimes Against Persons Bureau, on November 28, the day of the murder, and again on December 9. As required by Judge Metcalfe's previous order on the Brady motion, he handed copies of these statements to White as he released the witness for cross-examination. The court granted a brief recess, so that the defense could examine the statements.

White read them with interest, and found them useful enough so that, when court reconvened, he offered them as the first two defense exhibits, and confronted Turko with them. In her first statement, written the day of the crime, she had reported that the killer "was wearing a heavy dark coat with a large collar . . . I could not see his face but his hair appeared to be dark brown and at least collar length."

White asked, "Did you refer in that statement in any place to bushy hair?"

"No, sir."

"Is it a fact, Miss Turko, in your experience in the dark every color whether it's blonde, dark brown, blue, or whatever, appears to be darker than it would be if it was in a bright light?"

"Generally that is the case. I do have my flashlight on, though."

White then referred to her second statement on December 9. Once again she had said, "I could barely see inside the vehicle." What's more, White stressed, in this statement, as she had repeated in court today, she clearly reported that there was only one occupant in the vehicle.

For the past four months, David Harris had been enrolled in a "teen challenge" rehabilitation program affiliated with the Assemblies of

God. Along with sixteen other boys, he lived a regimented lifestyle on a ninety-two acre ranch in Floresville, Texas, near San Antonio. Now he appeared in front of the jury as a rather ingratiating sixteen-year-old boy, with a healthy tan.

But from the moment he began his testimony he belied his appearance. Mulder knew that Harris's credibility was the key to a conviction, and he attempted to steal our thunder by leading his own witness through a recitation of those incriminating facts that he knew the jury had to hear. Harris related the details of his crimes prior to the date in question.

Then he told the jury that he arrived in Dallas around noon on Saturday, November 27, and had just passed a Sears building, he said, when ". . . I saw a hitchhiker so I picked him up and he said he ran out of gas. So I was going to take him to get some gas and he told me, 'Thank you for picking me up, it was freezing out there.' "

"What did his hair look like?" Mulder asked.

Harris replied, "Bushy hair and a mustache . . ."

Following Mulder's directions, Harris identified me as the hitchhiker, but he noted that my hair, that day, "was a little bit longer and stuck out a little bit more."

After we spent the day together, Harris said, it was about 9:00 P.M. when we entered the drive-in theater, and *The Swinging Cheerleaders* was already showing. He said that we watched the rest of that movie and the first half of the next movie before we left about midnight. I was driving. It was some time later, on Inwood Avenue, when a police cruiser stopped the car.

Mulder asked, "What did Dale do?"

"He pulled over to the side of the road."

"What happened next?"

"He rolled down the window and . . . I said, 'Get out and show him your license,' because I didn't want him to see me in there."

"Why didn't you want to be seen in the car?"

"Because it was stolen and I was running away."

Harris demonstrated how he slumped down in the front seat, with his nose against the dashboard, so that the officer would not see him.

"All right," Mulder said. "What is the next thing you saw Dale do?"

"I saw him get the gun from underneath the seat."

"Did he say anything to you at that time?"

"I asked him what he was going to do and he said, 'I will handle this'. . . . Well, I was looking between the backseat and the front seat, between the bucket headrest, and I saw the officer walk by and he said, 'Let me see your license,' or something of that nature. And then Dale started shooting."

Harris told the jury that the officer fell after being hit with the first shot, and that I then pumped several more bullets into him before speeding away.

Mulder asked, "Did you say anything to Dale after he drove off?"

"I asked him why the hell he done that."

"What did he say?"

"He said, 'Don't worry about it,' that they didn't get a license or nothing."

According to Harris, I drove around for about a half hour before winding my way back to the motel. Then I just left him in the car and went inside my room. Harris found a parking lot, caught some sleep in the car and, in the morning, hightailed it back to Vidor.

Mulder continued his ploy of having Harris admit to the incriminating details, rather than allowing White to pull them out. He asked, "David, did you ever tell anybody that you killed that police officer?"

"Yes, sir."

"Who did you tell?"

"Hootie . . ."

"What did you tell them that for?"

"I thought it was making me big to their standards."

"But you are telling this jury today that it was Dale Adams, Randall Dale Adams that shot and killed that police officer?"

"Yes, sir."

My sister Nancy, supposedly sequestered in the hallway, was troubled to realize that she could hear everything that was going on in the courtroom. She wondered what good it was to sequester the witnesses when microphones amplified every word so that it could filter past the thin walls.

She heard Harris identify me as the killer and tears poured down her cheeks.

Out of the crowd of sullen, suspicious faces, a woman approached. She had a sympathetic look in her eyes. "Don't cry, honey," she said. "Is that your brother in there?"

Nancy nodded and sobbed, "Yes, but he didn't do it. They don't know him like I do. He didn't do it."

The woman sighed and said, "All the families say that. Let me take you downstairs and I'll show you all the people who didn't do it."

Nancy felt her cheeks flush with anger. "Get away from me," she growled. "Leave me alone."

Before delving too deeply into his cross-examination, White again argued for the right to introduce evidence concerning Harris's crimes after the murder, taking the court into an area that Judge Metcalfe admitted was "maybe fuzzy."

First the judge excused the jury, and then ordered the volume lowered on the witness microphone to prevent the jury from hearing any details of this line of questioning.

Under cross-examination, Harris admitted that he had burglarized a house trailer and committed the armed robbery of O'Banion's Convenience Store. He further admitted that, after he turned himself in to the Vidor Police, he signed a statement implicating his friends in the crimes.

Now that the facts were elicited for the court and the trial transcript, White sought to get them before the jury. Judge Metcalfe asked, "Mr. White . . . I would like to know how the later commission of a burglary and a robbery by this witness is material to this case?"

To White, the answer was obvious, and he could not comprehend why the judge failed to see it. "Your Honor," he sputtered, "I believe . . . that he is the perpetrator of the crime and I believe that the evidence will show he was on a criminal spree and he was committing one crime after another."

"In other words, you want to show he is a criminal generally, is that right, is that it?"

"Not just a criminal generally, but it's the specific time span from November 26th to December 19th that he was on a criminal spree committing a series of related crimes."

Mulder appeared willing to compromise. He said, "I'm rather in agreement with Mr. White as regards his past difficulties, those that occurred prior to the murder of the police officer . . . It's all right to go ahead and bring those out."

"I'm not concerned about that, Mr. Mulder," the judge said, "because I'm going to allow those anyway. But I am concerned about the burglary and robbery that occurred after the commission of this offense and prior to today and how they relate to the guilt or innocence of the defendant in this trial."

White tried again: "He has a propensity of committing crimes and blaming it on the closest person at hand."

Judge Metcalfe elicited an opinion from an appellate attorney who happened to be in the courtroom and determined that the additional crimes, committed after the murder, would only be relevant if they were tied closely to the murder in time and place. They were not, the judge ruled. He reaffirmed his position: He would allow the jury to hear testimony concerning Harris's criminal actions prior to the murder of Officer Wood, but not after.

Metcalfe went over Harris's previous statements to the police and instructed White, line by line, what he could and could not bring to the jury's attention. Then he gave Mulder a five-minute recess to explain all of this to Harris, so that the witness would not blunder.

The jury was brought back into the courtroom, but before White could take up his cross-examination of Harris, the court accommodated another prosecution witness. Bill French, owner of the Hines Boulevard Pawn Shop, had to close his store to come to court, so everyone agreed to let him speak his short piece and get back to work. To our surprise, the brief testimony gave us a piece of powerful ammunition to use against Harris.

On direct examination, French testified that I had pawned my eight-track stereo with him on November 27. Mulder did not ask him what time that transaction took place. But on cross-examination, White did ask, and French replied, "The best I can tell it was around noon or a little before."

With those words still hanging in the air, French was excused and Harris was recalled for cross-examination.

White immediately broached the subject of time. He referred to Harris's previous statement, in which he said that I had changed my shirt at the motel ". . . sometime between 2:00 P.M. and 3:00 P.M., is that correct, sir?"

"Yes, sir."

"And from that motel you asked him if he would be interested in going with you to pawn some items, is that correct?"

"Yes, sir."

"Do you have any conception of what time it was when you finally got your items pawned?"

"Around four o'clock I reckon."

White paused to let the jury digest the four-hour discrepancy between what Harris said and what the pawnbroker had told them only a few minutes earlier.

When White tried to get Harris to describe what he was wearing the night of the murder, the witness required some prodding. At first, Harris denied that he was wearing a fur-lined jacket, but White reminded him of his testimony at the January 21 hearing, where he said he wore "blue jeans and my blue fur-lined coat." Only then did Harris seem to remember the coat.

Now my attorney took Harris through the day once more, establishing that he had the means to commit murder, the gun, and since he was admittedly at the scene of the crime, he obviously had the opportunity.

White now moved toward the touchy subject of Harris's criminal record, in order to establish that the boy had a motive for gunning down Officer Wood. Judge Metcalfe listened very carefully, as did Mulder, ready to object if White crossed into forbidden territory. White got Harris to admit that he was on juvenile probation for a series of burglaries committed in 1975 and 1976, and for the theft of his mother's car. Then he asked, "Well, is part of that supervision if you were instructed—if you were to get in any further difficulties with the law that this supervisory status would be revoked and you would be placed in some kind of custody?"

"Yes, sir."

"And is it not a fact that knowing that if you got in trouble and were arrested that you would be kept in detention, that you burglarized Mr. Cunningham's house and stolen his car and come to Dallas and pawned some of the stolen items?"

"Yes, sir."

"And you knew this when the policeman approached you on that day, did you not, when the policeman was murdered?"

"Yes, sir."

There was the motivation.

White now sought to show that, following the killing, it was Harris, not I, who exhibited guilty behavior. He asked, "All right. Now, after this murder you are saying that Dale Adams here, the defendant . . . drove right on home and said forget it, is that your testimony?"

"Yes, sir."

"And insofar as you know he went in, went to bed and whatever?"

"Yes, sir."

White retraced Harris's steps back to Vidor. By the evening following the murder, the boy was back in his hometown, watching the ten o'clock news at Hootie Nelson's house. Lynn Brown was also present. White asked, "Is it a fact when the story of the policeman in Dallas came on the television you turned to these people and said, 'I wasted that pig'?"

"No, sir."

"What did you say?"

"I told them I was there whenever he got shot, that I did it."

"That you did it?"

"Yes, sir."

"Did you tell anybody else you killed the policeman?"

"Dennis Johnson and Randy Hayes."

When White finished his cross-examination, we were both satisfied. We wondered how anyone could not harbor a reasonable doubt concerning David Harris's story.

Others wondered, too. In the hallway, Mom overheard two uniformed policemen talking. "They don't have anything on this guy," one of them said. "Mulder's got his work cut out for him. He's going to lose this one."

Mom turned to face the speaker, grateful and relieved that he had come to the only possible conclusion. She smiled and introduced herself. "I'm Randall Adam's mother," she said, holding out a hand.

Shock registered on the faces of both officers. Abruptly they walked away.

The prosecution called Joe Perry, former owner of another pawn shop in Grand Prairie, who testified that I was the man who had sold him electrician's tools on November 27. Mulder elicited from him the fact that my hair was now shorter and neater than it had been that day.

On cross-examination White asked what time of day the sale had occurred.

"Between about ten and one," Perry answered. Once again we had cast serious doubt on Harris's timing of the day's events.

After the day in court, Mom returned to her motel room and jumped into the shower, as if it could wash away the frustration. She worried that she was becoming paranoid. It seemed as if everyone in Dallas responded to her with rudeness and suspicion. They could offer no proof, but she and her daughters were convinced that they were being watched constantly. What were they going to do—stage a breakout from the Dallas County jail?

Mom had always tried to live by the philosophy that if you treat people nicely, they will respond in kind; but it was not working in this environment.

The next morning the jury was sequestered once more as Judge Metcalfe conducted a lengthy hearing on the admissibility of my signed statement, the one that the Dallas newspapers had reported to be a "confession." Mulder called Detective J.W. Johnson to the stand.

The detective testified about the interrogation that he and Investigator Luther conducted following my arrest. He said that he and Luther had approached me at the job site about 10:00 A.M., that I agreed voluntarily to come downtown with them and that we arrived at the Crimes Against Persons office of the Dallas police department about 11:30 A.M. Following my arraignment, interrogation began about 1:00 P.M. He said we talked for a total of about five hours, during which time he provided me with a sandwich and coffee.

I tried to hide my discomfort from everyone in the courtroom. I was brought up to believe in the honesty of the police officer, yet something was very wrong here. How could Johnson say that the interrogation lasted only five hours? The way I remembered it, it was much longer.

"And did he in fact make a statement to you?" Mulder asked.

"Yes, sir," Johnson replied.

"Did you add anything in there that you thought should be in there or did you strictly go by what he wanted in the statement?"

"Strictly what he said he wanted in it." Johnson said that he took his handwritten copy of the statement to clerk-typist Carla Crenshaw, who prepared five typed copies. After reading it to me as I followed along on my own copy, he said that I signed all five copies in the presence of a witness, Crenshaw.

To my surprise, Mulder then produced a second statement and had Johnson identify it. The detective said that after signing the original one, I stated that I "left out the part about the pistol," and asked to prepare a second version. When it was retyped, according to Johnson, I signed five copies of the second version.

White and I were both confused. I remembered signing only one statement. Judge Metcalfe asked, "Mr. White, have you seen both of these?"

"No, I have not, Your Honor."

Mulder interjected, "He has been given both of these, Judge."

"I have been given one of them to the best of my knowledge," White said.

We had a few moments to study the copies. They were identical, except for the addition of a few paragraphs concerning Harris's firing of the gun at a Yield sign, for "target practice." White told me that we might as well not make an issue of the two statements, since they were consistent concerning the important details.

Still confused, White rose to cross-examine the detective. Accepting Johnson's time frame at face value, he asked, "You are talking about a man you had in custody from 10:30 A.M. to at least 6:00 P.M. and during that time he received a sandwich, coffee, an opportunity to go to the bathroom and you don't recall anything about wanting to make a phone call or talk to anyone?"

Johnson replied, "He did not ask me could he use a phone."

It's not true! I thought. I remembered asking many times. Could he have forgotten or was he just lying? I bit my teeth sharply into my tongue to keep from shouting out, "What the hell is going on here?!"

White took Johnson back over his story. According to Johnson, he and Investigator Luther were the only two officers with me during the whole time from 10:30 A.M. until 6:00 P.M.

White attacked that contention, asking, "Did ever . . . Gus Rose speak to the defendant in the time you and Investigator Luther were talking to him?"

"He may have."

"If he did talk to him that is something you didn't tell us a moment ago, it's a change you are making in your testimony?"

"No, sir, I don't know whether Sergeant Rose talked to him or not."

Still outside the presence of the jury, and for the limited purpose of countering Detective Johnson's testimony, White called me to the witness stand.

We challenged several details of the detective's story, the first point being that I had, indeed, asked to make a phone call—several times—but was not given the opportunity. There was no sandwich, I said, only a pack of vending machine cheese crackers tossed in front of me "and I didn't eat the crackers," I said. "I wasn't in any mood for food at the time."

I told Judge Metcalfe that the interrogation continued far longer than Johnson said, but I tempered my estimate so that it would not seem so outlandish in comparison to the detective's testimony. I was questioned until at least 8:00 P.M., I said, and during the course of the afternoon and evening, at least five different police officers were involved.

White asked if Johnson was there the whole time, and I replied that he had left sometime in the afternoon because "he said he had some Christmas shopping to do, he left and another police officer, Lieutenant whatever walked in and stayed with me until the end of the evening."

"And is it your testimony," White asked, "that even though you had requested an opportunity to make a phone call you were never granted that request and even though you had requested an appointed counsel you were never appointed counsel?"

"That's correct."

Mulder rose for his first opportunity to confront me directly, although his subject matter was limited to the hours surrounding my arrest and interrogation. He asked me a number of questions about Justice Cole and my understanding of my constitutional rights. Then he turned sarcastic. "You are a big boy," he said.

"Yes, sir."

"You have been in the service, kind of drifted around the country . . ."

White objected to this, and the judge sustained it. Mulder continued, "You didn't have to talk to the police officers, you knew that, didn't you?"

"Yes, sir."

"All right," Mulder said. "So let me hit the bottom line on this. Knowing that you had a right to remain silent, knowing that you had a right to a lawyer present with you to counsel with you during any interrogation by the state or by any police officers or lawyers representing the state, knowing that you had a right to terminate any interview or interrogation or conversation with police officers or lawyers representing the state at any time, and knowing if you made a statement that that statement could be used against you on trial for the offense for which that statement was made, you are telling the court that you did go ahead and make the statement even after you understood all those rights, aren't you?"

"Yes, I did."

"No question about that?"

"No question."

"That statement was voluntarily made by you?"

"That statement was voluntarily made, yes, sir."

"Nobody mistreated you, did they, Adams?"

"No, sir."

"They didn't starve you?"

"Like I said, I didn't even eat the crackers."

"I mean the mere fact you didn't get your milk and cookies for lunch didn't affect you one way or the other that day?"

"No, sir."

Mulder recalled Johnson to the stand to rebut my testimony. The detective reiterated his statement that I had not asked to make a phone call. When asked about the latest possible time that I might have signed the second statement, he responded that 6:30 P.M. was about as late as it could have been. He denied that he had left to go Christmas shopping.

Now White called Ray to the stand. My brother had driven back to Dallas the previous night from his current job assignment in Ponca, Oklahoma. Ray told the story of his own experience that same day, to give the judge a picture of how the Dallas police conducted the investigation. He said that police officers stopped at his job site around 2:30 P.M. on December 21, and asked him to come downtown to answer some questions. He went voluntarily. He was never placed under formal arrest, but he was questioned for seven or eight hours.

White asked, "Did you have the feeling during this entire seven hours that you could have had at any moment stood up and walked away without being placed under arrest?"

"No, sir," Ray replied, "I asked to leave two or three times."

"And what happened when you asked to leave?"

"They said they were getting a car and this was over a period of about two hours right at the last . . . I don't know whether I could have left or not if I had just walked out."

After hearing the testimony of both sides, Judge Metcalfe ruled, "The confessions of the defendant were freely and voluntarily made and they are admissible, they are admitted into evidence." It was incredible! Even the judge called these pieces of paper "confessions."

The jury was recalled, and Detective Johnson took the stand to formally introduce my statements into evidence and to read them to the jury. Both versions of the statement ended with the declaration: "I do not remember anything after I took a right on Inwood until I was turning left on Fort Worth Avenue."

Mulder then allowed Johnson to complete the unwritten scenario. Johnson spelled out for the jury that Inwood Avenue becomes North Hampton Road, the scene of the killing. On a map, he pointed out the 3400 block of North Hampton Road, which lies in a direct line between Inwood Avenue and Fort Worth Avenue. This was the very area covered by my statement, "I do not remember anything . . ."

Mulder seemed to think that the jury would see this as a tacit admission to murder. And he must have felt that he had proved his case, for when Johnson left the stand, the prosecution rested, after one and one-half days of testimony.

9

THE DEFENSE

THE DEFENSE OPENED its case on Wednesday afternoon, and one of White's major strategies was to contrast my behavior with Harris's in the days following the murder. He brought my brother back to the stand, this time in front of the jury.

Ray testified about the events on November 27 from his own limited perspective. He remembered that I brought Harris to the motel room briefly, but he was unable to say with certainty when I returned that night. "I was dozing on and off," he explained. "I'm not certain of what time that I woke up and talked to him . . . I think it was around ten o'clock but I can't be certain."

"All right. Is there anything that you would be doing that day around ten o'clock or any other time during the day that would connect your brother's arrival with a specific event?"

"Yes, sir, the 'Carol Burnett Show,' I think that I caught a portion of the 'Carol Burnett Show,' but the days was mixed up and I'm not certain."

White asked, "Did he come in and tell you he had killed a policeman?"

"No, sir."

"Did he act differently in any way?"

"No, sir, not at all."

"Did he tell you he had to move to another motel room?"

"No, sir."

"Did he tell you he had to leave town or go to another city?"

"No, sir."

"Did he continue going to the very same job?"

"Yes, sir."

"Had anything changed about your brother's life in those days from November 27th to December 21st?"

"The only thing I can think of was that he was planning on getting his girlfriend from Florida to come to Fort Worth and live, that is the—that is what he was looking forward to at that time."

Harris's actions, in the month following the killing, were quite different. Dennis Johnson, a seventeen-year-old student at Vidor High School, still in his sophomore year, testified that, on the evening of December 3 or 4, he and Randy Hayes picked up Harris at Bill's Gas Station in Vidor and that, during the course of the evening, Harris told them, "I shot, I even killed a police officer in Dallas."

"Did he use the word 'pig'?" White asked.

"Yeah, he did."

Twenty-four-year-old Lynn Brown, who described himself as a self-employed cabinet builder from Vidor, testified that he had seen Harris at Hootie Nelson's house on the Sunday night after Thanksgiving, had heard Harris boast that he had killed a "pig" in Dallas, and had seen the .22 caliber pistol.

"Did you leave shortly after that?" White asked.

"Yes, sir."

"Leave them there?"

"Yes, sir."

"Got out of that situation, did you?"

"Fast."

White had further questions for Brown, but they had to be taken up outside the presence of the jury. Scribbling notes in shorthand, my sister Mary found it both frustrating and confusing that Judge Metcalfe was so willing to sequester the jury. In her own law firm experience, this was unusual. Nevertheless, this was the only way that White was able to get certain testimony into the record.

With the jury box empty, Brown testified that he and Hootie Nelson had dropped Harris off before the boy burglarized a house trailer.

White asked if David Harris had attempted to blame the burglary on Brown.

"Yes, sir," Brown replied.

During his cross-examination of Brown, Mulder made a very big mistake. He began with a sarcastic question: "What is a nice guy like you hanging around with David Harris?"

White objected, the judge sustained, and Mulder started over.

He said, "You are a mere eight years older than he is, can't you find little boys your own age?"

Brown explained, "See, I was staying with Alvin Nelson, not David Harris."

Seeking to show that Brown's testimony was biased, Mulder made his blunder. He asked, "You are mad at him, aren't you?"

"Yes, sir," Brown replied.

Hearing that repartee, White scrawled a note to himself, but he waited for a time before acting upon it.

The jury was recalled and sixteen-year-old Randy Hayes became the third witness to testify that Harris had bragged of killing a Dallas police officer. Hayes corroborated Johnson's earlier testimony that Harris had made the boast while the three were in a car together.

Then White turned to Judge Metcalfe and announced, "Your Honor, I have a matter outside the presence of the jury I feel I should go into."

Once more the jury trudged into seclusion, obviously wondering what all the secrecy was about. Like me, they had probably thought that the purpose of a trial was to ferret out the truth, no matter what it was. This was simply an exercise in evasion.

White was frustrated, but he led Hayes through an explanation of what else occurred that evening, of how Harris had robbed O'Banion's Convenience Store. Once more White tried to get this testimony before the jury. He argued that Harris was the one who actually robbed the store, then later implicated his friends as accomplices. "He has a propensity," White noted, "of committing crimes and blaming it on the closest person at hand."

Judge Metcalfe again refused to allow the jury to hear this.

But White was now ready to play his trump card. He sought to recall Lynn Brown to the stand, to follow up on a line of questioning that Mulder had unwittingly opened during his cross-examination. Mulder had elicited the fact that Brown was mad at David Harris, and White argued that he was now entitled to ask Brown why. He knew the answer: because Harris had implicated him as an accomplice in the house trailer burglary. If he could get this information in front of the jury, he could begin to construct his "crime spree" theory.

White argued to the judge, "This burglary by David Harris which he blamed on the witness Lynn Brown follows the same pattern as the murder of the policeman, Robert Wood, which he is blaming on the defendant Randall Dale Adams. All this area is opened up by the state, it certainly would demonstrate a scheme and design and motive on the part of David Harris.

". . . Now that the state has opened this door I should be allowed to inquire into the facts of this burglary. It is a fact that this burglary is so clearly and completely parallel, the effort that David Harris has made in the case on trial here, that is to say, to commit a crime and to shift the burden of that crime onto another party."

Judge Metcalfe agreed only within narrow limits. He would allow White to ask Brown, in front of the jury, why he was mad at David Harris, but he would not allow him to develop the issue further.

The jury filed in, Brown resumed the witness stand, and White asked, "Will you tell the court and the jury now why you are mad at David Harris?"

"Because I'm charged with a burglary of breaking into a house and entering it and I didn't do it."

"And did this charge arise as a result of something David Harris said or did?"

Judge Metcalfe interrupted Brown's response and instructed him to answer yes or no.

"Yes," was all that Brown was allowed to say.

. . .

When court convened on Thursday morning, White called Ruby Scott to the witness stand. She was comanager of the 183 Drive-In Theater, in Irving, Texas. She had not been working on the night of November 27, but she did have the records of the scheduled movies, which we introduced as Defendant's Exhibit Number 8. These indicated that the first feature, *Student Body,* was shown at 7:00 P.M., followed by *The Swinging Cheerleaders* at 8:40 P.M. According to the schedule, *Student Body* was shown a second time, beginning at 10:24 P.M. and ending at 11:49 P.M. On weekends, such as the day in question, there would then be a late showing of *The Swinging Cheerleaders* if the attendance warranted it.

Both attorneys highlighted a major discrepancy in the stories told by Harris and me. Harris said we arrived during *The Swinging Cheerleaders* and left during *Student Body.* I said exactly the opposite. If Harris was correct, it could have been approaching midnight when we left. If my version of the story was true, we left the drive-in around 9:30 P.M. It all depended upon whom the jury chose to believe.

White now called to the stand Jim Shearn Bearden, the elected attorney of Orange County, Texas, and once more the jury trudged from the courtroom. Bearden testified that his office had several matters pending against Harris, and he declared that it was his decision as to whether or not Harris would be declared an adult for the prosecution of these crimes.

Judge Metcalfe asked, "Have you ever made any promises to David Harris in relation to this case?"

"I wouldn't know David Harris if he was in the courtroom," Bearden responded.

"Have you ever made any promises to anybody, Mr. Mulder, Mr. White, or anybody with relation to what you would or would not do on David Harris's pending cases?"

"No, sir."

"Okay," Judge Metcalfe said.

Mulder pressed the point, asking the witness, "Has any agreement been struck between you and David Harris or his lawyers or his parents or anyone representing David Harris as to what would be done with him after he testifies in this case?"

"No, sir."

Despite the denial, White knew that Orange County was dragging its feet on Harris's other cases, and he asked, in light of the additional crimes he was charged with, "has any action been taken by your office to revoke David Harris's juvenile probation?"

"I think a petition has been typed," Bearden replied.

"Is that the limit of the activity of your office?"

"Yes, sir."

"Have you made any steps to have—to having David Harris declared an adult so he may be prosecuted for this robbery?"

"No, sir. Mr. White, in Orange County my office does not recommend probation to armed robbery and the history of the juror in Orange County is—for a seventeen year old that they are going to probate the dickens out of him and there is not any need with the case load that I have of taking up the court's and state's time in attempting to do a case of that nature when in truth and reality he will get a slap on the hand and back on the streets."

In other words, I thought, no.

Assistant Orange County Attorney James Jenkins's testimony was also taken outside the presence of the jury. He underscored his boss's story. He stated that the petition for revoking Harris's probation was prepared months earlier, but not filed. He explained, "I was undecided as to whether or not to certify him or try to transfer him to district court for trial that—well, I'm sort of under the impression that the jury in Orange County would not convict a seventeen year old and give him prison time so—and then since that time David has been doing fairly well, I believe he is in some home and I understand he has plans to join the Navy when he is seventeen so it could very well be we would not file the petition to revoke his probation."

White asked, "And so even though Mr. Harris has committed a robbery . . . And so even though he caused her [clerk Judy Moore] to lay down on the floor at rifle point while he committed this robbery on December 5 of '76 you have never moved to revoke his probation or have him declared an adult for purpose of prosecution, is that your statement?"

"That's correct."

On cross-examination, Mulder sought to make it clear that this lenient treatment was not the result of Harris's agreement to testify against me. He asked, "Y'all haven't made any agreement with him as to what you are going to do if he cooperates with us or what you are going to do with him?"

Jenkins replied, "I have made no agreements whatsoever."

Now Judge Metcalfe called for the return of the jury, and allowed White to elicit from Jenkins the details of Harris's juvenile record prior to, but not after, the murder of Officer Wood.

The defendant almost never takes the stand in a capital case. It is often too risky for the defendant to place himself in a position where a sharp district attorney can cross-examine him and rip his story to shreds. But by now, neither White nor I had any doubts about our strategy. This was a simple case of Harris's word against mine. The jury had heard from Harris; now it would hear from me.

During my testimony, I made a point of looking directly into the eyes of the twelve men and women of the jury. I told my story as simply and directly as I could, knowing that my life depended upon it.

White took me over the events of November 27, and then he directed my attention to the two signed statements, introduced into evidence by the prosecution. He said, "On both of them, it says at the last line, 'I do not remember anything after I took a right on Inwood Avenue until I was turning left on Fort Worth Avenue.' You are describing this very day you have described to the jury. What do you mean?"

I replied, "They was asking me what happened at the time that I was driving and specifically I didn't know. And that is what I said I didn't know."

"Are you telling us that you don't remember being stopped by the policeman?"

"No, I do not."

"Were you stopped by a policeman?"

"No, I was not."

"Did you shoot a policeman?"

"No, I did not."

"Did you see anybody shoot a policeman?"

"No, I did not."

"Are you telling this court and the members of the jury that you are not guilty of this murder?"

For a moment I stared into the eyes of the jury. I was shaking inside but I did not want the tension to show through. I tried to compose myself, to make my voice as firm and clear as possible. "I am not guilty," I said.

White said, "I pass the witness."

Mulder rose to cross-examine me. He began by saying, "You thought you had it made, didn't you?"

"What is that?" I asked.

White objected to the argumentative nature of the question, but the judge overruled and allowed Mulder to continue.

Mulder said, "You got a new hair style I notice, Adams?"

"I have had a haircut, yes."

"I said a new hair style."

"It is the same, it is just a little shorter."

Mulder continued, "Now . . . you told your lawyer that your explanation for this last sentence is that nothing unusual happened when you turned right on Inwood until you turned left on Fort Worth Avenue."

"That's right."

"That ain't what it says, though, is it?" Mulder asked.

"It states that I turned right on Inwood."

"And what?"

"And that I do not remember."

"All right. It doesn't say that nothing unusual happened, though, does it?"

"No, it doesn't."

"You aren't saying that they deceived you or tricked you?"

"No, I signed—I'm not—I signed that statement."

"You sure did. But I mean you were so definitive about everything and you talked about this and that and going here and who bought the beer, who paid for this and that and then you get down here to the bottom, the crux of the whole thing, the police officer killed in the 3400 block of Hampton and you said, 'I turned right on Inwood

94

and I don't remember anything from the time I turned right on Inwood until I made a left turn on Fort Worth Avenue.' "

"They were asking specifics, yes."

"You could see this day coming, couldn't you?"

"What do you mean?"

"Right where we are now."

"No, I could see that it was coming after I was in the interrogation room, yes, I had already been arraigned."

"Yeah," Mulder said with relish. "Listen to me. I'm going to ask you one more time now. They put everything in this statement that you asked them to, didn't they?"

"I told them I had taken a right on Inwood, driven to Fort Worth, taken a left. They asked me if anything happened on the drive down Inwood and I said no. They said—they were asking me what I was talking about, they were asking me specific things. I didn't say—I said I didn't remember. I have driven that route I don't remember how many times."

"That is not what it says, is it?"

"No, that is not what it says."

"Were you drunk?"

"No, I don't think so."

"Were you high on dope?"

"No."

Mulder retraced the timing of the evening. I continued to assert that we had left the drive-in movie during the middle of the second feature, and arrived back at the motel around 10:00 P.M.

Finally, Mulder said, "You know you might get a little more leniency if you 'fess up and admit this?"

"There is nothing to admit," I replied.

Now White rose for redirect examination. He, too, zeroed in on the subject of my statement. "Were you scared that day?" he asked, referring to the day of my arrest.

"Very much."

"Are you scared today?"

"Very much."

"I don't suppose you dotted every 'i' and crossed every 't' on that statement, did you?"

"I wouldn't have known."

"Are those your words, your words or some words that a police-man put together after talking to you?"

"That is hard to say. We went over it fifty, sixty times, I don't know how many times, that is the way it ended up."

For the record, White wanted to talk about my hair also. He asked, "Was your hair as thin on top when you were arrested as it is today or have you had a chance to look?"

"I have been going bald for a while, I don't know. I would say it would have been."

"You have had some worries and some problems in the last two months, have you not, sir?"

"Yes, sir."

White elicited the information that I had never before been ar-rested or even questioned by the police concerning a felony. The only blot on my record was a youthful DWI offense.

On recross-examination, Mulder asked with a sneer, "You still want to stick with your story that you were home tucked in bed, don't know anything about the murder of this police officer?"

"Yes, sir," I replied.

"Do you remember anything about police brutality in *The Swing-ing Cheerleaders*?"

"No, sir."

"That didn't rev you up?"

"No, sir."

Now Mulder picked up a copy of my statement, and waved it at me. "This is your statement," he said, "it's what you dictated to that peace officer?"

"Yes, sir."

"You were happy with it at the time?"

"It came out that way."

"But yet after being interrogated about the death of a police officer and they questioned you for five or six hours and you don't even— you don't even deny killing him in this statement, do you?"

"No, I don't."

"Because when they pressed you on it you kept saying, 'I don't remember,' and you would hang your head, wouldn't you?"

"They kept pressing me about what happened between the time I turned off Inwood and the time I turned off Fort Worth Avenue and no, I do not remember the conversation or anything that happened during that."

"That is not what you said here, is it?"

"Yes, it is."

Mulder's voice rose: "You show me the word conversation in there, show me where it says anything about a conversation."

"It doesn't say anything about that."

"Take a hold of that," Mulder commanded, forcing the statement into my hands.

"It doesn't."

"Hold it up."

Judge Metcalfe interjected, "One thing at a time."

White rose and snapped, "I object to the badgering."

Judge Metcalfe said, "Let's have order. One thing at a time."

Mulder pointed out, "His hands are shaking so . . ."

"Yes, I'm scared," I admitted.

Again Judge Metcalfe called for order. He allowed everyone a moment to cool off, then directed Mulder to continue.

Mulder asked, "You are nervous because you are lying, are you?"

"No, I'm not."

When court was adjourned that Thursday afternoon, White's face beamed. His entire bearing was one of confidence and assurance. He told me that I had handled myself well during a difficult cross-examination. He was convinced that there was no way the jury could believe David Harris beyond a reasonable doubt.

In the morning, we would call a few more defense witnesses, then rest our case. By tomorrow afternoon, the closing arguments would be finished and the case would go to the jury. White *knew* that we were going to win, and that Mulder, for the first time in his stellar career, was going to lose.

I thanked my attorney for his work and wished him a good evening. Then I was taken back upstairs to my cell, for what I believed was my very last night in jail.

10

THE REBUTTAL
WITNESSES

I WAS AWAKENED very early in the morning by a guard who thrust a cup of coffee and a small gooey pastry through the bars at me. I shaved and tried to make myself as presentable as possible.

From off to one side, a voice cried out, "Hey, Adams!" It was my neighbor, the man with the small TV in his cell.

I shouted back, "What?" as I approached the barred front of my house.

"They're sayin' it's bullshit," he reported, "on the news, they're saying that the case against you is bullshit."

"Thanks," I said. "I know that already."

"They're sayin' the newspaper's sayin' that a good ol' boy is bein' railroaded."

I wondered if Doug Mulder was enjoying his morning paper.

When court convened on this Friday morning, the first order of business was to finish our defense case. White called Police Officer Teresa Turko to the stand and had her review her initial statement to police investigators, in which she said that the windows of the car were "very dirty and I could barely see inside." She admitted that nowhere in that first statement was there a mention of bushy hair. Instead, she described the driver as "wearing a heavy dark coat with a large collar." White showed her the second statement, dictated many days after the murder, and she admitted that this statement, too, made no reference to bushy hair.

Yet in her testimony for the prosecution, White asked, "you have used the phrase bushy hair, have you not?"

"Yes, sir," Turko admitted.

"And you have identified a hairdo, pictures of this defendant, Randall Dale Adams, have you not?"

"Yes, sir."

"Is it true you never used the phrase bushy hair until some-time after December 20, 1976, when David Harris came into this case?"

"December, yes, that would be right."

Now White called character witnesses, first my mother, then my sister Nancy. As Mom entered from where she had been waiting in the witness room, I could see that she was extremely nervous. Fortunately the questions were brief and relatively easy, merely attesting to the fact that I was a good hard-working boy with, as far as she was concerned, an honest reputation in the community. Nancy's testimony was similar. Mulder did not risk losing sympathy with the jury by badgering them on cross-examination.

Finally, after Nancy left the stand, White declard, "The defendant will rest, Your Honor."

The judge asked Mulder, "What says the state?" Mulder's options were to prepare for closing arguments, or to reopen the prosecution's case by calling rebuttal witnesses.

For once, the smooth first assistant district attorney appeared caught off guard by the sudden close of our case. He complained that White had told him the morning's testimony would take about two hours, but it had been much more brief than that. "I'm not prepared to proceed at this time," he said.

To accommodate the prosecution, the judge called a recess, and sent the jury off to its quarters.

As Mom and Nancy sat on a hard wooden bench in the hallway, they became aware of a rumble of activity, like the approach of a storm front. Prosecution assistants and police officers scurried about. The sound of voices drew closer, and were accompanied by a wave of news photographers, rushing ahead of the approaching parties to turn, kneel, and click their camera shutters.

"Mom, what's going on?" Nancy asked.

"I don't know," Mom replied. She glanced up to see a white woman, flanked by two black men, being escorted toward the courtroom.

When I returned to court, I sensed immediately that the air had shifted. White appeared very nervous. I whispererd, "What the hell is going on?"

"I'll talk to you about it later," he replied.

One of Mulder's assistants brought three strangers into the room and had them sworn as witnesses. The prosecution was required to notify us in advance of any and all witnesses who might be called during the initial presentation of the case, but this requirement did not hold for rebuttal witnesses. It seemed obviously unfair to me, but those were the rules and we were stuck with them. Edith James scribbled down their names and ran off to see what she could discover about them. The newcomers were sent to the seclusion of the witness room and, finally, Mulder was ready to proceed.

First, he recalled Detective J.W. Johnson to the stand for a quick question. Referring to my interrogation, Mulder asked, "Did he tell you what time he got back to his motel room where he was staying?"

"He said it was near one o'clock."

This was clearly hearsay testimony, and by now, even I knew that it should not be admitted, but White was too preoccupied to lodge an objection, and the judge simply let it pass without a comment.

Johnson was excused and, as Mulder called the first of his three rebuttal witnesses, I noticed that the glint had returned to his eye.

The white woman took the witness stand and identified herself as Emily Miller, married to R.L. Miller. Back on the night of November 27-28, she testified, she was working at the Fas-Gas service station, located at Hampton and Loop 12. She had closed her station at 11:30 P.M. that night and had gone to help her husband close the Fas-Gas station that he ran, at Illinois and Zang. They left that station about five minutes past midnight, bought a gallon of milk for her daughter's baby, and were driving home, traveling on Hampton.

Mulder asked if she noticed anything unusual.

"Yes," Mrs. Miller replied, "as we stopped for a red light I turned to my husband and I told him, I said, 'Look at that nut coming with no lights on his car.' " She then saw a police cruiser pursue the car.

"And what did you observe next?"

"Well, as I'm the nosy type, I guess . . . I told him to slow down so I could see who was in the car." They crept past the scene in the opposite direction. Mrs. Miller remembered that the car in question was a small blue compact, a "Ford product."

"Did you get a look at the driver of the compact car?" Mulder asked.

"Yes, I did."

"Would you notice him if you were to see him again?"

"Yes, I would."

"Look around this courtroom and tell this jury over here under oath whether or not you see that man in court today who was driving the compact car."

"Yes, I do."

Mulder asked her to step down from the stand and point out the driver. She complied and pointed a finger directly at me. Then Mulder asked, "Is there any question in your mind but what that is the man that you saw, that man?"

"No. His hair is different but that is him . . . That night his hair was out like an Afro, why I noticed that, my son-in-law has an Afro like that, like this man right here had."

"Now, I will ask you, Mrs. Miller, if you saw a police officer at the scene?"

"Yes, I did. It was Officer Wood, I knew him because he had dropped my daughter home before on occasion."

It was only with supreme effort that I kept my body from shaking visibly. How had Mulder come up with this woman, someone who not only happened to be driving past the scene at the time of the murder, but who also said she knew the victim? Her testimony was strong and sure. Why had Mulder saved her as a rebuttal witness? That was the one question I was able to answer. He had saved her, I realized, so that he would not have to tell us about her. My mind was reeling, but I forced myself to concentrate on what this woman was saying.

After they proceeded down the road a short distance, Mrs. Miller continued, her husband heard a noise, which he said "sounded like bullets." She replied, "Well, that policeman probably got shot." In court, she added, "But I really didn't believe it or I would have turned around."

Mulder asked if they drove past the scene again later that night.

"Yes," Mrs. Miller said, after dropping off the gallon of milk for her daughter's baby. "We were having a family argument that night between the two of us and we were really just driving around talking because we didn't want to go home and talk about this so we drove around and we came back and I seen the ambulance and I seen the squad cars."

The next day they read about Officer Wood's death in the newspaper. Mrs. Miller said she wanted to go to the police then and there with their information, but her husband said sarcastically, "Why don't you stick your nose in it?" That afternoon, Sunday, she again was driving past the scene. She happened to stop at a traffic light next to a squad car, and informed the officer that, according to the newspaper account, they were looking for the wrong car. It was a Ford, not a Vega, as reported in the papers. The officer put her in touch with the Crimes Against Persons Bureau, which is how she ultimately became a witness.

White rose for cross-examination, but he was at a loss. I could see that he, too, was shocked by the strength of this woman's testimony. Even he was having difficulty hiding his emotions. He had no idea who this woman was, or how to attack her story, and he had no alternative except to finish.

He began by pursuing her curious statement that she had known the victim. Mrs. Miller explained that Officer Wood had once stopped her fourteen-year-old daughter, but instead of issuing a ticket for driving without a license, he had brought her home and delivered a lecture.

That line of questioning seemed to go nowhere, so White tried another tack. He questioned why Mrs. Miller and her husband were driving around West Dallas, a predominantly black neighborhood, in the middle of the night.

Mrs. Miller replied, "My husband is black, you know."

"No, I didn't know."

"Well, he is black and he knows West Dallas and he has people there. And you are trying to tell me it is real dangerous because everybody is black over there. I don't know what you are getting at. But white people are just as dangerous as black people."

Having slammed into a stone wall, White sat down.

Mulder called R.L. Miller to the stand. He was, indeed, a black man, dressed in a leisure suit with an open collar. He said he was presently employed as a sanitation truck driver in Hutchinson, Kansas. He testified that he and his wife Emily were on the way home from work when they had passed the small compact car stopped by the police cruiser. He estimated that they were driving at "twelve, fifteen miles an hour, it wasn't very fast, creeping," and were "ten, twelve feet" from the other car.

Referring to the driver of the car, Mulder asked, "And did you get a good look at him?"

"Yes," Miller replied.

"All right. What type of hair did he have?"

"Curly, kind of bushed up."

Following Mulder's direction, R.L. Miller also pointed me out as the driver of the car.

On cross-examination, White managed to chip away at a few

minor details, getting Miller to admit that the murder car was on the shoulder of the southbound side of the four-lane road, and that he was, therefore, a minimum of sixteen feet away, rather than the "ten, twelve," he had originally said.

White asked, "Can you see into the interior of a dark automobile from across the two-lane highway, can you, that is my question?"

Miller answered, "If the window is down you can."

Still searching for the motivation behind this surprise testimony, White asked, "You and your wife knew there was a reward offered in this case, did you not?"

"Well, not really."

"You didn't know that?"

"No."

Michael Randell was called to the stand. He was a tall, twenty-nine-year-old black man who said he was once a professional basketball player with the Denver Nuggets, and was now the manager of the Colbert-Volk Clothing Store. He testified that he had been playing basketball at the North Hampton recreation building at 3710 North Hampton, until it closed at 10:00 P.M. Then he spent the next two hours "messing around." About 12:30 A.M. he was on his way home to his wife and two children when he passed a small, dark, compact car that had just been stopped by a police cruiser. He said he remembered the time as about 12:30 A.M., because he had promised his wife he would be home by 1:00 A.M. and had just checked his digital watch. The policeman was approaching the car as Randell drove by.

Mulder asked him to describe what he saw.

"Well," Randell said, "I saw two individuals. While the driver was slumped down in his seat I noticed—he kept looking back like this towards the police car, I guess, but he was moving his head back and forth like this." He demonstrated.

"You were able to see that driver and look right at his face?"

"Right."

Randell, too, pointed to me as the driver of the murder car.

It was ghastly to see the finger pointed directly toward my eyes, and it required supreme effort not to stand up and scream in frustration. I thought of Mary, sitting behind me in the courtroom, and how awful it must feel to see your own brother singled out so unmistakably as a cop killer. I felt only momentary relief when I remembered that Mom and Nancy were out in the hall, and did not have to see this.

Mulder asked, "Now, did he look any different then, Mr. Randell, than he does now?"

"Yes."

"What was different about him then?"

"He had a nice looking Afro, large 'fro."

Randell said he had driven on, and had thought nothing of the incident until he read about the cop killing in the newspapers. He said he had called the police "one or two days later" to tell them that they were looking for the wrong type of car. Instead of a Vega, they should be looking for a "Ford product." Something sounded strange. Randell, like Emily Miller, had described the killer's car as a "Ford product." The term was a bit formal and not consistent with the rest of their vocabulary. What it sounded like, I realized, was a phrase that had been suggested to them, implanted in their minds, and rehearsed.

White had his chance to throw a few questions at Randell, but they were ineffectual. He asked Randell what he had told the police when he first called them. "Did you tell them it was a black male or white man?"

"He wasn't black. I told them it was an individual, I don't know what it was, it could have been a Mexican or anything, but I know he wasn't black."

White sat down, more confused and agitated than ever.

With the brief cross-examination over, Mulder asked if Randell could be excused to return to his job. Judge Metcalfe countered, "Do you know where you can reach him?"

Mulder asked Randell, "You will be on the job all day today?"

"Yes."

Metcalfe excused Randell and then formally asked Mulder, "What says the state?"

"Your Honor and ladies and gentlemen of the jury," Mulder said, clearly pleased, "at this time the state of Texas would rest its case."

Judge Metcalfe called a lunch recess, and asked to see the attorneys in his office.

. . .

The hallway outside the courtroom exploded with reporters, clamoring for access to the single pay telephone. My sister Nancy spotted White in the crowd and tried to get some explanation. What happened? She had been able to hear much of the testimony, even out here in the hallway, but it was so confusing. Who were these people who had identified her brother? White, whose quiet confidence had been soothing until now, appeared extremely upset, pale, apprehensive, *vulnerable*.

Nancy overheard one police officer say to another, "They've got him by the balls."

After the recess, Judge Metcalfe conducted a hearing outside the presence of the jury on what was obviously the subject of the conference in his chambers. White wanted the chance to discover more about the three rebuttal witnesses. In particular, he wanted to know if the witnesses had been coached, if their identification of me had been tainted by being shown photographs or viewing a lineup.

White called Emily Miller back to the stand and asked, "Did you at anytime after November the 28th and before today have the occasion to view either photographs or a lineup in which the person that was supposedly driving the vehicle that was stopped on Hampton Road was supposed to be in that lineup?"

"Yes," she answered. She had seen a lineup of suspects and then she had also viewed photographs.

Concerning the lineup, White asked, "Did you identify the person you see here?"

"Yes," Mrs. Miller replied. "I recognized him at the time."

To be absolutely sure, Judge Metcalfe asked, "Did anybody down at the police station or any officer or district attorney, did they ever suggest to you who to identify?"

"No, they did not." Mrs. Miller said the same was true when she was handed a group of photographs. "I picked them up and looked at them and said, 'This is your man right here.' "

The judge gave White the option of having Mrs. Miller repeat this testimony before the jury, but since it strengthened her original identification, White said, "I will waive further appearance of this witness."

Still outside the presence of the jury, White called R.L. Miller, and elicited the fact that he had not viewed a lineup. Instead, he said he had picked out my photograph from a group shown to him by detectives who flew to Hutchinson, Kansas, and interviewed him on April 21, only last week, some five months after the crime. White then agreed to have this witness excused.

Judge Metcalfe issued his ruling, finding that the in-court identifications by the eyewitnesses was not tainted by their having viewed a lineup or photographs.

It was late afternoon by the time Judge Metcalfe recalled the jury and gave them a friendly lecture. "I'm going to release you until nine o'clock Monday morning," he said. ". . . I think it would do well that you and everyone else connected with the case get a good weekend's rest and come back fresh Monday morning at nine o'clock and we will go into the reading of the court's charge and the final arguments. . . .

"I want to admonish you again not to discuss anything about this case with anybody or allow anybody to discuss the case with you. And with reference to any publicity or matters that might be in the press about this case, let me make a suggestion to you. It will probably do you well if this weekend, and I'm not saying anything will be in the news media about the case, I don't know, but it might do you well to have somebody else in your family go through the paper before you look at it just to make sure there is nothing in there, or take it out. . . .

"It might do you well to stay away from watching the news on television just as a precaution. Maybe confine yourself to the baseball game or something. Please go out of your way to make every effort to avoid anything you might hear, see, or read outside of this court-room that might in any way pertain to this case. It is only with your cooperation in this matter that we are able to have a fair trial in this case.

"With that in mind, if you will be back Monday morning at nine o'clock."

. . .

Sitting in my cell on Friday evening I wrote to my Aunt Lou and
Uncle Ray in Illinois:

> The state rested their case Wednesday about noon,
> and we started my defense. We tore the state's case
> up, and I was feeling good, but today the state
> brought in three witnesses who "just came forward"
> and said they happened by at the time.
> They said they could tell who killed the p/o, then
> identified *me*. All of them were just driving around
> at the time. It was two men and a woman. One of
> the men and the woman knew the p/o killed, and
> the other had heard of him. They were very well
> *programmed* in their stories . . .
> My lawyer is still very hopeful, but said the woman
> is dangerous. I wonder how much the state paid
> them.

At about the same time I was writing the letter, Edith James happened to arrive for dinner at the Adolphus Hotel Coffee Shop, not
far from the courtroom. There she saw the Millers having dinner
with Michael Randell, along with a blond woman whom she assumed was Emily Miller's daughter. The young woman was holding
a baby that appeared to be mulatto.

She reported this to White, and my two defense attorneys wondered what Randell and the Millers had to talk about.

Before court Monday morning, Mulder and White met with Judge
Metcalfe in his chambers. There, Mulder finally submitted the results of the psychiatric examination that he promised to have per-
formed on David Harris. Judge Metcalfe concluded that Dr. Grigson
had found nothing unusual, especially insofar as it concerned Harris's ability to testify in court.

. . .

partner I didn't see her. The window on the driver's side of the car was down and I saw that the driver had about a 3 inch afro. He was either a Mexican or a very light skinned blackman. He was wearing dark clothing but I could not make out the color. We passed the cars and I did not know about the shooting until the next day.

Everyone in the courtroom knew that either Randall Dale Adams or David Harris killed Officer Wood, and both of us were white as snow. This statement, given to police five days after the murder, proved to White's satisfaction that Mrs. Miller's identification of me as the driver of the car was worthless.

Over the telephone, Detective Johnson read White the contents of Michael Randell's police statement, and White concluded that this, too, was vague.

My attorney, feeling ever more downtrodden, resolved to put Emily Miller and Michael Randell back on the stand or, at the very least, get these statements in front of the jury. In a whirl of activity, he issued subpoenas to bring the witnesses back into court.

With the jury still sequestered, court finally reconvened, and Judge Metcalfe noted with a sense of weariness, "It is now 12:05 P.M. and we were to argue this morning at nine o'clock . . . I understand, Mr. White, you have another request to reopen, is that correct?"

"Well, Your Honor," White said, ". . . it has come to my attention that Emily Miller and Michael Randell have given written statements. . . . This morning I made known . . . my request that I had information that such statements . . ."

"Pardon me before you go further," Judge Metcalfe interrupted. "The record will reflect this is Monday, and that the testimony was closed Friday. Go ahead."

"Yes, Your Honor. Mr. Mulder at this time has now allowed me to examine visually one of these statements, namely that of Mrs. Emily Miller and Michael Randell read to me over the telephone. . . . Those two statements distinctly refer to someone other than a white man as being the person they believed to be and identified as the killer in this case.

"I feel that . . . I should be allowed to introduce this evidence before the jury."

Mulder argued that the statements were not inconsistent with the testimony of the witnesses. He said that Randell's statement described the driver of the murder car as a man with a large Afro, and said nothing about race. He admitted that Emily Miller's statement said that she believed the individual to be either a very light-skinned black or a Mexican, but he recalled that when, on Friday, "she testified looking at the defendant, she didn't know to this day whether he was a light-skinned black or Mexican."

Judge Metcalfe said he recalled that, too. I certainly did not.

"Let me say," Mulder argued, "it is innately unfair at this time for him to offer witnesses' testimony when they are not here to explain anything in this statement. He agreed to let the witnesses go and I have been advised today that the witness Emily Miller left Sunday for Belleville, Illinois, wherever that is."

Before ruling on the admissibility of the statements, the judge said, "Now, my first question, Mr. White, is whether or not Michael Randell or Emily Miller are available at this time to testify."

White replied, "Your Honor, I have issued subpoenas for both of them as of this morning at approximately 10:00 A.M. It is not my knowledge—within my knowledge at this time whether they are available or not."

It was well within Mulder's knowledge. Regarding Michael Randell, he said, "I called there for him and they said he is ill today. I called his house and no one answered." As for Emily Miller, he expanded upon his previous statement: "She told us Friday that she was leaving for Belleville, Illinois, and I went out to her apartment out on Ewing just about eleven o'clock this morning . . . and I was advised by her next door neighbor that she had moved out and they had moved boxes out and she had gone."

With the witnesses unavailable, White still sought to introduce their statements into evidence. Judge Metcalfe dealt first with Randell's statement. "You could have inquired Friday about that," he said.

White answered, "I was unaware of that statement."

Concerning Emily Miller, the judge asked if White had investigated the accuracy of Mulder's report that she had skipped off to Belleville, Illinois.

"I have only been informed of that in the last few minutes since we have been in this courtroom," White said. He argued with passion, "Judge, I feel it is vital that her statement be admitted since she refers to a person who would be of a different race from my client . . . And that no matter how Mr. Mulder attempts to conceal this from the jury of the people—the fact is she has referred to a party of a different race than my client and I think it would be significant to the jury. . . . I believe the state held these witnesses from their case in chief, did not list them on their indictments so I would not have any opportunity to investigate them. I believe the state was aware she was going to be leaving town Friday." All of this, White said, made the evidence of Emily Miller's statement "so paramount, so critical, there is no getting by the state's failure to provide it to the defendant."

Mulder countered, repeating his contention that it would be "unfair to the witness, not to me or not to the state, but to the witness, to allow a statement to come in when she is not here to explain it, and had he asked for that statement I'm sure it would have been furnished, no question about that."

White now said the very words I wanted to shout through the courtroom. "Your Honor," he raged, "I think Mr. Mulder's argument . . . is incredible. He has got a person on trial for their life, a person who might receive the electric chair and he is worried about being unfair to a witness. Mr. Mulder knew about this statement, the defendant and his counsel did not. . . . Mr. Mulder is trying to convict an innocent man. Mr. Mulder ought to join me in offering that statement for the consideration of the jury. He is afraid of the truth. He is afraid to have an innocent man walk out of this courtroom when he is charging him with capital murder."

The argument was full-blown now. Mulder, his own hackles raised, said, "He doesn't know what my responsibilities are. I believe this is apparent to the court that I ran him on two polygraphs, your choice and our choice, and ran that boy too and the boy passed and he failed miserably every time."

"That is quite enough," Judge Metcalfe lectured.

"That is the truth," Mulder said.

After Judge Metcalfe calmed the attorneys somewhat, he issued a lengthy lecture on the matter at hand. He noted that White had a right to seek to reopen his case, but that he was attempting to call two witnesses who were unavailable. He noted that the prosecution had failed to provide the statements of Michael Randell and Emily Miller in a timely fashion, but he also noted that White had failed to request any such statements on Friday, prior to cross-examination, which was the proper time to lodge the request.

"There are times when the request to do something late can be allowed," he said, "there are times when the request to do something late cannot. I will not grant the request because to do so with regard to recalling Emily Miller and Michael Randell I am convinced it will impede the trial and will interfere with the due and orderly administration of justice. In short, simply I'm not going to send this jury home or back to work, tell them sometime later this year that we will call them back together and resume the trial. I see absolutely no point in that." He admitted the statements into the evidence of the trial record, but would not allow the jury to see them.

As far as those twelve men and women were concerned, the testimony of the three rebuttal witnesses now stood unchallenged.

11

THE THREE QUESTIONS

IN HIS CLOSING argument to the jury on Monday afternoon, White did his best to dispose of the testimony of the rebuttal witnesses. He theorized how difficult it would be, at night, in a moving car, to make such a positive identification. He also attacked Turko's testimony, pointing out that her courtroom declaration that the killer had "bushy hair" contrasted with her earlier, written statement that the killer wore a coat with a fur-lined collar.

He covered numerous other points before he came to the crux of the matter: "Everybody knows one of these guys did it. It is not a wildly complicated case because you boil it down to one thing, a policeman was killed, one person killed him.

"Who was more believable? Which testimony was more believable, a man who stays in Dallas, never leaves his job or his place of abode or a person who has committed burglary after burglary, theft after theft, lie after lie, bragging of killing the police officer?

"David Harris is really something else. Think about this. He commits a burglary at four o'clock, gets the keys, gets the money ready because at eleven o'clock he comes back, tries to ease the car out in the driveway with manual force. The car won't move but David Harris already committed a burglary and knows he is wanted for it. He hid out with Hootie drinking beer and he has the nerve to go up to a house he has already burglarized once that day, open the door with the keys he has got, get inside that car, turn on that car, and drive it away.

"Nerve? Ladies and gentlemen, nerves of steel. Nerves that would kill, nerves that would kill a police officer and stand in front of you and deny it.

"Ladies and gentlemen, David Harris is the demon seed if I have ever seen it . . ." White then uttered a prophecy: "If we don't get him this time he will kill again."

Now my attorney's words grew ever more hostile. The rage that had been building within him burst forth in front of the jury. He nearly shouted the accusation, "We have got two murders in this case," causing everyone to sit up and take notice. "We have got David Harris who's killed a policeman . . . and we have Doug Mulder who is trying to commit murder today. Doug Mulder is prosecuting an innocent man . . . and only you have the power to stop it. . . .

"I ask you not only to write not guilty on that verdict but to go upstairs with me to the grand jury and present this evidence when David Harris turns seventeen in October of 1977 and have him indicted for murder because he deserves it. And I hope Mr. Mulder will try him the way he has tried an innocent man because that is the only way that Doug Mulder can redeem himself for this crime he has perpetrated here in the courtroom."

White's words were still ringing through the room when Mulder rose to respond. Calmly, he told the jury, "I don't feel I need any redemption from the likes of Mr. White, nor do I intend to answer many of the maniacal remarks and accusations he has made, not only against me but against witnesses in this case. I know David

Harris's background. . . . And I have never asked that you take him into your hearts or into your homes. But I ask you to evaluate his testimony in light of the other sworn testimony and in light of the physical evidence in this case."

He spelled out for the jury what they would have to do to find me not guilty. First, they would have to believe that I was telling the truth. Second, they would have to believe that Teresa Turko, David Harris, Detective J.W. Johnson, Emily Miller, R.L. Miller, and Michael Randell were all lying. It was one against six.

He summed up his feelings toward me by declaring, "He's a liar. He's not worthy of your believing him."

Then he concluded, "Ladies and gentlemen, we have proven this man's guilt beyond any reasonable doubt and I will ask you to so find based on the believable evidence in this case."

The case went to the jury at 5:30 P.M. on Monday.

Some two hours later, the foreman sent a note to the judge, requesting that the jurors be taken to the scene of the crime "to evaluate the lighting conditions." Obviously, the jury wanted a chance to assess the reliability of the three rebuttal witnesses who claimed that they could identify a stranger at night, while driving past in an automobile as much as four lanes distant. Judge Metcalfe refused this request as unnecessary.

Another hour passed, and the foreman send a second note, requesting a transcript of the testimony of the Millers and Mr. Randell. It was clear to everyone that the debate centered upon the reliability of the final three witnesses. If the jury had placed its trust in David Harris's testimony, it would have convicted me already.

By late evening, Judge Metcalfe called a halt to the deliberations. He ordered that the men and women of the jury be sequestered for the night at the nearby Adolphus Hotel. They were to resume their work at 9:00 A.M. the following day.

In a note the next morning, the jury advised, "We are in disagreement as to whether or not the prosecuting attorney or the defense attorney in the examination of Mrs. R.L. Emily Miller asks Mrs. Miller if she identified Randall Adams in a lineup prior to this trial and ask for her answer."

Judge Metcalfe prepared a response, but before he read it to the jury, he allowed the attorneys to debate its contents. What the judge proposed to tell the jury was: "In answer to your request the reporter cannot find anything in her notes relevant to your inquiry."

White objected that this was incomplete. He wanted the judge to tell the jury, flat out, that there was nothing in the testimony to indicate that Mrs. Miller had viewed a lineup. He knew where the jurors had picked up this information. It had been disclosed in hearings outside the presence of the jury. Someone on the jury had either eavesdropped on that testimony or, perhaps, read it in the *Dallas Morning News* on Saturday. White said, "It is obvious and transparent that members of the panel have been engaged in reading newspapers and educated themselves to the media about this trial rather than getting all their evidence through sworn testimony in the court. For that reason I move at this time for a mistrial."

Judge Metcalfe said simply, "Motion for mistrial is overruled. Your objection is overruled, your exception is noted. Bring out the jury, please." He read them his prepared answer and sent them back into the jury room.

"Mrs. Foreman," Judge Metcalfe asked, "has the jury arrived at a verdict?" By now it was early Tuesday afternoon. I stood alongside White and James. My knees felt weak.

"Yes, they have," responded Juror Fain.

The verdict was read: "We, the jury, find the defendant guilty of capital murder as charged in the indictment."

The courtroom erupted with noise. Mulder began to accept congratulatory handshakes.

Judge Metcalfe declared a lunch break, and told the jury that we would resume immediately after the meal to continue with the punishment phase of the trial.

As I was led from the courtroom I glanced back toward my family. Mom, through her tears, mouthed the words, "I love you, Randy." I choked back my own tears, trying to maintain dignity.

Now I was a convicted cop killer, and one task remained for my twelve peers. They had to decide whether I would live or die. Like a strong uppercut to the jaw, the realization hit me that these people really were going to try to kill me.

No one was hungry, but Nancy and Mary were worried about Mom and wanted her to eat. They ushered her into an elevator and, only after the door closed, realized that Judge Metcalfe was there, too. He held an open newspaper in front of his face.

"Hold your head up, Mom," Nancy whispered. "We haven't done anything wrong, and neither has Randy."

Another elevator passenger said to the judge, "I bet you're glad to get rid of that dog that you had."

Metcalfe said nothing, but he raised the newspaper higher.

Only minutes later, heartbroken, scared, and exhausted, my family stood on a corner outside the courthouse, waiting for a stoplight to change. Suddenly an immense black sedan sped out from the underground parking garage. As the car pulled adjacent, it paused, as if the driver had recognized the pedestrians. A peal of raucous, vicious laughter enveloped Mom and my sisters, and then the car drove off.

Mary stared at the retreating form of the car, her mouth open in both amazement and revulsion. Fresh tears careened down Mom's cheeks. Nancy wanted to throw something.

They had recognized everyone in the car. Mulder was driving, and his assistants Winfield Scott and Stephen Tokely sat in the back seat. Riding shotgun, apparently heading off to lunch with the three prosecutors, was Judge Metcalfe himself.

White explained that the witnesses for the prosecution during the penalty phase would consist of the two psychiatrists who had interviewed me the previous month. We were both onto the game now, aware of how justice was meted out in Dallas County, and we had little doubt as to whose side the psychiatrists were on.

Much was happening all about me in the courtroom, but none of it seemed based in reality. I found myself almost hoping for a death penalty decision, for I believed that the appellate courts were likely to review that sentence with care. And I was certain that we were going to appeal. I thought: we're going to appeal the hell out of this case. So bring on the psychiatrists. Let them say whatever they will.

White warned me that it would be tough, but he advised me once more to keep my feelings in check. "Don't panic," he said. "Don't show emotion."

Mulder spent several minutes reviewing the professional qualifications of Dr. John T. Holbrook, who had first worked for Henry Wade as one of the ten doctors who had testified against Jack Ruby during his trial for the murder of Lee Harvey Oswald. Back then, Holbrook had testified that Ruby did not suffer from "psychomotor epilepsy," which, the defendant contended, had rendered him temporarily insane. In the late 1960s, Holbrook began the first psychiatric program within the Texas Department of Corrections. Since 1973, he had been in private practice, but was called upon frequently as an expert witness, both by prosecution and defense attorneys.

Mulder had the doctor briefly describe his conversation with me. When Mulder asked for his conclusions, Dr. Holbrook reported that he could not get me to describe any emotion.

"What does that mean to you as a psychiatrist?" Mulder asked.

"He has the profile and characteristics of the sociopath or anti-social personality."

Mulder asked if the doctor could "lay it out for us in four-letter Anglo-Saxon words."

"Well . . . they form no close social or emotional contacts with anyone and they tend to live pretty much as loners. They tend to have little or no regard for the general institution of society and they act strictly in terms of their own personal needs, that which makes them feel good at the time, whatever that might be . . ."

"What type of murders do these sociopaths commit?"

"Well, when they commit murder it is usually to make them feel good or it is a matter of convenience to eliminate a witness or to give them time. It is also a purely practical matter to them from their point of view of the circumstances, it has nothing to do with passion or commitment as we understand that."

Mulder asked if Dr. Holbrook would expect such a person to panic after a killing.

"No," Dr. Holbrook said. "They may feel good for as long as ten or fifteen minutes . . . they may cycle for two hours before they grow tired and want to sleep a while. Then they begin to start their predator-like behavior again . . . they begin a series of thoughts . . . I think I will kick the cat or do something to the old lady or I won't pay my bills and then they begin to build up again towards some arrestible kind of criminal behavior."

What kind of worker does a sociopath make? Mulder asked. Dr. Holbrook replied that a sociopath is a good worker, almost indefatigable. "So they could work at a job all day," Mulder asked, "and creep at night on anything they might want to do?"

"In the criminal population or in the case of a business executive he could work all day and figure out how to grind somebody up the next day."

Had Dr. Holbrook interviewed me at this moment, he would most definitely have found emotion. I struggled to follow my lawyer's advice and conceal my anger, but it was very, very difficult. The worst pain was knowing that my family had to hear this pompous drivel.

Now Mulder asked a critical question: "Will Adams, Randall Dale Adams, will his condition improve or get better with time? Is this a stage he is going through that he is going to grow out of?"

The psychiatrist replied, "I would expect little or no change."

"He will constitute a continuing threat to society, there is a good probability?"

"Yes."

"All right. Now, Dr. Holbrook, during your examination and evaluation of Randall Dale Adams, did he demonstrate any remorse or sorrow?"

"I could find no indication of any remorse or sorrow relative to any event in his life." What that demonstrated, he said, was a lack of conscience.

But, I wondered, could it not also demonstrate a lack of guilt?

Dr. James Grigson testified that he had, at the direction of Judge Metcalfe, visited me in the hospital division on the eighth floor of the Dallas County jail, where he conducted what he said was "a complete psychiatric examination." He said that the significant part of the examination "was the absolute absence of any type of guilt or remorse, regret feelings . . . I diagnosed him as being a socio-pathic personality disorder." He said this was characterized primarily by the absence of conscience and by the ability to manipulate.

Mulder asked, "There on the scale of sociopathy, where does the defendant Randall Dale Adams fit?"

"I would place Mr. Adams at the very extreme, worse or severe end of the scale. You can't get beyond that."

On cross-examination, White asked the very question I wanted to ask: "You have to assume, do you not, sir, that he took another person's life to make that deduction?"

Dr. Grigson answered, "Well, even without that he is the same person. I don't really know what all Mr. Adams has done, but I know he is a sociopath."

That was the extent of the prosecution's case.

My mother approached the witness stand full of righteous indignation. She had had enough of this court and its manipulations. Until this moment, she had been afraid that any aggression on her part, any bitter emotion shown by her or her family, would hurt my cause. Now she resolved: I'm going to tell my part, whether they like it or not. But she did not know quite where, or how, to begin.

White helped her. He asked gently, "Mrs. Adams, I will ask you if your relationship with your son, Randall Dale Adams, is a close and healthy relationship?"

"Yes."

"Have you ever had any problems with him in your relationship between you and your son?"

"No, sir."

"Ever in your life?"

"No, sir." The words were spoken quietly, but they were punctuated by huge droplets of tears that rolled down Mom's cheeks.

It brought so much pain to my heart! No longer could I keep my feelings in check. They were about to burst forth in a tirade that would prove to the jury, once and for all, that I was quite capable of showing emotion.

But murderous rage was not what White wanted me to exhibit. He saw the agitation growing in me, and he paused in his questions to huddle at the defense table, counseling me to calm down. We had a quiet, but heated argument. "Get her off the stand," I whispered. "Don't make her go through this."

He tried to reason with me, but I cut him off.

"I don't care what they do to me," I said through clenched teeth. "Just get her off, *now!*" I said this loudly enough for Nancy to hear, and I am sure many others heard it also.

White said, "Pass the witness."

Mom did not wait for a question from Mulder. Her months of private pain now erupted with a shriek aimed in the direction of the jury, "My son didn't do this terrible thing!"

Judge Metcalfe admonished, "Mrs. Adams, answer the questions you are asked."

"He did not do this, Judge," she sobbed.

Mulder said, "Judge, we have no questions."

"Step down," Judge Metcalfe ordered. "Wait back in the witness room if you will. Let her take a cup of water with her."

Mom sobbed softly, "My son didn't do this."

I wanted to rush toward her, but dared not. Mary and Ray moved forward from the spectators' area to help her. Companion tears coursed down Mary's face as she clutched Mom's arm. Ray, whose eyes appeared ready to erupt with fire, took her other arm. Together they led her away down the central aisle and through the rear door of the courtroom, her mouth still chattering in an accelerated attempt to be heard, to be believed.

Nancy watched them go, and felt enormous pride. This family was spunky, she knew, and she realized with a sudden start that the State of Texas would never beat us. Sure, Mulder & Co. were winning this initial battle, but they had no idea how tough this family could be. Nancy was saddened by the certain knowledge that we were in for a protracted war, but she was just as certain of ultimate victory. No emotion? Indeed! She whispered, "Way to go, Mom."

I glanced at White and found him smiling.

. . .

Judge Metcalfe charged the jury with the responsibility of answering three questions: (1) Was the murder of Robert Wood done deliberately and with reasonable expectation that death would occur? (2) Is there a probability that the defendant will commit further criminal acts of violence that would be a continuing threat to society? (3) Was the crime unprovoked by the victim?

Under Texas law, if the jury answered "yes" to all three of those questions, I was to be sentenced to death. If it answered "no" to any one question, then the sentence was to be life imprisonment.

Stephen Tokely presented the first portion of the closing argument for the state, tackling those three questions one at a time. Drawing heavily upon the testimony of the two psychiatrists, he characterized me as the embodiment of evil. "Dr. Holbrook said," he recalled for the jury, "that his psychopathic personality is there and it simply is waiting for something to trigger it. To me that indicates he is like a time bomb with a short fuse just waiting to go off if the right set of circumstances occurs . . . He has absolutely no regard for other person's lives and it doesn't matter who they are . . . And when it hits him he will kill again."

As Tokely droned on, I found it difficult to pay attention. My heart was in the hallway behind the courtroom.

But I listened closely when White rose for his closing statement. Judge Metcalfe asked if he wanted a warning when his forty minute time limit was about to expire.

"No," White said sadly, "I won't need a time warning. Ladies and gentlemen, I'm not going to take forty minutes . . . I can hardly talk at all to be quite honest about it."

He addressed his attention merely to question two, and the psychiatrists' contention that I would pose a continuing threat to society. He reminded the jury of testimony they had heard concerning my life. I had proven myself to be a responsible individual, a contributing member of society, a hard worker, a good soldier. But the district attorneys and their cohorts, the psychiatrists, he charged, "have taken all the good things in Dale Adams's life, his Army record, holding a job, being close to his family, faith in God, knowing right from wrong and saying that is just clichés, it doesn't mean anything. I think it meant something before this happened, I think it will mean something in the future." They had taken the simple evidence of a quiet life, and made it seem, somehow, more sinister than that of my chief accuser, an admitted thief.

White expressed the belief that no reasonable individual could conclude that I was a continuing threat to society and, therefore, they had to answer no to the second question.

White sat down and I studied the jury. Their eyes told me that they were not buying it.

Mulder had the last word, and he made the most of it. He began, "I think, ladies and gentlemen, I would be somewhat remiss at this time if I did not for a moment at least comment on Mrs. Adams's testimony. I'm sure she had some impression on you as she did on me. She is certainly the defendant's mother who has come to plead for his life and certainly no one can fault her for that. But she is perhaps just as blameless, just as innocent of any wrongdoing as this young policeman's mother, her son was so wantonly slaughtered. And I remind you that to spare his life based solely upon an emotional plea from his mother would be just as wrong to take his life based upon an emotional plea of that young man's mother who demanded an eye for an eye and a tooth for a tooth and a son for a son."

These lawyers, I thought, have a way of twisting everything. I don't show emotion and thus I am a sociopath. Mom shows emotion and the jury is told to disregard it.

"Now, we don't come down here and ask for death in a case of this nature based upon emotion," Mulder continued. "We have based our case on facts and the fact of the matter is that whether his lawyer likes it or not, this man is a cancer on society."

Mulder spoke for a time about the victim, Officer Robert Wood, who "died as a soldier fighting a war against crime. . . . Police officers go out and they detect crime, they apprehend and arrest criminals. And I guess it could be said that they are the front lines in this war against crime. . . . You know, being a soldier in this war on crime is not looked upon with the same patriotic fervor that there once was. There is no ribbons or ticker tape parade, generals don't come home and run for President. But you see, the dead are buried just the same. The war goes on.

". . . We are a nation of laws, a country of laws, a state of laws. We have laws that are designed to protect the citizenry. Our laws in turn are enforced and protected by that thin blue line of men and women who daily risk their lives by walking into the jaws of death, sometimes to walk back out again and sometimes to perish.

"Let the traffic ticket come your way and my way. I think we all tend to forget just how much we count upon and depend upon that thin blue line. I know when we are victimized by crime or when crime's ugly shadow is cast in our doorstep to whom do we look? Upon whom do we lean? Behind whom do we seek protection? That thin blue line.

"But you know, have you ever stopped and thought who protects the police officer? Who protects the police officers? Who picks up their banner when they fall in battle and with whom must they of necessity expect the faith to be kept? With whom must these police officers out here who are protecting you, with whom must they of necessity expect the faith to be kept? You see, their faith and their trust rests solely with your conscience and your courage. So I beseech you, don't break the faith with these men out there who are dedicated to your protection.

"Don't give this man a life sentence when he has earned death. . . . And I ask you don't turn your back on Robert Wood, don't break the faith with Robert Wood."

I glanced at Judge Metcalfe and saw tears welling in his eyes.

It took the jury less than a half hour to reach its decision. Judge Metcalfe read the answers to the questions one by one:

"We the jury unanimously find and determine beyond a reasonable doubt that the answer to special issue one is yes . . .

"We unanimously find and determine beyond a reasonable doubt that the answer to special issue two is yes . . .

"We the jury unanimously find beyond a reasonable doubt that the answer to special issue three is yes."

I saw what was happening. I heard the words. I understood the implications fully. But nothing seemed real. All I could think was: What the hell is this? How did we get here? Behind me, I could hear Mom sobbing.

White asked if I could have a few moments with my family before the guards took me away.

Judge Metcalfe said no.

I was taken from the courtroom, as Mulder, surrounded by a sea of blue uniforms, accepted congratulations from the family and friends of Officer Robert Wood.

Even as I was led off in chains, Officer Wood's widow Toni was telling reporters, "I'm relieved . . . I would have been disappointed if they had found him guilty and then not have given him death." She noted that her late husband "believed in the death penalty."

A reporter asked her if she had been disturbed by White's arguments that Dallas police had arrested and charged the wrong man. She replied, "I had faith, every bit of faith in the Dallas police department. I thought they had the right man. I think they deserve a lot of credit for all they've done in this case."

White countered this by proclaiming, "I still believe my client is innocent and with a new trial, he'll be found innocent."

"Mom," Nancy said when the family returned to its motel, "I know you want to be by yourself. Mary and I are going to the restaurant for a little while."

Mom said nothing. She merely got out of the car and walked to her room.

Inside, as she sat on the edge of the bed, a numbness crept over her. She did not cry. She could not pray. She simply sat in stunned, empty, heart-broken silence.

She was still sitting there alone when Mary and Nancy returned to check on her. She said to her daughters, "You know, I never thought that one of my children would ever get into any trouble that I couldn't fix, that I couldn't make better. I guess I was wrong."

Neither of her daughters could think of anything to say. All they could do was stay close. They sat on the bed with her.

Finally Mom said with a deep sigh, "I wish your father was here."

Nancy was quick to protest, "No you don't, Mom. Think about it. Would you really want Dad to go through this?"

Mom was silent for a moment, then she said softly, "No, I guess not."

. . .

David Harris returned to the "teen challenge" program. Probation for his earlier crimes was due to end in July, and Orange County authorities said they did not know what, if any, action would be taken against him for his later offenses.

"David's a likable kid and we'd like for him to get his life straightened out," declared Keet Goforth, his juvenile probation officer.

His mother told the *Dallas Morning News*, "David's changed a lot, but he has a ways to go." She said that he now talked about wanting to become a police officer.

Meanwhile, I was taken back to the Dallas County jail to await transfer to death row.

12

THE SIDESHOW

THE FAMILY CAME to visit before they returned home. Ray came along and announced that although he would continue to live in Fort Worth, officially, his work would keep him on the road and out of Texas much of the time. He would come to see me as often as he could.

"Try not to worry," I told everyone. "Try to pretend I'm in the service, or away at school."

When they piled into their car and turned north, Mom said to Nancy and Mary, "Leaving Randy here in Dallas is the most difficult thing I've ever had to do."

. . .

The fog that had descended upon me in the courtroom followed me to my eighth-floor jail cell, and hovered. For a time I sat quietly, trying to figure out what had happened. In those first few days I was so paranoid that I even suspected that my own attorney, Dennis White, was a part of the one-sided game being played against me.

It would be some time, I was informed, before Texas got around to transporting me to death row. I was to remain here in the Dallas County jail indefinitely, until the trial transcripts were prepared and certified as correct by both the prosecution and the defense. And since the trial had been an extended one, this could take as long as a year.

At first, this sounded alright with me; I was in no hurry to get to death row. But I realized very quickly that now that I was *officially* a cop killer, the guards seemed to operate on the assumption that death in the electric chair was too good for the likes of me. Some were determined to make whatever time I had left on this earth as miserable as possible.

I kept this information from Mom when I wrote to her on May 7, only five days after my conviction:

> *Doing fine* and feeling good . . . Been reading the Bible and praying. God has given me peace, and assurance that things will work out O.K. . . . I'm also going to check into some home study courses, while here. Maybe I can prepare myself for school, for when I get out . . .
>
> Love ya, and the family, and my best wishes to you all. It was good to see Ray. I was worried about him. I'm glad he got out of town. They would have been looking to put something on him, too.

I also decided that it was time to burn the bridges with my girlfriend in Florida. I added in my note to Mom:

> Tell Kathy, if she calls, that I love her, but will not write anymore. It would not have worked anyway.

Only a week passed after the trial before I was taken back to Judge Metcalfe's courtroom for the official sentencing procedure. Unwilling or unable to look me in the eye, the judge intoned the words that state law required him to say, sentencing me to die in the electric chair.

Two days later, White came to inform me that he was filing a motion for a new trial, based upon evidence that had come to light during the previous week.

He had regained his cool professional demeanor, but he had fire in his eyes, and he was ready to fight back in the way he knew best. His new evidence was the result of a frenetic week of work by Edith James and himself. He showed me the introduction to the seven-page motion. which declared:

> New testimony material to the Defendant has been discovered since the trial, in that: Perjury was committed by eyewitnesses Emily Miller and Robert L. Miller about matters of their background and activities that were of such common knowledge that the most cursory investigation by the District Attorney would have discovered such perjury.

Even a legal neophyte such as I could read between these lines. White had always believed in fair play and expected to see it personified in the American judicial system. Until he came up against the Doug Mulder definition of justice, he had believed the district attorney's office to be populated by honorable men and women. Now the scales had fallen from his eyes. He was incensed at Mulder's reliance upon the three rebuttal witnesses, and his motion spelled out specific points where they had lied.

He showed me sworn affidavits attached to the motion, gathered from the Millers' former coworkers. One declared: "Robert told his wife, Emily, in my presence that they wished they had paid more attention when the murder occurred, they could probably get a lot of money, because there is always a reward when a policeman is murdered." Another declared that Robert Miller "said the car's windows were either dirty or fogged up and he could not see inside."

A third affidavit, referring to Emily Miller, proclaimed, "I would not believe anything she said."

White told me that he had spoken with yet another Fas-Gas employee, who refused to sign an affidavit, but told him off the record that Emily Miller was "the lyingest son of a bitch I ever met."

Michael Randell lied when he stated that he was playing basketball in the North Hampton recreation building until 10:00 P.M., and had remained in the area for the next two hours, "messing around." How did we know this? Because Jessie R. Jones, the recreation leader at North Hampton, swore to that fact that the gymnasium closed at 5:00 P.M. on Saturdays.

White charged that Mulder's use of three rebuttal witnesses was devious. They should have been primary witnesses, allowing us an opportunity to investigate and a fair chance to rebut. White called this "flagrant" and "calculated." To me, that sounded like a legal language cussing out.

Having dealt with the Millers, Randell, and Mulder, White now turned his wrath upon Judge Metcalfe himself, pointing out numerous judicial errors. The court erred, he said, in not permitting the jury to hear about the Dallas police department's Internal Affairs Division investigation of the victim's partner, Police Officer Teresa Turko. Such evidence might have elicited doubt in the jury's mind as to how well Turko could see inside the car.

The court erred further, White said, when it refused to let us present evidence concerning crimes committed by David Harris after the killing, when it refused to allow nineteen members of the Vidor Independent School District to testify to defects in David Harris's character, when it refused to allow the jury to see the earlier signed statements of Emily Miller and Michael Randell, when it did not allow the jury's request to view the crime scene, and when it failed to declare a mistrial after the jury exhibited its knowledge that Emily Miller had viewed a police lineup.

White held nothing back. "Furthermore," he wrote, "the statutes of Texas for jury selection in [a] capital case are repugnant to the Constitution of the United States and the Constitution of the state of Texas . . ."

I was overwhelmed by the amount of evidence White had managed to amass in only a few short days, and I was pleased and impressed by the enormity of his anger, more so when he suggested that, beyond this criminal appeal, we file a civil lawsuit against Wade and Mulder, charging violation of my civil rights under the Fourth, Fifth, Sixth, Eighth, and Fourteenth Amendments, and asking for $5 million in damages.

I signed the appropriate papers.

We had a further discussion about money. There was no way my family could continue to pay out fees to lawyers, and the appeals process in a capital case was certain to be lengthy and costly. White said he was eager to continue on the case, and asked if I wanted to ask the state of Texas to pay the legal fees for my appeals. I said yes, and signed the necessary pauper's oath.

The day after White filed his motion, a reporter from the *Dallas Morning News* located Emily Miller. She was not in Belleville, Illinois, after all, but at the Alamo Plaza Motel in West Dallas. She lashed out at White's criticism of her testimony, and the affidavits obtained from her former coworkers. "They are all liars," she said. "The whole kickback here is these people think my husband and I got a big reward out of this deal. We did not get one dime."

The paper reported, "Dallas police have stated that $20,000 in reward money was paid to a woman in Vidor who provided information which led to Adams' arrest." Obviously this was not Emily Miller, who lived in Dallas.

The story appeared on Friday, May 13, and later in the day Mrs. Miller held a press conference to further counter the attacks on her character. She introduced her daughter, Ricki Lynn Aguilar, and her son-in-law Charles, and said that they were the reasons she was looking so closely at the car that night. She worried that the driver was her daughter, who had no license. Finally, she said, she and her husband were tired of being "harassed" by newsmen.

On May 20, 1977, a hearing was held in Dallas County Criminal District Court Number Two on our motion for a new trial. Judge

Metcalfe presided. We faced the nearly impossible task of persuading him to declare that he had made enough mistakes during the course of the trial to overturn the verdict of the jury.

No longer was I naive. No longer did I expect an unbiased search for the truth. I did, however, expect common courtesy and a sense of decorum, but what I witnessed was more like a carnival side-show.

Our first witness was William Barrow, supervisor of self-service operations for Continental Oil Company, the parent of the Fas-Gas stations. Checking his records, he testified that Emily Miller had been dismissed on November 13, 1976, two weeks before the night in question; the official reason was for failure to show up for work. It was clear that she was not employed by Fas-Gas on November 27, as she had testified.

Barrow's records showed that R.L. Miller was still employed by the company on the date in question, but that he was fired on December 6 for failure "to follow company rules."

Ricki Lynn Aguilar, Mrs. Miller's daughter, had also worked for Fas-Gas. Barrow said she was fired on November 11.

Elba Jean Carr, a former coworker of the Millers, took the stand, and White asked her what R.L. Miller had told her a few days after the murder. She replied, "Robert said he didn't see anybody, said he just saw the car had been chased and he thought it was a black car and the paper stated it was a blue car." Nevertheless, she said, "Mr. Miller said that they probably could get a lot of money out of this."

After she read in the newspapers that the Millers had testified in the trial, identifying me as the driver, Mrs. Carr said she had called the district attorney's office on Saturday, April 30, to tell Mulder that she believed the Millers were lying. She spoke to some unidentified person, but was unable to reach Mulder.

She tried again at 8:30 A.M. on Monday, May 2, but never spoke to the first assistant district attorney. In frustration, she called White and finally found someone who would listen to her. This was how White had learned of Mrs. Miller's prior written statement. The information had come too late to help us at trial, but White realized that it was basis to move for a new trial. He and his secretary went to Mrs. Carr's home on May 5 and secured an affidavit.

On cross-examination, Mulder said to Mrs. Carr, "You are just really a kind of nosy busybody who . . ."

James interrupted with a machine-gun volley of words, "Object to the attack on the witness, the ad nauseam attack on the witness, totally uncalled for, argumentative, improper cross-examination, badgering the witness."

"Overruled," Judge Metcalfe said.

Mulder continued, and elicited the fact that, on the very Saturday morning that Mrs. Carr had first attempted to call Mulder, she too had been fired from Fas-Gas. With a sarcastic tone, he asked, regarding Emily Miller, "You don't know really what she saw, do you?"

"No, sir."

"They just might not have wanted you sticking your big fat nose into . . ."

Again James objected, and Mulder conceded that "big, fat nose" should be stricken from the record.

Judge Metcalfe called a ten-minute recess so that the attorneys could cool off.

White introduced business records from the Adolphus Hotel, showing that the Millers were housed there for several days during the trial, and that the tab had been picked up by the state of Texas. That made them paid witnesses, White contended, and it was information that should have been supplied to the defense, because it added to our effort to discredit the witnesses.

White had subpoenaed Dallas police department records concerning the Millers, and he offered these into evidence. They showed that on December 3 and 4, 1976, the Millers were questioned at their residence concerning a domestic disturbance. It was December 3 when Mrs. Miller first "came forward" with her testimony concerning Officer Wood's murder, five days after it had occurred.

Clifton Eubanks, manager of Fas-Gas station No. 1 on Fort Worth Avenue, reported a conversation R.L. Miller had with him following the murder: "He was telling me about it that he had passed by and that he couldn't see inside the window or see, it was dirty or foggy and he thought the car had backfired when he passed by."

The elusive Emily Miller herself took the stand and gave an immediate indication that she was going to be a hostile witness. When White asked for her address, she snapped, "Dallas, Texas."

"Well, do you have a more specific address?" White asked.

Mrs. Miller replied, "That isn't none of your business."

White moved on, only to find that the state objected to nearly every one of his questions concerning Mrs. Miller's statement to the press, and her motivation for testifying. The judge sustained those objections. My frustrated attorney got her to admit that, on the night of the murder, she was not employed by Fas-Gas, but she denied that she had ever discussed the killing of Officer Wood with Elba Jean Carr.

White asked if she was staying at the Adolphus Hotel on Monday morning, May 2, but the court would not allow her to answer the question. "Your Honor," White complained, "I had a subpoena issued for this witness on that morning and I believe I should be allowed to inquire as to her whereabouts at that time."

Mulder said, "I think the record shows she was not there."

When Judge Metcalfe finally allowed White to pursue his line of questioning, White asked, "Where were you on the Monday morning after the trial of this case?"

Mrs. Miller responded, "Well, I don't feel—I don't ask you where you were staying and living and it ain't none of your business where I'm staying."

The judge instructed her to answer.

"I don't know," she said. When pressed, she admitted that she might have moved to the Alamo Plaza Motel by that time, but she added, "I could have been at K-Mart on May 2nd."

"Did you receive a subpoena on May 2nd of 1977?"

"I received a subpoena over at the Alamo Motel on Fort Worth Avenue, me and my husband together."

White was on his feet asking the questions, and I did not have an opportunity to point out to him the implications of what Mrs. Miller had just admitted. If the Millers had received subpoenas on Monday, May 2, why had they not showed up in court? Did Mulder know they were still in town?

. . .

After a recess, White called Dr. James Grigson to testify about his examination of David Harris. The psychiatrist said he had found Harris competent, but, "Due to his previous record it was my opinion that if he continued along these lines that he would become an overt sociopath."

Mulder tore this down on cross-examination. He asked, "Did you find the Harris boy to be believable?"

"Yes, I did."

"Did you find Randall Dale Adams to be unbelievable?"

"Yes, I certainly did."

R.L. Miller returned to the stand and denied that he had said anything about the murder to Mrs. Carr because, he said, "she runs her mouth just like my wife."

White attempted to ask Mr. Miller several additional questions, but was not allowed.

On cross-examination, Mulder asked, "Y'all did tell me you were leaving town, did you not?"

"Yes, we did."

"And going up to Hutchinson, Kansas, or Illinois one or the other?"

"Yes, sir, and I can tell you what was the delay."

Mulder did not want to go into the subject of why the Millers were still in town on the very day when he had advised the court that they were gone.

Michael Randell took the stand. White attempted to question him about how he could have been playing basketball until 10:00 P.M. at a recreation center that closed five hours earlier, but once more the judge would not allow him to pursue the line of inquiry.

"Your Honor," White finally complained, "I wish to note on the record that my inability to question three witnesses, I have just identified the two Millers and Mr. Randell, make my motion for new trial impossible to pursue."

That, I thought to myself, is exactly why the judge is not allowing you to ask the questions.

We had further evidence to show that the Millers had motivation to lie. White had learned that Emily Miller's daughter was a defendant in a robbery case that had occurred in January of this year, 1977. At the time of my trial, that robbery case was also pending in Judge Metcalfe's court, under the prosecution of Assistant District Attorney Winfield Scott. On May 10, one day after Judge Metcalfe sentenced me to die in the electric chair, Scott presented a motion to dismiss the charges against Mrs. Miller's daughter. Henry Wade endorsed the motion, and Judge Metcalfe signed it. White contended that the Millers had made a deal with the district attorney's office, to have the charges dropped in return for their testimony against me. Both Mulder and Scott denied knowing of any connection between the two cases until after my trial was over.

After hearing all of our points, Judge Metcalfe immediately declared, "Motion for new trial is overruled."

Then he said, "Now, let me make an observation to you, Mr. White. Appeal in this case is of course, mandatory under the law. If you wish to give formal notice of appeal at this point in time you can do so."

White did, and the judge said he would inform the Texas Court of Criminal Appeals in Austin that the case was on its way to them. He asked if White planned to continue to represent me.

"Your Honor," White said, "the defendant filed a pauper's oath for the appeal. His representation will be under the control of the court."

"That being the case," Metcalfe replied curtly, "I will appoint Mr. Mel Bruder as attorney on the appeal. . . ."

Just like that, without anyone asking my opinion in the matter, White was off the case, and Mel Bruder, whoever he was, was my new lawyer.

White told me that Bruder was an ex-assistant district attorney. That information left a sour taste in my mouth.

I was certain that the guards searched out the hottest cell in the Dallas County jail. In the middle of the summer, with no explanation, they moved me from the eighth floor to the twelfth floor.

My new house was a detention tank fashioned completely of metal, including the door, with a tiny window in it that could be opened and shut only from the outside. There were no external windows.

Outdoors, the summer heat pushed the thermometer above 100 degrees nearly every day. Indoors, it must have soared to 120 degrees. The cell held a sink-commode structure, but the plumbing did not work very well, and the stench was overpowering. I was allowed to shower once a week.

Other inmates were housed on the twelfth floor, but I was isolated at the end of an extended catwalk, far removed from any other occupied cells. Half of the time the commissary man never bothered to come down to me. Here, I could scream my lungs out, and no one gave a damn.

It was going to take a great deal of resolve, I knew, not to go crazy here.

I wrote to Mom and my sisters and some of my friends. I wanted Mom to hear from me at least once a week, but what could I tell her? Hi, Mom, today I ate breakfast, paced my cell, sweated like a pig, longed for someone to talk to, ate lunch, paced my cell, whistled, tried my hand at writing a poem but tore up the paper in frustration, ate dinner, paced my cell, paced my cell, paced my cell . . .

The days were excruciatingly long.

Nothing happened. I was in limbo, awaiting the preparation of my trial transcript. I heard nothing from the mysterious Mel Bruder, and I supposed that you get what you pay for.

A single bright spot shown through, in the form of one of the guards, a certain Captain Messenger. He seemed kindly disposed of me, and allowed me out of my house whenever he could so that I could make a collect call home to Mom. He was the one guard who had followed the case closely enough to be convinced that I got a raw deal and he told me, quite openly, that he was pulling for me to be granted a new trial.

White and James remained as my attorneys for the civil suit, *Randall Dale Adams v. Douglas Mulder and Henry Wade,* which was filed in the U.S. District Court for the Northern District of Texas, Dallas Division. Actually, I held little hope that it would accomplish much, but at least it would be heard by a judge other than Donald Metcalfe—a federal judge, at that.

District Attorney Henry Wade called it a "publicity stunt" and said that my claims did not "amount to anything." He noted, for what seemed to me to be the millionth time, that I had failed a polygraph test, and Harris had passed.

A Dallas County assistant district attorney filed a motion on behalf of Mulder and Wade to dismiss the lawsuit. He contended that officials of the district attorney's officer were immune from civil liability—that, while performing their duties of administering the law they, themselves, were above it. Beyond this, he charged, ". . . plaintiff's allegations have no basis in fact . . ."

In a more comprehensive brief filed eleven days later, the same assistant district attorney asserted that if perjury was committed at the trial, it was encouraged, not by Mulder and Wade, but by the defense attorneys. I could only assume that he was calling me a perjurer for denying guilt. He concluded his brief with a request that the judge not only dismiss the lawsuit, but allow Mulder and Wade to recover their costs of defending it from the petitioner, me.

U.S. District Judge William Taylor, Jr., listened calmly as Emily Miller admitted that she may have misled the court on a few minor details but she remained firm in her identification of me as the driver of the car, and the murderer of Officer Wood.

On July 11, Judge Taylor announced that he agreed with the contention that the district attorney's office had immunity. He threw our lawsuit out of court, and ordered that the defendants could recover their costs from me.

There was, of course, no way for them to get any money from a condemned man who had recently signed a pauper's oath. Henry Wade and Doug Mulder would have to be satisfied with killing me.

Ray came to see me as often as he was allowed, if he was not out of town on a job assignment. He always called home first, so that he could relay the family's latest news, and he always left a bit of money in my jail account. The visits were strained. We had to bend down to talk to one another through a small screened opening, and straighten up to see each other through a tiny glass window.

We talked about his girlfriend, or his job, or the news (Elvis died in August), but we avoided talking about me.

Time passed one dreary day at a clip.

Almost every day I tried to write home. The opening line was easy: "I'm in good health and my spirits are up." Following up these patent lies with news of any substance was the difficult part.

Sometimes I worked on a single letter for a full week before I had a page or so to mail.

Nancy, Mary, and their husbands talked frequently among themselves about Mom. They were not sure how long she could stand the strain. They could see the skyrocketing blood pressure in the flush of her fair skin. They could see the melancholy and the fear just behind her eyes. There was little they could do for me now. What, if anything, could they do for her?

Mom could not keep herself from reading every prison book and watching every prison movie. "Mom," Nancy warned, "don't pay attention to those things. They bring you down too much. And if you crash, the whole family will fall apart."

Mom knew that she was right, but she persisted; she simply had to get some idea of what life was like for me now.

13

THE SHANK

ONE DAY NEAR the end of 1977, I was called out of my cell and told that my attorney was here to see me. I really did not know what to expect, but I reasoned that the attractive woman with shoulder length light brown hair who waited in the attorneys' visiting room was not Mel Bruder.

She explained that she was Bruder's associate. He was tied up on another case at the moment and she was here to handle some details.

A stack of papers lay on the table in front of her, on the other side of the bars. "I have a whole bunch of things for you to sign," she said quicky. She slid a paper under the bars and said, "First, here's a writ . . ."

I said angrily, "Look, if this man doesn't want to stop up here and talk to me, then I don't want to talk to him either." I stood up, turned around and pounded on the door, yelling to a guard, "Get me out of here."

A week passed before Bruder came to see me in person. He was fortyish, with close-cropped brown hair. The dark suit covering his heavyset frame appeared as if it had not been pressed for quite some time. He explained in a calm self-assured voice, "I don't have time to come and see everybody. Sometimes I have to send other people. You don't need to take me if you don't want me, but I've been assigned to the case. If you want me, you better talk to me."

I signed the necessary papers, and we began to speak in earnest.

We met several times after that, in order for him to familiarize himself with the case and prepare a brief for my direct appeal to the Court of Criminal Appeals. My initial skepticism gave way. This man appeared to know what he was doing, and seemed genuinely concerned about the obvious errors in this case.

Not once during these meetings did he ask me whether or not I had killed Officer Wood. For his purposes, it was irrelevant.

"Pack up," a guard said one Friday morning just after New Year's Day, 1978.

Quickly, I gathered my humble store of belongings. I was ushered into an elevator and taken to the tenth floor, placed into what was known informally as "Dallas death row." It was a tank with five narrow one-man cells, each opening onto a dayroom containing a metal picnic table-bench structure bolted to the floor, a TV, and a shower stall.

There were four other inmates in the tank when I arrived, two of them white and two of them black. But I had only been there for about an hour when the guards took one of the white prisoners away.

I was anxious for human company, but I forced myself to act and speak with caution. I had no idea who these other men were.

The white man was a surprisingly friendly sort, and I spent much of the day getting acquainted with him. Mike Berry was in his mid-forties, an accountant by trade. A few weeks after his divorce became final, he had gone to his ex-wife's house. While he was there, her new boyfriend called and told Berry that he was on his way over.

"I hope you come," Berry threatened, "because I'm going to blow your shit away."

Minutes later, Berry went to answer a knock at the front door with a .357 Magnum pistol in his hand, cocked. Before he could open the door, whoever was on the other side kicked it in. Berry fired the pistol, realizing as he did so that his target was not his ex-wife's boyfriend, but a Dallas police officer, summoned by the boyfriend to investigate what was going on inside the house.

When he realized what he had done, Berry put the gun to his own head, but just as he fired, his ex-wife's brother lunged toward him, yelled "Mike, don't!" and hit him on the back of the head with a huge glass ashtray. The bullet merely grazed the side of Berry's forehead, and his survival provided Doug Mulder with another notch on his belt.

Berry was already a veteran of death row on the Ellis unit, outside of Huntsville, Texas, and he was back in Dallas only for a brief court appearance. He advised me, "Don't let your attorneys tell you to hang around here in Dallas. Go on down there. Number one, you're going away, so get it over with. Number two, I believe you'll like it much better. They don't mess with you down there."

He explained that most of the "bosses" on death row were young, college-age kids, and if you did not give them a hard time, they left you alone. "Here," he said, "you've got some assholes who want to take everything out on you. There, most of the guards just want to put in their eight hours and go home, and they don't want to go home with a bucket of piss thrown all over them."

The two black men housed with us were Charlie Washington and Roland King. Washington was about as tall and skinny as I was. King was short and stocky, muscular. I knew nothing about them except that they seemed to stick together, and they both had a detached, crazy sort of look in their eyes.

Berry was taken away on Friday evening for transport back to Huntsville, and I was left alone on the unit with Washington and King. The weekend passed uneventfully, and I enjoyed the opportunity to watch some television, even though Washington and King turned on cartoons whenever they could find them.

The two black men were still asleep on Monday morning as I ate breakfast and took a shower. I was toweling myself off, keeping one ear tuned to a morning news show on the dayroom television, when something caught my eye. "What the hell is that?" I muttered aloud. I walked over to the TV and stood on tiptoe to reach what I realized was a homemade knife, a "shank" in prison terminology. It had been filed down from a spoon to an extremely sharp blade. The wicked-looking point was several inches long and filed to a razor edge.

I tried to reason this out. I doubted if the shank belonged to Washington or King. They were dumb, but not dumb enough to leave a knife sitting on top of the TV. The only other conclusion was that one of the guards had planted it there, and I did not wish to take that line of reasoning any further. I only knew that I wanted it *gone*. With my towel, I wiped the blade clean of fingerprints. Then I ran to my cell and put on some clothes.

With the shank hidden in my towel, I edged into a vacant cell, which opened onto the hallway. I pushed my shaving mirror out between the bars to glance in both directions, to make sure that no one was watching. Then I threw the offending knife out into the hall, as far away as possible.

A couple of hours later, I was lying on my bunk reading a book. My head was turned away from the cell door, but I suddenly sensed a presence in the room. I turned my head around and saw the two black men. Washington, standing in front, said, "Get out of that bunk. I think I'll whip your ass."

"Do what?" I replied, tossing my book down.

"I told you to get your ass up."

I swung my legs off the side of the bunk and, as I did so, Washington launched a right-handed uppercut. I tried to duck back, but he caught me in the nose, sending me spinning backward.

He was confident enough to take his time. He ambled toward me, with King behind him in the narrow cell. The whole front of my face ached, but I knew what I had to do. In one movement I scrambled to my feet and landed a solid kick directly in Washington's groin. He bent over in pain, and I grabbed him in a head-lock, pushing him backward and pummeling him in the side at the same time. Through blurred vision I could see that his body was pushing King back against the doorway.

"Get the fuck out of the way, Charlie!" King yelled.

Washington grabbed at my legs and tried to flip me to the floor.

I managed to stay upright, but he got me turned around. King jumped on my back and clobbered me in the head several times. I lashed back at him with my elbows and heard my voice screaming for the guards.

"Git in yer house!" yelled the voice of a guard.

The two black men released their grips.

"Git! Git outta hyar!" another guard yelled.

King scampered away, leaving a trail of blood spatters. Washington sank to the floor, moaning, holding his groin and gasping for air.

Blood poured from my nose, streaming down my face and onto my T-shirt. As a guard took me off to the medical unit, he noted, "We have trouble with those two all the time. We move them somewhere and they jump on whoever's there."

An unsympathetic doctor cleaned up my bloody nose and cracked lip. The partial plate I had gotten while in the Army was cracked too. The doctor declared the damage to be minor and ordered me back to lockup.

But I was not taken back to Dallas death row. Instead, I was marched off to a station known as the control picket, where an officious guard informed me that I was charged with instigating a riot.

"Well that's kind of strange," I said. "Why don't you go up to the tenth floor and see where all the blood is."

"Huh?"

"It's in *my* cell. What the hell did I do, yell, 'Hey, come in here, I'm gonna whip your ass'! Come *on*, people."

Jail officials must have realized that they could never make this charge stick, for it was the last I heard of it. They moved me back to the eighth floor, back to isolation. My new house was only recently vacated by a man who was convicted of killing his daughter. He had been shipped off to the prison farm system near Huntsville to begin serving a life sentence.

I sat in my cell nursing my wounds, trying to analyze the situation. Were Washington and King mad at me for getting rid of their shank? No, that story did not wash. They certainly would not have attacked me if they thought I had their knife. Most likely, they did not even know about it. I could only conclude that the two black men were the type who would naturally gang up on a lone white man, and I was sure that someone knew this before I was left alone in there, and before someone planted a knife in the unit.

Someone had set me up. Who? Why?

You're going on into this prison system, I reminded myself. You're going much deeper. These are not nice people you are dealing with.

January deteriorated even further than that, when the Dallas Cowboys beat the Denver Broncos in the Super Bowl. The city went wild, and that included my fellow inhabitants in the Dallas County jail.

For a time my sleep patterns were totally disrupted. I was up all night and asleep all day. The relatively cold weather of the Dallas winter bothered my arthritis a bit, but more nagging was an ear infection. It took several trips to the medical unit to clear that up.

But as time inched past, things seemed to stabilize, proving, I guess, that you can get used to about anything.

Through her pastor, Mom learned of a clergyman in Dallas, Louis Berceril, known as Brother Louie, and she asked him to visit me. He was an ex-convict who had made his peace with the Lord and dedicated his life to helping other prisoners do the same.

Brother Louie was a stocky muscular man of Mexican descent. He did not look much like a man of the cloth, especially when he removed his suit jacket, revealing his prison tattoos. He came to see me frequently and was a great source of solace. He provided me with numerous religious books to read, and finally was able to find a small TV set to loan to me. In an effort to improve my mind, I watched an educational TV station, picking up some basic knowledge concerning science and English.

One Sunday the newspaper featured an ad from Sears, depicting models posing in the year's "new swimsuits." I cut out the pictures and taped them to my wall. Even better was the local television coverage of tryouts for the Dallas Cowboy cheerleaders. I hated the Cowboys, but I could cope with their cheerleaders.

Over time I realized that one effect of this whole mess was to bring a measure of maturity. I wrote to Mom, "When I'm free I'm coming home to stay. I think my roaming days are over."

. . .

In July, Bruder filed a seventy-five-page brief with the court of criminal appeals in Austin. It listed forty grounds of error, covering all of the points that had incensed his predecessor, Dennis White.

Perhaps Bruder's strongest argument was his contention that my death sentence was unconstitutional because the court disqualified a total of thirteen jurors who expressed some philosophical objections to the death penalty, but never said they would automatically vote against it. He based his argument on the *Witherspoon* decision, and his brief quoted from its eloquent argument:

> . . . a jury that must choose between life imprisonment and capital punishment can do little more— and must do nothing less—than express the conscience of the community on the ultimate question of life and death. Yet, in a nation less than half of whose people believe in the death penalty, a jury composed exclusively of such people cannot speak for the community. Culled of all who harbor doubts about the wisdom of capital punishment—of all who would be reluctant to pronounce the extreme penalty—such a jury can speak only for a distinct and dwindling minority.

Now it was up to the court of criminal appeals to decide whether the jury that decreed my death was truly speaking for the people, or only for "a distinct and dwindling minority."

Bruder advised me that it would probably take the court six to nine months to render a decision. When the conviction was overturned, as we were sure it would be, Dallas County would then have six months to decide whether to retry me or set me free.

Putting that all together, I calculated that I would be released some time late in 1979 or early 1980.

14

THE ROW

IT WAS ABOUT 4:00 A.M. on July 27, 1978, well more than a year after the end of my trial, when I woke to realize that two men, dressed in business suits, were standing outside of my cell. One of them asked, "Randall Dale Adams?"

"Yeah."

"Pack up your shit. You're gone."

"Where?"

"We're here to transport you to death row."

They threw a pair of pants, a shirt, a pair of socks, and some shoes in through the bars. Then they thrust a cup of coffee at me.

One man ran off to attend to the paperwork. The other watched as I gathered my belongings.

They put me in handcuffs and leg shackles, and shuffled me out toward the searcher's desk. There, the guard checked my appearance against the photograph on my file folder.

Soon I was in the backseat of an unmarked car, my chains secured to a large ringbolt attached in the center of the floor. Up front, one of the two men activated the radio as the other headed for a freeway entrance ramp. Behind us, a Dallas County police cruiser pulled into position. Once we hit the open road, the driver floored the accelerator and we sped through the Texas countryside at eighty-five and even ninety miles per hour.

The man riding "shotgun" chattered constantly on his police radio, reporting our current whereabouts. Whenever we reached an exit near a county line, the police cruiser tailing us pulled off, but another was waiting to take up position. We made the 180-mile trip from Dallas to Huntsville in what must have been record time.

Huntsville serves as the hub for more than thirty prison units that dot the surrounding countryside. The Texas Department of Corrections (TDC) Diagnostic Unit is located in the midst of the city, about five minutes off of I-45, and here is where we stopped.

Every TDC inmate is processed through Diagnostics whenever he is moved. A regular prisoner may live here in a two-man cell for weeks as clerks shuffle his papers, physicians check him out, and psychiatrists evaluate the state of his sanity. But a condemned man has priority. I was in and out of Diagnostics within the hours of the morning, and shunted into a TDC minivan. My destination was the Ellis unit.

Along with its nearby twin the Eastham unit, Ellis is reserved for those prisoners considered the most dangerous. Each unit is a small city in and of itself, capable of being more or less self-sufficient.

"Catch the wall!" one of the gray-uniformed guards yelled, as he pushed me from the warden's office into the three-quarter-mile-long central hallway of the Ellis unit. It was the tail end of a lunchtime, so the hallway was crowded. Prisoners clad in white shirts and slacks—like painters' uniforms—moved to and from chow, back and forth to work, or perhaps on commissary errands. They responded immediately to the guard's order, facing the concrete block.

Someone dared to turn his head. "Don't look at this boy," the same guard yelled. "He's a dead man."

I was led to the first of many finger-like wings stretching at right angles off the hallway. This was J-Line, or death row. A sign bolted to the wall above the entrance blared the message, painted by hand on wood: Abandon Hope All Ye Who Enter.

I stepped under the sign and into a rectangular cage. The door was locked behind me. My handcuffs and leg shackles were removed and I was ordered to strip. When I was buck naked, someone threw me a pair of boxer shorts and prison coveralls. I dressed, the inner door was unlocked, and I stepped into my new home, which the state of Texas hoped would be a short-term final residence.

J-Line held three tiers of sixty cells each. Until now, only one of the tiers had been designated as death row, but Henry Wade, Doug Mulder, and their counterparts throughout Texas had been very busy. I arrived shortly after prison officials determined that it was time to expand death row to the second tier of J-Line.

My house was a one-man cubicle, about nine-by-twelve feet, with brick walls on three sides and a barred door in front. At the rear, through a window grate, I could see a small catwalk that ran the length of the tier. My cell was freshly painted, and there was much construction activity evident. Officials were in the process of moving the remaining regular inmates from J-Line and renovating it for incoming condemned men, such as myself. All in all, it was a bit larger and brighter than my previous accommodations.

Television sets were mounted on brackets in the hallway outside of every third cell, and I was situated so that I could watch either to the left or the right. It did not matter, for all the sets were tuned to the same channel. The cell had a radio speaker built into the back wall, with a selector allowing me to choose among rock and roll, country and western, and soul music. Someone told me I would get outside into the courtyard for one hour a day.

I was too late for lunch, but a kindly guard knew I was coming and had saved me a tray. The food was surprisingly good and plentiful—roast turkey and dressing, beans, greens, and some kind of peppers, cornbread, milk and coffee, and cake for dessert. I ate my fill, then lay on my bunk for a time, trying to orient myself. I wrote a quick note to Brother Louie in Dallas. Authorities informed me that I had ten days for someone to come to pick up the personal effects I had left behind, or they would be donated to Goodwill. I knew that Reverend Berceril would take care of it for me.

I wrote to Mom, to give her my new address, and to tell her not to worry.

But I could not stop worrying myself. Despite the good food and the brighter environment, this was death row. What lay ahead?

Slowly, I drifted into troubled sleep.

On Saturday morning, I woke to the sound of birds chirping outside. Looking through the bars and across the catwalk, I could see through an outer window that a bit of rain had fallen overnight, but dawn brought a beautiful summer morning. Before long, a trusty came around to serve a breakfast of scrambled eggs, bacon, toast, and coffee. I thought, Mike Berry was right. This is much better than the Dallas County jail. I fantasized about calling to have a pizza delivered.

As others awoke, men called out morning greetings to one another, shouting down the line, across the hall, and between the tiers. The exchange of pleasantries was interrupted by a late sleeper who began a dialogue with the man in the cell across from him. It went something like this:

"Shut up!"

"Go to hell."

"C'mon guys, I'm trying to sleep."

"Fuck you!"

"Up yours."

This would-be sleeper rushed to the front of his cell and rattled the bars, occasioning more curses and threats to various portions of the anatomy. These men were all condemned to death. How could the guards or anyone else issue any kind of meaningful threat to get them to behave?

TDC had an answer to that question. In midmorning, an "intern" appeared in the halls with a dispensary cart filled with cups of varicolored pills. I did not know whether he was a prison employee or a trusty. Men eagerly reached through the bars of their cells, crying out, "I'll take a pink one today," or "Gimme a couple of greens." All requests were accommodated freely, and soon death row grew quiet.

Then, from somewhere down the hallway, I heard a man carrying on a loud friendly conversation with someone. I tuned my ears to his words and tried to solve a mystery. It sounded as if the man had a visitor in his cell, but I did not think that was allowed.

"Shut up, Brooks!" yelled the man in the cell next to me.

"Who's he talking to?" I called out.

There was a pause. My neighbor knew that I was a newcomer, and he exhibited the wariness of the veteran con. Finally he explained, "Aretha Franklin. Brooks talks to her every day."

After a time I found myself acting as an intermediary, carrying on a conversation with a prisoner below and behind me, who wanted to talk with a man on my tier, but farther off to the side. The two men were fall partners, both on death row for the same crime.

It was mid-morning when I noticed a slim black man standing in front of my cell. He was dressed only in a towel, but he held an open Bible in his hand. He quoted a scripture passage to me and then moved on, repeating his sermonette for my neighbor's benefit.

When he was gone, my neighbor told me that I could expect a daily visit from the Preacher as he made his way to the shower stall at the end of the tier. The Preacher was believed to have raped and murdered anywhere from ten to fifteen women, all of them white.

I spent one precious hour outside that day, in the sunshine of the courtyard along with ten other inmates. We could play basketball or volleyball or just sit in the sun and associate with one another face to face. It was a nice surprise to find that one of the other men in my exercise group was Mike Berry.

However, I took an immediate dislike to Charlie Brooks, Aretha Franklin's bosom buddy. Aside from being crazy, he was a mean-spirited black man who made no attempt to conceal his hatred for whites.

As Berry had told me during our brief conversation in Dallas, most of the death row guards were reasonable men, interested in doing their jobs with as little hassle as possible. They were locked inside a cage full of dangerous men, and if you did not appear to offer a threat, they appreciated it and treated you accordingly.

But there were a few guards here who were as capriciously vicious as those in Dallas. One of them was the intern. For weeks, I watched him hand out whatever pills an inmate requested. Then one day, his attitude changed. Perhaps he was only acting on a whim, or perhaps he held a grudge against his victim. At any rate, when the inmate across from me and one cell down pleaded for a red pill, the intern responded with a sneer, "Fuck you," he said, and moved his cart off down the cell block.

The inmate raged at the intern's back, without satisfaction. Within a half hour he was in withdrawal. He thrashed about his cell, screaming and banging his head against the brick walls and iron bars. I heard the sounds of uncontrollable retching. The guards let him suffer for a while before a team of them entered, overpowered him, and injected a shot of the powerful tranquilizer Thorazine. He was "gone" for many hours. Late that afternoon when he woke up and began screaming again, the guards hit him with another Thorazine injection. Then they lashed him to his bunk and strapped a football helmet onto his head.

Soon, two familiar faces appeared on the row. I saw Roland King march past me to a cell down the line, and a few minutes later Charlie Washington was brought in, and placed nearby, within shouting distance. The last time I saw him, blood was dripping from my nose, but he was doubled over in pain from where I had kicked him in the groin.

I let him get settled, and then I initiated a conversation. "Charlie?" I called out.

"Who the fuck are you?"

I told him and we spoke briefly and not unkindly with one another.

Before long, our conversation was interrupted by the arrival of the commissary man. Washington bought a couple tins of a mackerel concoction called Jack Mack. He made himself a sandwich for breakfast that stunk up the entire wing. He was in hog heaven, and no longer felt like talking.

That afternoon I found him in my exercise group, a faint aura of

Jack Mack still clinging to him. Out here in the yard, we decided to let bygones be bygones. He admitted that the guards back in Dallas had designated him and King as informal "enforcers." Whenever they wanted somebody whipped, they put him in the cell block with Washington and King, and left them alone for a while.

Now I had a chance to learn more about the two. Washington had tried to hold up a liquor store at gunpoint and found himself staring down the twin barrels of the clerk's shotgun. It was a stand-off, and the other man blinked. Washington qualified for the death penalty by committing murder in the course of a felony.

It was King, he told me, who was the crazy dude. High on booze and drugs, and desperate for cash, King broke into a church one Sunday night, tied up the old preacher and his three women collection counters, tossed them all into a car, and drove to an isolated spot in the country.

He sat in the car for a time, getting higher, wondering what to do with his hostages. Over a period of hours he raped each of the three women, starting with the youngest. Finally, he grabbed the old man and dragged him off into the woods to rape him also. When the preacher fought back, King killed him. Now figuring that he had nothing to lose, he shot the women also. But two of the women survived to testify against him. He received a death penalty sentence in one case and, for good measure, a life sentence on one of the other counts.

Hearing this, I was happy that King was not in my exercise group.

Most of the time, we lived in our underwear, for there was simply no reason to get dressed. We were confined to our cells for nearly twenty-three hours of every day, let out only for a shower and exercise. Weeks and months went by with no visitors, no interference whatsoever from the outside world, and so we made friends, as best we could, with one another.

Whenever anyone was carted off for a few days for a court appearance, guards made use of the available space. Because of these absences, as well as the ongoing construction work, there was a constant shuffle in living arrangements that allowed for a bit of variety among one's neighbors.

For a time, my next-door cell mate was a fellow named Buster Watkins, known to everyone as B.W. He had been convicted of the murders of several women, and had a couple of death sentences hanging over his head.

B.W. and I rigged up a way to play chess. I drew the board pattern onto a square of cardboard and hung it out between our cells in front of the bars. It was difficult to see the far corners of the board, but we trusted one another to play honestly.

Another neighbor, briefly, was Billy Fletcher, an ex-cop, who had adopted the habit of stopping a pretty woman on the highway, issuing her a warning, and taking note of her address. Within a day or two he would break into her home and rape her. Ultimately, he killed the daughter of a former state senator. As an ex-cop, he needed special protection. He never left his cell without an escort of at least three quards.

During the second week of August, I finally received a copy of the transcript of my trial. When I first saw it, I was surprised at its brevity. I had expected something massive. I had the time, of course, to study it very carefully, and I was disappointed to realize that a mere written transcript could not reflect many of the tricks that Mulder had used to obtain his death sentence against me.

Bruder wrote to tell me that, despite its failings, there still was plenty of ammunition here to cause an appellate court to order a reversal, and I agreed. I believed that any objective reader would be forced to that conclusion—but the dry words on official paper could not convey the nuances that had so obviously swayed the jury and subverted justice.

The first phenomenon of the row is denial. The state had declared its intention to execute me, but I did not believe that it could ever happen.

But death row is a house of sorrow, and the issue of existence hangs heavily over each inmate. You can only deny reality for so long. After a time, the best you can do is try not to dwell upon it.

I wrote in my journal:

> I was told repeatedly by the Correctional Officers
> and inmates that "only the dead live here." And it
> is true that a lot of dead souls are being housed
> here . . .
>
> I was astonished that the "mark of Cain" was not
> tattooed upon my forehead or burnt into my arm for
> the world to see. It could not have been any worse
> than what the state had already done to me and my
> family . . .

Somewhere I read a description of what it is like to be electrocuted. Back in 1946, seventeen-year-old Willie Francis actually survived a trip to Louisiana's electric chair. He reported later that his mouth tasted like cold peanut butter and that he saw blue, pink, and green dots in front of his eyes. A year after this experience, Francis took another trip to the electric chair, where the state of Louisiana finished the job.

Death became a shadowy specter hanging at the edges of my mind. I tried to banish it, but it hovered, never very far from consciousness. I tried to pass the time and hoped, paradoxically, that it would not pass. Determined to hide this from Mom, I kept my letters light; nevertheless, I still had to use an official TDC letter form that blared the message, "TO THE PERSON RECEIVING THIS LETTER: Mail is opened and inspected in compliance with TDC Rules and Regulations." Sometimes, to soften the impact, I drew a "smile" face below my signature.

Although I was careful not to overdo it, I found myself accepting an occasional dose of medication from the intern. Some days, some nights, I just had to get the hell out of this place, and a pill was the only available transportation.

A novel floated around from inmate to inmate. It was written by a former death row guard from Florida, and the plot dealt with three men and two women whom Florida wanted to execute on the same day. The author had witnessed a number of executions, dating back prior to 1972, and he wrote with eerie insight about the procedures that occur within the days leading up to an execution.

We all knew how it worked, and often—too often—I sat in my house quietly, reviewing the drill in my mind: Three days before my death, a heavily armed troop of guards would come, shackle my legs and chain my arms, and usher me none too gently into a prison van. They would drive me forty-five miles to a special facility in Huntsville, deep within a maximum security wing of the Walls unit. That cell, rumored to be thirteen steps away from the death chamber, is where I would spend the last seventy-two hours of my life.

At first my mind dwelt upon a word-picture burnt into my memory ever since the jury selection phase of my trial. I heard the echo of the district attorney's voices as they described the process to numerous prospective jurors: "They strap him into the chair. Then they fire so much juice into his body that the eyeballs explode and the blood runs down his face. His fingernails pop off and his toenails pop off and he bleeds from every orifice of his body."

It became apparent, however, that that grisly scenario would not come to pass, even though the end result would be the same. If TDC and the state legislature had its way, they would scrap the old electric chair and one of us here on the row, perhaps I, would become the first person in the U.S. to be executed by lethal injection. Guards would strap me onto a gurney, insert an IV needle into my arm and begin to drip harmless glucose into my veins. Then at some moment, when the warden of the Walls Unit gave the signal, they would add cyanide to the mixture.

My friend and fellow death row denizen, Mike Berry, took issue with this change. When the *Dallas Times-Herald* printed an editorial declaring that lethal injection was a more humane form of capital punishment than the electric chair, Berry wrote a letter to the editor:

> I strongly object to the use of the word "humane" when used in conjunction with the death penalty or the taking of a human life in any form whatsoever . . . It is downright hypocritical to refer to the deeds committed by those on death row as "heinous" while referring to lethal injection as a form of execution as "most humane," and all in the same paragraph.

It did not matter all that much to me. Dead is dead.

I had always considered myself a nonviolent person, but I wondered if I could maintain that final shred of dignity. How would I react when the guards came to my door? Would I stand passively and allow them to cuff and shackle me? Would I walk those final steps in peace, stare into the eyes of my executioners, and declare, "You people are wrong, dead wrong, but if this is what we have to do, let's do it"?

Or would I fight? As the death squad walked into my cell, would I challenge them? Would I tell them, "You're going to have to drag me out of here, because I'm not going on my own!"

Either way, I vowed, before they carry out Execution Order Number 602, I will insist upon my right to a few final words. Because I *do* have something to say.

Way back in 1964, the U.S. Supreme Court had rendered a decision allowing inmates the right to challenge state prison practices in federal court. Eight years later, TDC inmate David Ruiz decided to do just that. He drafted a thirty-page handwritten petition complaining of inhumane living conditions. Foolishly, Ruiz took the letter to Warden Billy McMillan to have his signature notarized. According to Ruiz, the warden said, "I'm going to tell you what I think about inmates' rights . . . This." He tore up the petition.

Ruiz rewrote the petition and managed to get it to U.S. District Judge William Wayne Justice. The judge eventually combined that complaint with several others that he had received, creating a picture of overcrowding, poor working conditions, poor security, inadequate medical care, and abuses (including vicious beatings and murders) perpetrated by inmate supervisors known as "building tenders." If successful, this class-action lawsuit, known as *Ruiz v. Texas,* was likely to result in the most sweeping changes ever ordered by the federal government within a state prison system.

The U.S. Justice Department had entered the case in 1974 as a "friend of the court." Among other abuses, its investigators found that, in the general population facilities, as many as four prisoners were crowded into nine-by-five-foot cells. In their legal brief, Justice Department attorneys noted, "They literally live on top of each other, watch each other defecate and have absolutely no privacy."

TDC slowed the process of the suit with every available legal maneuver, and it was not until 1978 that Judge Justice was prepared to formally convene the trial that would develop a record of systematic abuses.

We became a part of this investigation. One morning the guards coerced everyone to get dressed, warning that we were about to receive a special visit from a group of court-appointed observers, here to inspect the conditions of life at Ellis. Berry shouted up to me the news that he had fashioned a small sign to display at the front of his cell. It proclaimed: *Homo sapiens.*

When the visitors arrived, the Preacher obliged them with an impromptu sermon.

The national press covered the issue of the pending inmate lawsuit, and Mom, alert for anything regarding prison life, heard about it. She wrote, inquiring in a worried tone what was going on. I replied:

> Texas is the only state that makes a profit on its prison system. That's one of the reasons it looks so good on the outside and on paper, but the inside that most people don't see is what's so bad. Here where I'm at isn't too bad . . . but elsewhere it is overcrowded, the food is worse, the working conditions are bad and they don't have the guards to protect most of the inmates from each other. Texas only has 1/3 the guards that other states have even though it is the biggest in the U.S.

I reminded Mom that this was one of the better aspects of living under a death sentence. It was meager comfort to her, I knew, but at least on the row we were fed better, isolated, and more strictly supervised.

Periodically we voted on the TV programming, and the results were predictable: cartoons when they were available, soap operas in the afternoon, action shows in the evening. And if any kind of sports programming was on, we watched it.

This eventually became so boring that I altered my daily routine. I began to wake up earlier, about five in the morning, to savor the quiet time. I made myself a cup of coffee and stared out the window, watching a large dark-colored snake make his regular, early morning rounds. The chain link fencing surrounding J-Line was a favorite spot for birds to nest, and was, therefore, a happy hunting ground for a snake in search of eggs.

During those next few hours of solace, I read ten chapters of the Bible. I started with Genesis 1, and resolved to go the whole way through—if I had enough time.

Later on, when the cell block settled into its noisy routine, I drew a pillow over my head and tried to take a nap.

The *Ruiz* trial began in Tyler, Texas, on October 2, 1978. Simultaneously, soft grumblings among the inmate population turned into louder and louder arguments, and finally burgeoned into open revolt. Hundreds of inmates in various TDC units proclaimed work strikes and hunger strikes in order to enhance the publicity surrounding the court proceedings.

My vantage point was limited, but I knew that here at Ellis, among the general population, hundreds of inmates had gathered in the exercise yard, refusing to work, and refusing to return to their cells. On the Row, we were confined to our houses and denied exercise privileges until things cooled off.

Mom flew to Dallas and met with Mel Bruder before Ray drove her down to the Ellis unit to see me on October 27. She told me that Bruder had no news concerning the appeal, other than to report that the court was still sitting on it.

During the conversation, Mom mentioned that she was going to contact the famous Houston attorney Richard "Racehorse" Haynes to see if he would be willing to defend me in the event that the appeals court ordered a retrial. This was fine with Bruder, for his specialty was appeals, not courtroom theatrics.

At one point Bruder mused, "You should have had Mulder for your attorney. He could have pulled his tricks in your favor."

Mom responded, "But that's not justice."

My appellate attorney asked, "Justice? What is justice?"

I finished reading the Bible in late January, and decided to go through it again, reasoning that I would understand even more of it the second time. I talked to the prison chaplain about being baptized again, to affirm my faith. My mind was ripe for some philosophical conversation.

Three cells down from me was an American Indian named Thomas Barefoot. During brief encounters in the exercise yard we got to talking. Barefoot was convicted of killing Harker Heights, Texas Police Officer Carl LeVin and had received his death sentence partly as a result of punishment phase testimony by the same Dr. Grigson who had condemned me.

To me, Barefoot did not appear to be a continuing threat to society. He was, in fact, a recent convert to Christianity but, unlike the Preacher, he was quiet about it. We had some good discussions about why we were here, and what grand plan God had in all of this. We could not fathom why we were thrust into this situation, but we had faith that there was some purpose to it all.

15

THE SHORT-TIMER'S CALENDAR

ON JANUARY 31, 1979, with the issues before them for only two months and the holiday season intervening, the Court of Criminal Appeals ruled on my appeal, wherein Bruder had identified forty separate instances of error. The court's opinion made for gut-wrenching reading, for it systematically tore apart all forty points.

The appellate court held that, while pending charges such as those David Harris had faced in Vidor are admissable to show the bias and motive of a witness, Dennis White had failed to make that specific objection during my trial; therefore, Judge Metcalfe was correct in suppressing this evidence. This was incredible! Before, during, and after the testimony phase of the trial, White had argued the vital importance of this testimony as it fit into his "crime spree" theory. If the evidence is true, what difference does it make?

Likewise, the court contended that White had not followed up vigorously enough on his attempts to question Police Officer Teresa Turko, in front of the jury, concerning the investigation of her positioning by the Dallas police department Internal Affairs Division. The court's opinion cited a bit of conversation between White, Mulder, and the judge, which was conducted at the bench, out of the hearing of the jury, and out of my own earshot too. Here, Mulder had suddenly withdrawn his objections to this line of questioning, giving White a free hand to pursue the theme. It was the court's opinion that White did not take advantage of Mulder's sudden spate of generosity, and on this point, I had to agree.

One of our strongest points was the failure of the district attorney's office to show us, in a timely fashion, Emily Miller's initial statement to the police, describing the killer as "a Mexican or a very light-skinned black man." But instead of pointing an accusatory finger at the assistant district attorney, the court chastised White for waiting too long to ask to see the statement—even though he had not known of its existence until three days had passed and Mrs. Miller was supposedly on her way to Belleville, Illinois. At any rate, Judge E.F. Dally, writing the court's opinion, declared, "After examining the entire record, we cannot say that Emily Miller's written statement creates a reasonable doubt as to appellant's guilt."

On perhaps our biggest issue, that the court's method of selecting jurors violated my constitutional rights, the court concluded tersely, "We have reviewed the *voir dire* examinations . . . and concluded that the trial court was correct in its determination."

Finally, the appellate court addressed the issue of whether or not the death penalty was too severe in my case, and it used, as a basis for its opinion, the professional determinations of the court-appointed psychiatrists. Judge Dally wrote: "At the punishment hearing, Dr. John Holbrook, a psychiatrist, testified that he had examined appellant and determined that he has the profile and characteristics of a sociopath. Holbrook also testified that he would expect little or no change in this diagnosis in the future and that, in his opinion, appellant would commit criminal acts of violence in the future that would constitute a continuing threat to society. Dr. James Grigson, another psychiatrist, gave similar testimony. This testimony, when considered with the evidence of the crime itself, which was a particularly senseless and motiveless killing, is sufficient to support the jury's determination that appellant would constitute a continuing threat to society."

The court ruled nine to zero to uphold my conviction and death sentence.

This latest development mobilized my family. Visits were allowed only once every two weeks at Ellis, but Mom corresponded with the warden and worked out a deal. Since she lived so far away, she would be allowed to visit me on a Friday, at the end of one visiting period, and see me again on Monday, at the beginning of the next period. She had no reason to tell the warden how she planned to spend her weekend.

In the second week of February, Mom flew to Dallas along with her friend Marlene, who was also the assistant pastor at her church. Ray met them at the Dallas airport and drove them in his company's pickup truck to Huntsville. The next day, a Friday, Ray brought them out to the Ellis unit. Only two visitors were allowed inside, so Ray remained in the truck in the prison parking lot as Mom and Marlene came to see me. Mom brought me up to date on the family news, and Marlene prayed with me.

Then Mom and Marlene hightailed it to Houston. Mom was determined to see Racehorse Haynes in person and cajole him into taking my case. Somehow she obtained his home telephone number and called him on Friday night. He answered the phone himself and listened patiently. Mom introduced herself, told him she was in town only for the weekend, and asked for an appointment.

"Come to my office tomorrow at two," he said, "but ask to speak with Sissy, or you won't get in."

On Saturday afternoon, when Mom found herself face to face with the legendary defense attorney, she had to work hard to restrain her tears. She wanted to remain dignified, to keep this conversation on a professional level, but it was difficult. The words that she had rehearsed simply tumbled out. "Mr. Haynes," she implored, "we need help. We can't offer you the money that you are used to getting, but would you please take my son's case?"

Haynes knew the broad details of my case, and he believed that my appeal had merit. But he appeared tired as he pointed to a mountain of paperwork and replied, "Mrs. Adams, you see here? I am tied up with this millionaire's trial and there is no way I can take your case."

The business at hand, for Haynes, was securing the acquittal of Fort Worth businessman T. Cullen Davis, who had been accused of trying to hire someone to murder the judge in his divorce case. Mom knew this, but she hoped desperately that Haynes could devote some of his time to me. Her face fell.

Haynes tried to be consoling. "If I were you," he said, "I would keep Mel Bruder on the case. He's a very good appeals attorney." Haynes suggested that if we wanted someone else, we might try Randy Schaffer, another Houston-based lawyer with whom Haynes had worked in the past.

Mom noted the name, and filed it away.

On Monday she returned to see me, and this time Ray was with her. When I saw him, I thought he had put on a bit of weight.

Ray was mad. Over the weekend, someone had stolen the company pickup truck right from under his nose. He happened to glance out of the window of his motel room just in time to see the truck leaving the parking lot. He chased after the thief, yelling out his rage, but could only watch the truck disappear into the distance, carrying many of his personal effects. He reported the theft to the police, but they had not yet located the truck.

Mom was forced to rent a car for the remainder of the weekend. After our visit, Ray drove Mom and Marlene back to the Dallas airport and returned the rental car there.

On March 21, Bruder filed another petition with the Court of Criminal Appeals, asking for a rehearing on my case. That was quickly denied, paving the way for Judge Metcalfe to recall me to Dallas.

At 1:00 P.M. on April 5, 1979, I once more stood before Judge Metcalfe in Dallas Criminal Court Number Two. The ceremony was informal, designed mostly to put the facts on the record and, perhaps, to provide District Attorney Henry Wade with another opportunity for a press conference.

Judge Metcalfe ordered me to stand. His stern gaze served as a warning against any outbreaks of emotion.

I rose, with Bruder at my side, and heard the judge decree that May 8, 1979, was the date of my death. The words filtered into my consciousness, but they did not sound real.

"Does the prosecution have anything to say?" the judge asked.

"No," Mulder replied.

"Does the defendant have anything to say?"

"No, Your Honor," Bruder said. "But I would like to have about ten minutes with my client."

"Yes. Your request is granted. Court is adjourned."

In the holding area behind the courtroom, Bruder told me that he would immediately file an application for a stay, asking U.S. Supreme Court Justice Lewis F. Powell, Jr., to delay my execution in order to allow the highest court in the land to hear the grievances that Texas had summarily rejected. He had the application all prepared, awaiting my signature.

I scanned the papers. The legal wording had a strange plaintive tone. After briefly raising the multitude of issues surrounding my case, Bruder wrote, "Wherefore, the petitioner prays that a stay of execution be granted. . . ."

Indeed, I did pray, for if Justice Powell refused the request, I had thirty-three days to live.

I spent another week in the Dallas County jail, and the one bright spot was a visit from Captain Messenger, the guard who had befriended me here earlier. He was assigned to another of the local jails now, but he took time off to see me before I was shipped back to the Row. He wished me the best, and expressed the hope that the appeals process would stay the execution date and, ultimately, vindicate me.

He was a good man.

It was Friday the 13th when I was returned to death row. In my absence, the living quarters had shifted once more and I was shunted into a new cell, with new neighbors.

When I stepped into my house, I saw something lying on the floor. It appeared to be a booklet of some kind. I stopped to pick it up and immediately realized that TDC's version of the welcome wagon had paid me a visit. In my hands was a "short-timer's" calendar, a desk calendar with most of the leaves ripped out, so that it contained only twenty-six pages, beginning with this day, April 13, 1979, and ending on May 8.

As I held it in the palm of my hand, its feather weight was a tangible reminder of how fleeting is this commodity of time. I knew that all around me was a justice system full of guards, police officers, district attorneys, judges, and politicians who believed it was high time that they got the execution ball rolling again. They had this new tool at their disposal, lethal injection, and were itching to use it.

The next morning, the sight of the short-timer's calendar greeted me as I awoke. I tried to avoid looking at it, but felt a compelling urge. I resisted for a time, but soon I picked it up and, very slowly, pulled off a single page and crumpled the paper in my hand.

Down the hallway I heard Candy Man scream out to someone. I knew him by reputation. Ronald Clark O'Bryan was a short obese fellow convicted of lacing his own son's Halloween treats with poison, in order to collect on insurance.

Suddenly the entire world seemed mad. I now had twenty-five days to live, and I was locked in amidst a society of misfits. What was I supposed to do with this one precious day?

One of my new neighbors was Henry Martinez Porter, a Hispanic from Fort Worth. I asked if he played chess and he said yes. So I hung my cardboard chess set out between the bars and we spent a few hours playing and swapping stories.

Back in Fort Worth, Henry had pulled off a string of jewelry store robberies, and believed that the police had no evidence against him. But one day he was driving through town when a patrol car stopped him. He had a few anxious moments, but the police officer merely issued a warning for speeding, and let him go. Then, Porter told me, as he pulled back into traffic, he noticed that the patrol car was following. He watched carefully in his mirror, hoping that the car would veer off, but it did not. After about a mile, the officer suddenly activated his lights and siren.

Porter reasoned that the officer had radioed in a license plate check, and that his run of successful robberies had come to an end. That police officer died much like Officer Wood, lying by the side of the road in a pool of blood as Porter sped away.

He headed for Austin, and holed up at a friend's house. It was about 4:30 A.M. when the front door blew open. Porter shot and killed the two officers who raced inside.

"By now I'd killed three cops," Porter said. I could hear him slap a hand against the side of his head as he added, "and it hit me too late. Why'd I shoot the first cop? 'Cause I thought he was on to us." Much later, at his trial, Porter realized that the officer had simply forgotten to return his driver's license, and was trying to do so.

Porter was sentenced to death three times over. His own case was embroiled in the appeals system, but he knew it was only a matter of time before he was executed, unless some court somewhere put an indefinite hold upon Texas's plans.

As we played chess, we talked a bit about Small Paul. It was his case that seemed to hold out the best hope for all of us.

James "Small Paul" Burns stood only about 5'5" tall, and he was kind of chunky. Nevertheless, he possessed the traditional haughty attitude of the good ol' white boy from Texas. Here's the story, the way I heard it. One night, some years before I had the chance to make his acquaintance in the recreation yard, Small Paul found himself on a barstool, sitting next to an older man, expensively dressed, who inadvisably flashed a fat wallet whenever he bought another round of drinks. The man was obviously drunk and just as obviously homosexual; Small Paul found these to be ingratiating circumstances. He allowed the old man to seduce him into his car. They drove off to some isolated location, whereupon Small Paul robbed him, beat him unconscious, and left him sleeping in a drunken stupor.

As it happened, a few weeks later the same pitiful man walked into the same bar and sat down next to Small Paul, showing no sign of recognition. They repeated the scenario. Late that night he tied the old man to the grille of his car and beat and raped him. This time the man died.

Small Paul's appeal was similar to mine in one key point. His attorney argued that he had been denied due process because three of his potential jurors were excused for cause after they expressed some misgivings about the death penalty and refused to take the required oath. Porter told me that only yesterday, as I was enroute back to death row, Small Paul had won a victory. A three-judge federal court panel had overturned his conviction and ordered a retrial. A story in the *Houston Post* quoted defense attorney Marvin O. Teague declaring, "It may well knock out every death penalty case." But Teague also predicted that Texas would fight the decision "with every weapon in their legal arsenal."

Indeed, the state immediately appealed to the U.S. Fifth Circuit Court of Appeals, and vowed to take Small Paul all the way to the Supreme Court, if necessary. Here at the Ellis unit, there were many interested spectators.

My mind became the arena of a great debate. Bruder held out hope that the Supreme Court would not allow Texas to kill me until it had a chance to review my case. The odds, he said, were good that I would not die on May 8, and one portion of my brain tended to agree.

But there was another voice within me that argued, why should the Supreme Court or anyone else listen to me? To them, I was merely another Charlie Washington or Roland King or Candy Man or Henry Martinez Porter. Long ago I had lost the constitutional right of the presumption of innocence. To them, I was a cop killer.

By now, six years had passed since the U.S. Supreme Court had voided all of the old death penalty laws. Since that time, only the suicidal Gary Gilmore had been executed. Not one death row prisoner in the entire country had been executed against his will, and everyone here placed his hope in that fact.

But more than once I said aloud, "Randall, you're the one they're not going to care about."

Over and over I replayed it in my head and the more I dwelt upon it, the crazier it seemed.

The events of that fateful day of November 27, 1976, were burned into my memory, now that I had relived them so many times. It was still early morning when David Harris stopped his car in front of the gas station, to ask if I needed help. By now I could recite the timing of everything that happened throughout the remainder of the day. From this vantage point, in dark retrospect, it all seemed so ridiculous. Why had I bothered to spend the day with the kid? Why did I not dump him when he started brandishing the pistol? I was guilty of stupidity, perhaps, but was that a capital offense?

Then there was the nagging question of time. Harris agreed, more or less, with my account of the events of the day, but he said that everything happened two or three hours later and the jury believed him, not me.

There were so many instances where my memory differed from the memories of others.

During my interrogation, I remembered that I had asked, repeatedly, for the opportunity to call my brother Ray; Detective Johnson testified that I had not asked to use a phone.

I remembered Johnson leaving to do some Christmas shopping; he said he never left.

This recollection was especially vivid: Detective Gus Rose standing over me, pointing his service revolver between my eyes, demanding that I sign a confession; Rose would later characterize this as "a friendly conversation."

The smallest details were blurred. I remembered the detectives bringing me a pack of cheese crackers; Johnson said they brought me a sandwich.

I remembered signing one statement at the end of my interrogation; Mulder introduced two signed statements into evidence.

I remembered three brief sessions with the lie detector, all administered by the same man; Mulder said I had failed two tests administered by two different men.

I remembered spending about an hour and a half with Dr. Holbrook; he said our interview lasted three hours.

Sometimes it seemed as if I was the only rational person left on the earth, but in the darker moments, as the short-timer's calendar grew evermore slim, the numerical weight of the evidence pressed upon me, smothering me. Were they right? Had my mind ceased to function in a logical manner? Was I, indeed, a sociopath who, in Dr. Holbrook's words, "could work all day and figure out how to grind somebody up the next day"?

I woke from fitful sleep on May 5. There were a mere three pages left on my short-timer's calendar. This, I knew, was the day when they must come for me, to move me to the death cell in Huntsville only a few steps away from the execution chamber.

As I waited the arrival of the guards, I wrote in my journal:

> Most people have never had to look upon the face of death. He stands just past your shoulder and watches your every move. But when you turn, he has fled. Yet you know that soon he will reappear, and when you turn to look again, he will stand his ground; claim you for his own; draw you into his shadow with an embrace as cold as ice.

What is it like? Do you simply cease to exist, pass into nothingness? Is there a superior being out there who gathers you unto Him? I did not know, and I did not feel that I was ready to find out.

I believe that everything that happens to man is known by someone or something, and I could not escape the conclusion that this mysterious entity was watching me now, very carefully.

Why had my life come to this?

What was the purpose? Surely there must be one.

Was this no more than a joke played out for the amusement of the gods? Or was there some deeper consideration, one that I could not discern?

I believe that man has a soul that survives his body, but it worried me that the soul, after death, might experience some sort of alteration, so that it does not know, or does not care, about mortal considerations. If it was time for me to walk into that execution chamber, I wanted some assurance that, somewhere, somehow, I could look back and figure out how it occurred, and why. I wanted to be able to follow the course of events after my death, to see what happened to my persecutors. Does the disembodied soul harbor vengeance? I hoped so.

"I want to stand in the gap for Randy," Mom said. Her friends gathered around her in a protective, womb-like circle. The pastor anointed her brow with a dab of olive oil. All about, her friends joined hands, drawing into a tight circle of prayer. Mom cried out, "God, I know you send guardian angels to all of us. Please, keep Randy's angels around him all the time, and if You see danger approaching, put Your arms around him. Keep the danger away."

Mom knew Who would have the last word. It wasn't Mulder or Metcalfe or the governor of the state of Texas or even the Supreme Court of the United States.

16

THE HANGING JURY

ON THE MORNING of May 8, with a certain sense of glee, I pulled off the final page of my short-timer's calendar. Here I was, still on death row at Ellis. No one had come to tell me anything, but neither had they come to take me to Huntsville.

I did not know what had happened, but something or someone had thwarted Texas's plans.

It was not until May 10, two days *after* I was scheduled to die, that I received a letter from Bruder. It advised me: "I received word yesterday from the clerk's office of the Supreme Court that Mr. Justice Powell stayed your execution until the filing of a petition for certiorari, and that the stay will continue in effect until the petition for certiorari is determined by the Supreme Court."

Slowly I began to climb out of the pit that was meant to be my grave. My eyes were opened to life in a new way. I was sure now that there was some reason for all of this, but I wondered if I would live long enough to understand what it was.

I sent Mom a Mother's Day card, and wrote in it:

> Please don't worry too much, because everything is in God's hands and the Lord is watching over.
>
> It's like the little girl who prayed for rain one night to help her flowers. The next day was sunshine and bright. She got ready for school and took her umbrella. One of her friends asked her what she was doing with an umbrella on a day like this. She told him she had prayed for rain and didn't want to get wet *when it did!*

As I awaited word on what the entire Supreme Court would do, time ran out on a short-timer's calendar in Florida.

In late 1972, and early 1973, while a fugitive from the California prison system, John Arthur Spenkelink and another career criminal, Joe Szymankiewicz, had roamed the country on a random crime spree. That ended on February 3, when, in a cheap motel room in Tallahassee, Spenkelink bludgeoned Szymankiewicz and shot him twice.

At his trial, Spenkelink claimed self-defense, but the victim's wounds had all been inflicted from the back. Six years and twenty-two appeals later, it was time for him to die.

In recent years, Spenkelink had spent his time on Florida's death row reading the Bible, as well as the works of the mystical Edgar Cayce, and had coined the phrase: "Capital punishment means those without capital get the punishment."

His mother, speaking of Florida's Governor Robert Graham, wailed, "How can he kill my son, my only son?!"

On May 31, 1979, at 9:50 A.M., the U.S. Supreme court rejected Spenkelink's appeal for the fourth and final time. Twenty-eight minutes later Spenkelink was dead, after three separate surges of 2,250 volts of electricity shot through his body.

When we heard the news on J-Line, we sensed that some of the guards and prison officials were jealous. To a man, we regarded this as far more serious than the execution of Gary Gilmore. Gilmore had wanted to die; Spenkelink had wanted to live.

In the eyes peering out of cells around me I saw a new realization, a message: *this is not a game.*

It seemed obvious that the courts were ready to sweep away the morass of technical objections raised by myself and every other death row inmate in America. We were about to see a flood tide of executions, and we were all caught in the undertow.

A change in the rotation of the exercise groups gave me a chance to get acquainted with Excell White, one of the first men in America to receive a death sentence under the new laws. The tall, skinny, sad-looking man had been here for a half dozen years.

I knew a lot about him already, for he was one of our most controversial residents. Every six months or so, White sank into a depression and ordered his attorneys to drop his appeals. Several times, the date of his execution had been set. But each time, special interest groups such as the ACLU and the NAACP lobbied him to resume his fight for life. And each time he relented, beginning the appeals again. As it happened, this was an effective way to prolong the entire process, and the authorities were beginning to suspect that White had planned the strategy all along.

White confided to me that another inmate had threatened that if he dropped his appeals one more time, he had better let Texas execute him, or he'd be a dead son of a bitch in the yard someday. He warned, "You're getting the courts pissed off at all of us."

The more I learned about Texas and its law enforcement system, the more it seemed like a hideous joke.

For instance, Texas had a law regarding habitual criminals, requiring that anyone convicted of a third felony must receive a life sentence. This was applied with full force to an unfortunate man who was convicted of three felonies, wherein he had swindled a total of $250. For that paltry sum, he was given a life sentence. Yet, at about the same time, a former Texas judge, having received an eight-year sentence for taking a substantial bribe, was freed after only three months, under the provisions of something called "shock probation."

The legal system seemed far more interested in politics than justice. In its current session, the state legislature was considering a bill that would authorize a life sentence for a police officer convicted of violating the civil rights of a person under arrest. Liberals proclaimed that it was a necessary tool to discourage police brutality; conservatives argued that it would hamstring the already beleaguered police. A dozen state legislators, unwilling to go on record on either side of this controversial issue, simply went into hiding. Their absence prevented the legislature from acting upon anything. The Texas Rangers were assigned the task of finding these legal ostriches, but I suspected that they did not look too hard.

And now, for the very first time, it seemed that Henry Wade's stranglehold on Dallas County weakened a bit. He got himself involved in a public feud with maverick Judge Tom Price. Charges and counter-charges flew about the press, and made for interesting reading in the newspapers. Some said that Wade had turned over too much authority to his chief assistant, Doug Mulder, and had lost control of the office.

One news report noted that eight of Dallas's ten felony judges were former assistants of Wade, and, all told, a whopping total of six hundred practicing attorneys in Dallas had once worked for the man. No wonder the Dallas Bar was such an exclusive club.

For some time, the U.S. Supreme Court had been concerned about the issue of jury selection in a capital case. They were eyeing Small Paul's appeal in the Fifth Circuit Court, and waiting for the moment it might get to them. But when they studied Bruder's brief on my case, they, in effect, told the lower court to forget about the issue. In December 1979, the justices announced that they would consider the process of jury selection in *State of Texas v. Randall Dale Adams,* and their decision was likely to affect, not only myself and Small Paul, but as many as half of our immediate neighbors, and countless other death row inmates around the country.

It was the first time in three years that the Supreme Court decided to grant a full hearing on a death penalty petition and it brought attention to my case from several circles.

A film crew from Dallas Public Broadcasting Service showed up at Ellis, intent upon interviewing me concerning the pending Supreme Court hearing. The reporter assured me that he had cleared the interview with Bruder, but he had nothing in writing to prove it. I suffered an attack of nerves. What if these TV boys twisted and turned my statements? What if this adventure into publicity somehow angered the members of the Supreme Court, and influenced them against me? At the last moment, I declined to speak with them and the crew had to settle for an interview with the warden.

My case was considered so critical that the NAACP Legal Defense and Educational Fund, Inc., filed an amicus curiae (friend of the court) brief to supplement Bruder's opinions. That brief quoted from a U.S. Fifth Circuit Court of Appeals decision in 1970, which declared "The stark reality is that one improperly excluded juror may mean the difference between life or death for the defendant." In my case, the brief argued, "Not one but several venire members were unconstitutionally excluded. . . . The jury selection process here 'stacked the deck' against Randall Dale Adams."

Melvin Bruder argued before the Supreme Court on March 24, 1980. He spelled out the heart of the issue, Section 12.31(b) of the Texas Penal Code, which required a prospective juror to swear that the mandatory penalty of death or imprisonment for life would not affect his deliberations on any issue of fact.

Bruder noted that the Supreme Court, in its 1968 *Witherspoon* decision, had set specific guidelines for jury selection in capital cases, designed to insure that the composition of the jury maintained "a link between contemporary community values and the penal system," so that it reflected "the evolving standards of decency that mark the progress of a maturing society." *Witherspoon* declared that the exclusion of prospective jurors "simply because they have voiced general objections to the death penalty or expressed conscientious or religious scruples against its infliction," denies the accused due process of law. Bruder reminded the justices that their own language in *Witherspoon* declared that a selection procedure that culls "all who harbor doubts about the wisdom of capital punishment" produces "a hanging jury," a "tribunal organized to return the verdict of death," "a jury uncommonly willing to condemn a man to die."

Bruder expressed his agreement with the Supreme Court's previous position that it is acceptable to exclude jurors who state unequivocally that they cannot vote for the death penalty under any circumstances, for this makes it impossible for them to adhere to the juror's oath that they uphold the administration of the law. But a juror's personal views on the death penalty are irrelevant, he argued, if that juror indicates that he or she can subordinate those views to the task at hand.

In his brief to the court, Bruder concentrated on seven of the most glaring instances where the Texas statute had been applied in my case, instances where prospective jurors stated that they would not automatically vote against the death penalty, but who, for various reasons, declined to take the required oath.

"It was never unmistakably established that any one of them was so irrevocably opposed to the death penalty that he would automatically vote against its imposition regardless of the evidence," Bruder argued. Therefore, he said, all of these jurors were qualified under the Supreme Court's *Witherspoon* standard. Yet they were dismissed by Judge Metcalfe because they could not fulfill the requirements of Texas law.

The result, Bruder contended, was that when I walked into that courtroom on April 26, 1977, to begin the testimony phase of the trial, I faced "a hanging jury," a "tribunal organized to return a verdict of death," "a jury uncommonly willing to condemn a man to die."

Afterward, Bruder wrote me, prophesying cautiously that we had "a good chance" of winning. He predicted that Justices Brennan, Marshall, Stewart, and Stevens would vote for me, while the Chief Justice and Justices White and Rehnquist would vote for the state. He guessed that one of the remaining justices, Powell or Blackmun, would vote with us, giving us at least the five votes we needed.

Mom and I wasted no time laying plans for a retrial. Following up on Mom's initial conversation with Racehorse Haynes, we both wrote to him, hoping that his work on the T. Cullen Davis case was winding down and that he would reconsider taking my case in the evermore likely event that the Supreme Court would send it back before Judge Metcalfe.

Meanwhile, church services came to death row. On the first Sunday, about fifteen jumpsuit-clad prison parishioners gathered in the day-room at the far end of J-Line. A gentleman in a business suit introduced himself as a chaplain and proceeded to hand out a supply of battered hymnals.

"Dear heavenly Father," he intoned, "thank You for allowing us to gather together here . . ." He ignored the chuckles, announced a page number and led us in a hymn.

Then he instructed us to open our Bibles to the first chapter of Genesis. We followed as he read through the chapter. Briefly the chaplain summarized what we had read, led us in a second hymn, offered a benediction, and sent us back to our cells.

On the following Sunday we covered Genesis, chapter two.

By the fifth Sunday, as we were making our way through the fifth chapter of Genesis, I could stand it no more.

I interrupted the chaplain's reading. "May I ask a question?" I said.

"Certainly."

"Do you know where you are?"

This was not the question he anticipated. He paused for a moment and then replied hesitantly, "Yes, of course, this is the Ellis unit."

"More specifically than that," I pushed.

"Death row," he said.

"That's correct. Do you realize that everybody here is under a death sentence?"

"Yes."

"Do you understand that many of us don't have a lot of time, much longer to live?"

"Yes. I understand that, too."

"I've been coming here for five weeks," I said, "and we are now up to Genesis, chapter five. I don't think any of us are going to be around by the time you get to Revelations!"

The chaplain's posture shifted dramatically. His words dribbled off into a recitation concerning the vicissitudes of life—his in particular.

I returned to my cell and watched Larry Bird shoot basketball.

Not long after that, out in the yard one day, Mike Berry and I were in the midst of a chess game. Various others in our exercise group were playing volleyball or walking in the sun. Everyone always had a cheerful "Hello, Papa-san" greeting for the effusive Berry.

The Preacher happened by, and he interrupted us with a Bible reading.

I was in a mood to challenge this flaunting style of religion and I baited him, asking him if it was God who had told him to hide in the bushes, wait for all those white women to come by, then rape and murder them.

"That was before I was saved," he said softly, but a faraway glint entered his eye.

"You're a racist," I declared.

"Huh?"

"How come you only attacked white women?"

"They couldn't describe me," he reasoned. "We all look alike to them." His face grew solemn. "But I've been forgiven," he said softly. He turned to walk away, and over his shoulder he called, "Woe to them who lust after women."

On a Sunday evening in June, Dr. John Holbrook checked into a room at the Boots and Saddle Motel in Mexia, Texas, about eighty miles southeast of Dallas. He was there to work on a case. The fifty-six-year-old psychiatrist had become disenchanted with his practice, and had told friends he was planning to reenlist with the U.S. Air Force as a colonel.

About 12:30 P.M. on Monday, motel employees found his body alongside a vial of prescription drugs and a bottle of alcohol. He had left a note in the room, and investigators discovered that he had left another note back at his Dallas home. Holbrook's friend

181

and attorney, Jack Ayers, declared that the notes revealed "no suicidal intentions," and said that officials speculated that death was caused by a massive coronary. However, initial autopsy reports indicated "no obvious cause of death."

Dallas District Attorney Henry Wade commented, "As far as I'm concerned, he was one of the most outstanding psychiatrists that I've ever had the pleasure of working with."

Judge Donald Metcalfe said that Holbrook "related to jurors very well. He had a knack of being able to talk in a very understandable manner. He will be missed."

On June 25, 1980, three months after Bruder had argued my case in Washington, a guard stopped in front of my cell and asked if I had been listening to the radio. I told him no. Turn it on, he said, because KHUN, the light-rock station out of Huntsville, had just reported that the U.S. Supreme Court, by a vote of eight to one, had overturned *Texas v. Adams*. The only dissenting vote was cast by Associate Justice William H. Rehnquist.

Even before I could tune in the radio, a TV station broke in with the bulletin, reporting the words of the majority opinion, written by Associate Justice Byron R. White. The court declared: "We repeat that the state may bar from jury service those whose beliefs about capital punishment would lead them to ignore the law or violate their oaths. But in the present case Texas has applied the law to exclude jurors whose only fault was to take their responsibilities with special seriousness."

It was more than one hundred degrees outside, but I felt a cold chill crawl up my back.

We saw a news report quoting Assistant State Attorney General Doug Becker, who said that there were now 131 persons on death row in Texas, and he estimated that 20 or 25 would benefit from the Adams decision.

Death row rocked with shouts and cheers.

As soon as I could pull myself away from the television, and from the comments tossed my way from all sides, I sat quietly on my bunk for about fifteen minutes and prayed out my thanks.

I was the first death row prisoner in Texas to win a Supreme

Court petition since the new laws came into existence after 1972. For the first time in four years, I felt like a winner. For me, I knew, the decision meant not only life, but freedom. My conviction was overturned and Texas would either have to let me go or grant me a new trial. And I was *sure* that we could win at a new trial, particularly if we landed Racehorse Haynes.

It was comforting to hear press reports that Henry Wade had vowed to retry me. He would follow the court's new guidelines for jury selection, he promised, and he would convict me again. Then he would execute me.

I relished the chance to once more confront Henry Wade and Doug Mulder and David Harris and Emily Miller, to prove that the Dallas authorities, contrary to the opinion expressed in the newspaper editorial, had known exactly what they were doing.

A few days later I received a letter from my first attorney Dennis White, informing me:

> Mel Bruder is announcing today that Racehorse Haynes will try your case. I will be glad to try your case again, or to assist Mel Bruder or Racehorse Haynes or whoever is available, in a re-trial of your case. Obviously I know, and we all know, more about your case now than at the first trial. I hope and trust my faith in your innocence will be vindicated on re-trial and you will be found not guilty and be set free.

It was difficult to cool my heels on death row. I was a veteran at doing time now, and it should have been easy. I should have known that much time would pass before anything happened, but it was so difficult to wait. For a month I heard nothing from Bruder, nothing from Racehorse Haynes.

Finally, on a Friday morning early in August, guards came for me about eleven in the morning. In handcuffs and leg shackles, trussed up to a belly chain, grasping my few possessions as best I could, I crawled into a van and was carted off on the forty-five-mile ride to TDC's Diagnostics Center in Huntsville. There, I was placed into a hospital cell holding tank. I was used to such treatment, and I knew that these guards had no alternative but to continue to regard me as a convicted cop killer, but inside I felt vindicated and very, very innocent.

I tried to keep the indignation out of my voice when I asked, "Why are you putting me here?"

"We don't know," a guard answered. "They told us to put you here."

"Well, I'm supposed to be going back to Dallas for retrial."

"The only thing I can tell you is that you'll be here until they come to pick you up."

I spent the weekend in the holding tank, making supreme effort to maintain a sense of patience, theorizing that Texas knew it was losing the battle against me, and thus was trying to exact every available ounce of revenge. I passed the time by musing upon a defense strategy for the new trial, formulating questions for my lawyer to ask once we finally had the opportunity to cross-examine Emily Miller properly. I wondered if Mulder would risk putting David Harris back on the stand. Could they even find these people, four years later?

On Monday morning I was ushered into the office of a psychiatrist, who announced that it was his job to assess which prison I was going to next.

Not prison, I protested. To the Dallas County jail. For retrial.

It was the psychiatrist who began to explain that once again I had underestimated the abilities of Henry Wade and his good ol' bunch of lawyers from Dallas.

The Dallas district attorney's office had a problem. Could it afford to take its chances with a retrial and finally give us an opportunity to impeach the witnesses in front of a properly impaneled jury? On the other hand, how could Dallas set me free, without an attempt at retrial, after two psychiatrists had characterized me as an irredeemable sociopath primed to kill again?

The powers that be in Texas were suddenly thrown into turmoil, and they now knew that they might have to face Racehorse Haynes at the defense table.

What they did not know was that Haynes had taken himself out of the picture. He wrote to my mother, expressing his regrets, explaining that he was "booked through 1981."

That letter was in the mail between Houston and Columbus when we realized that Dallas had found an answer to its dilemma. On July 9, 1980, District Attorney Henry Wade, Judge Donald Metcalfe, and Dallas County Sheriff Carl Thomas sent a letter to the Honorable Connie Jackson, Chairman of the Texas Board of Pardons and Paroles, noting:

> This case took in excess of six weeks to try. There is no reason to believe that a re-trial would be any less of a drain on judicial and prosecutorial resources. The reluctance of Federal courts to permit execution of a death sentence except in those cases where the prisoner is willing has been demonstrated.
>
> Accordingly, it is the considered recommendation of the undersigned trial officials that the Board of Pardons and Paroles recommend to the Governor of the State of Texas that the punishment of Randall Dale Adams be commuted to imprisonment for life.

The board made that recommendation, and on July 11, Governor Clements signed an executive order "granting" me:

> THE COMMUTATION OF SENTENCE FROM DEATH TO LIFE IMPRISONMENT IN THE TEXAS DEPARTMENT OF CORREC-TIONS.

Quite neatly, Texas had sidestepped a retrial. Bruder put it succinctly in a comment to the press: "It stinks."

In the summation of his argument to the U.S. Supreme Court, Bruder had declared that the flawed system of jury selection "requires a reversal of the judgment of the Court of Criminal Appeals insofar as it imposes the death penalty." In my opinion, he should have demanded that the justices also call for a retrial.

In Texas, the jury—and only the jury—can answer those three questions that determine the sentence in a capital case. By commuting my death sentence to life imprisonment, it seemed to me, the governor arbitrarily assumed the power of the jury. It was now the view of the state of Texas that it had fulfilled the dictates of the Supreme Court by allowing me to live. It had decided not to kill me, merely to lock me away forever.

The only way out was to start working through the state courts once more, demanding a new trial. Bruder warned that this was a high-stakes decision. If I won a new trial and was again convicted, I could find myself back on death row.

It was an easy call; of course I would file for what was legalistically called a "remand on the commutation issue." I expected no relief from the Texas courts, but I had to start there before I could take my case back to the Federal courts.

Meanwhile, the reality was this: for three and one-half years I had lived under a sentence of death, in comparative isolation. Now, as a lifer, I was to be thrust into the general prison population. At the Diagnostics Unit I became TDC #307231, and it appeared that I would retain that designation for a long, long time.

PART TWO

1980 – 1989

HOUSE OF PAIN

17

THE HAM

TWO OFFICERS FLANKED me as I shuffled inside the back gate of the Eastham unit. After a brief stop at the searcher's desk, they escorted me into a small room, the office of Building Major Burleson.

He was a sitting off in one corner, a Stetson perched on his head and boot-clad feet propped across the surface of his desk. For many minutes he ignored me. I stood before him like some kind of hogtied rodeo trophy as he continued reading the papers he held in his hand.

"Adams," he drawled, "Texas should've executed you."

"Well, sir," I replied, trying to keep my voice full of respect, "they still may get their chance. I'm going to file another appeal. I want a retrial."

"You're not under a sentence of death anymore," he responded, "you're doin' life, and you're doin' it at the Eastham unit. I'm gonna tell you now, if you step outta line, I'll finish the job Texas started."

He paused to emphasize his words. His eyes locked upon mine.

"Please," he continued, "step outta line."

We stared at one another silently for many moments before he turned to a guard and said, "Get his ass out of here."

Newsweek once called TDC the worst prison system in America, and Eastham—the Ham—the worst unit in the system. The official address is Lovelady, Texas, which is a euphemism for 13,000 acres of cotton and peanut fields in the eastern portion of the state. Rattlesnakes, sand fleas, and fire ants are about the only other forms of life dumb enough to live there.

Long before I arrived on the scene, TDC boasted about the self-sufficiency of its prison system. At its various sites, inmate laborers raised hogs for others to butcher and still others to cook. Crews of inmates cultivated all manner of vegetables as well as fruits and nuts; they were especially proud of their annual watermelon crop. Inmates planted, cultivated, and picked cotton; others sewed the fibers into prison uniforms. At times when normal food supplies were scarce, an inmate crew would head for one of the lakes within the TDC grounds and dynamite a supply of fish. Inmates handled all the maintenance tasks, including the repair of TDC vehicles. Even the very security of the prison was left largely in the hands of the convicts themselves.

The result was considered, by some outsiders, as a model prison system—and it was, if you evaluated its financial balance sheet. TDC not only paid for itself but actually returned a multi-million dollar profit to the state each year.

In Texas, the Ham is where they throw you when they consider you too low for the other trash heaps. It holds about 2,500 inmates, and the vast majority are hard-core, repeat offenders, convicted of multiple violent crimes. Once in a while, the system gobbles up a younger, more naive prisoner, and I think that is probably done for the amusement of the others.

There is almost no concept of rehabilitation. This is punishment, not correction.

The way the crow flies, Eastham is only a few miles from the Ellis unit, and it appears as if you could heave a Texas rock from one to the other. But the two gigantic buildings are separated by Lake Livingston and it takes forty-five minutes to drive the roads that meander between them.

Eastham is purposely set in the center of the entire TDC correctional system. If you managed to slip out of the three-story building and make your way across the ten-foot high fence and its coils of sharpened barbed wire at the top, no matter which way you ran you would soon find yourself in the midst of another prison compound, whether Ellis, Coffield, or the juvenile facility, known as Ferguson.

I found that the building itself was a mirror-image of Ellis. Its main feature was a long central hallway, from which 110-foot long cell blocks radiated out like fingers. The first apparent difference was the overcrowding. Cells originally intended for a single prisoner now housed as many as three, sometimes four. There was no separate catwalk where guards could patrol safely and observe the entire area, but as far as TDC was concerned, there was no real need to do that. At the Ham, there was only about one guard for every seven hundred inmates, so the guards avoided the tiers altogether. Daily life at the Ham was controlled by inmate supervisors, known as "building tenders."

I was assigned to L-Line, which consisted of three tiers of twenty-one cells, averaging three inmates each. A single guard controlled L-Line and four other lines, so it was impossible for him to supervise adequately. Thus, L-Line was the personal kingdom of its head building tender, known as Jimmy Joe. He stood about 5′10″ and his face wore the permanent flush of too many late nights and too much booze. That face looked about ten years older than his forty-five years, but there was no denying that he kept his body in shape. Working out was a passion with him.

Jimmy Joe's lieutenants were drawn from the toughest, meanest inmates, and they managed the affairs of L-Line with precious little assistance from the guards. Each of the assistant building tenders worked an eight-hour shift under Jimmy Joe's supervision. On good days, they managed to keep things under control so that Jimmy Joe would not be bothered. Jimmy Joe did not like to be bothered.

As he did with every new arrival, Jimmy Joe gave me a welcome lecture. "I'm gonna tell you *once* how this place works," he said. "Any squabbles, you bring 'em to us. Anything goin' on that's not right, bring it to us. Not the guards. Us."

Jimmy Joe knew that I had just walked off death row, and the Ham was one of the few places in the world where that reputation was a plus. He sniffed me out. He introduced me to his day shift tender, and my face brightened. It was Happy Eddie Thompson, whom I remembered from the Dallas County jail. Happy Eddie told Jimmy Joe that I was an okay guy, a cop killer, and Jimmy Joe flashed a look of respect.

After he led me to my new house, Jimmy Joe pointed to the two bunks. "The dude on the bottom," he said, "he's a kid. He's my punk. If you want him, use him."

I did not want the building tender, or anyone else here, to have any doubts about my sexual orientation, so I replied, "I appreciate it, but it's not my religion."

I sat alone in the cell throughout the day, using the only available chair—the toilet. I kept my back to the wall and my eyes and mind on alert. This was a new and very dangerous environment, and I needed to observe it very closely.

My biggest fear was that trouble would find me inadvertently. I would be forced to walk the halls of the Ham alongside men of minimal intelligence, many of them lacking any moral sense, and some of them certifiably crazy. Around me, I knew, was an invisible arsenal of knives and other weapons. Anything could happen, anytime. Someone might be after someone else, and I might just find myself in the way.

I knew that I would have to steer clear of the organized power groups among the general population. These were the Texas Syndicate and its rival, the Mexican Mafia, both made up almost exclusively of Hispanics, the self-explanatory Texas Aryan

Brotherhood, the Texas Mafia, and the black gangs, the Mandingo Warriors and the Brotherhood Self-Defense Family.

Here, simple survival was a victory.

Happy Eddie stopped by to tell me about my work assignment. All able-bodied newcomers were sent to work in the fields. I would be on White Line, in Three Hole. In times past, Eddie explained, there was a White Line, a Black Line, and a Mexican Line. Prisoners were segregated by race, in the fields as well as in the cells. Segregation was gone now, but the lines retained their old names. It was merely coincidence that I drew White Line. Three Hole meant that I would ride on the third of the flatbed trailers that carried us out to the fields.

He asked if I wanted to buy any soda pop, snacks, coffee, or tobacco. Jimmy Joe allowed him those concessions on L-Line. I could pay with scrip drawn from my modest account in the prison bank, or he would be happy to extend me credit. If I wanted a bag of coffee now, I could pay him two bags later.

Happy Eddie discussed the routine calmly. He explained that the best way to gauge Jimmy Joe's mood was to pay attention to his footwear. If he was wearing his spit-shine shoes, he had no time for you, because he was on his way to see the building major, or he had important business elsewhere. The time to approach Jimmy Joe was when he wore his everyday house boots; if you had a problem, he might even try to help you with it. But when you saw him wearing his scuffed-up, blood-spattered combat boots, your only hope was to run like hell in the opposite direction and hope that he wasn't mad at *you*.

The various cell block gates were used as a sort of communication system between the building tenders, Eddie said. If a serious fight broke out between two inmates, the turnkey would slam the cell block door shut—hard. To the tenders up and down the halls, this was a signal to shut down their own lines and "secure the farm." On the other hand, if Jimmy Joe was simply administering a "touch-up," there was no signal. He was just "getting the man's heart right," and needed no assistance.

Eddie said that his favorite event was Saturday morning "house-cleaning," when he and the other building tenders effected an "attitude adjustment" upon anyone who had given them or the officers trouble during the week. The weekly ritual began about 8:00 A.M. with the sound of slamming cell block doors reverberating through the air, and it lasted until after lunch. One by one, the tenders came for their victims, and dragged them off to the dayroom. From anywhere in the cell block you could hear the dull thud of boots impacting upon flesh and the accompanying cacophony of obscenities and yelps. The unfortunate victims almost always went directly to the hospital ward, and never returned to their old cell blocks.

If a prisoner died at the Ham, it was no big deal. The state paid little attention, and questions from nosy relatives went unanswered. TDC seemed to have developed an efficient system for losing the paperwork. If the victim had no family, his mortal remains were consigned to a plot of ground in Huntsville known as "Peckerwood Cemetery."

Finally, Eddie advised me to rest up today, because starting first thing tomorrow morning, I was going to learn what work was all about.

Sometime in the afternoon Happy Eddie was relieved by another assistant building tender, Skinny Gates. Cautiously we checked out one another. He only weighed about 140 pounds, but he carried them with a swagger. He also carried a deep scar on his forehead where another inmate, some time ago, had slashed him with a razor. I watched and listened as Skinny went about his business during the dull hours of the early afternoon. Part of the time he paced up and down the line, lecturing the empty cells, or merely conversing with himself. Suddenly, as he ranted, the pitch of his voice rose. The words spouted out faster, though perhaps more coherently. At other times he was quiet and morose. I concluded that he had at least three distinct personalities, and I wondered which was the most dangerous.

It was late in the afternoon when Skinny yelled out, "One Row, in and out." A guard, sitting in a protective cage at the hallway entrance, cranked open the doors to all the cells on this first tier, and the other inmates came trudging in from their day of work.

My body tensed. Only a few hours ago Major Burleson had threatened my life. Had he seen to it that I was assigned to a cell populated by some crazed murderer who would be happy to do the job that the Texas courts had not been allowed to finish? And who else might want to get rid of me? My name was not exactly a household word around the country, but in the last month or so I had become well known throughout TDC. Someone might want to earn a reputation for himself.

Even outside enemies might reach into the Ham to get at me. Rumor held that the going rate for murder was about two hundred dollars. For that paltry sum—a fortune in here—you could find someone to do the job.

Two men stepped into the cell, and we introduced ourselves warily. One was an old fisherman who had killed a guy in a barroom brawl. The other was a baby-faced kid. Why TDC had chosen to send him to Eastham was a mystery to me, unless officials were aware that the hard-core inmates needed a constant supply of fresh meat.

As the newcomer, I was relegated to the floor. The fisherman relaxed on the top bunk as the kid stretched out on the bottom. But before long, something troubled me. I noticed Jimmy Joe walk past several times, his eyes assessing the situation.

It occurred to me that he was waiting to see how long I was going to remain on the floor, and I realized that I had to make a power play, or Jimmy Joe might get the wrong idea. I had been careful to assure him, respectfully, that men were not my "religion." Now, obviously, he was wondering if I had misstated the case.

I had been in jails and prisons for nearly four years now, and like any other heterosexual convict, I long ago had to make a decision concerning my sex life. Like many others, when I had to find release, I played solitaire.

This was something Jimmy Joe could not quite understand. He would knock out your lights if you called him a "fag," but he reasoned that sex with another man was the only sex available, so it was simply the practical, necessary choice. He prided himself on being always a "pitcher," never a "catcher." The kid, his personal punk, was a "catcher," and if I allowed him to retain the priority of the lower bunk, what did that make me?

I decided to play it straight with the kid. First I offered him a friendly cup of coffee. Then, as he sipped at it I said, "I know you're Jimmy Joe's punk and I know that because he told me so and he also told me to use you if I wanted to."

The kid's eyes grew wide. The fisherman eavesdropped, unwilling to comment.

"I'm gonna tell you now, I don't care if you're a punk. It makes no difference to me. I don't like boys. I don't like men. I like women. And I ain't going to use you in that way and I want you to understand that. But we've got a problem. I know that Jimmy Joe is wondering why I'm letting some punk have a bunk while I'm on the floor. So it comes down to this. Either I whip your ass and kick you off that bunk or—and I would rather do this—we do it diplomatically. I'll buy it from you. So, why don't you just sell me your bunk?"

"Man, I don't wanna sell my bunk," the kid protested.

"I don't have any choice," I told him. "I'm going to sleep there tonight and you're going to sleep on the floor. I'm willing to give you a b-bag." A "b-bag" is about $2.25 worth of Maxwell House coffee. "Take it or leave it. Tonight I'm in the bunk."

The kid slept on the floor that night and he was drinking fresh coffee in the morning when Jimmy Joe walked by. He grinned and nodded in my direction.

After a surprisingly good breakfast that featured pancakes garnished with a thin syrup, I heard an authoritative voice shout through the main hallway, "One Hole!"

"Cap'n Shepard," the fisherman explained to me. "He's the boss of White Line."

All along the main corridor of Eastham, turnkeys at the cell block gates repeated, "One Hole!" and cranked open the dayroom doors.

When "Three Hole" was called, I found my way into a line of men shuffling single file past Captain Shepard's wary eyes. We reached the searcher's desk, where my name was checked off by Mr. Reimenschneider, field boss of Three Hole. His face appeared stern under the crew cut of his sandy blond hair.

I walked quietly, trying to do nothing that would attract attention, as we filtered through a doorway leading out to the "back slab," a large asphalt-covered lot on the opposite side of Eastham's main entrance. I followed the others toward a flatbed trailer, the third of twenty-two linked together like the cars of a circus train, attached to a single gargantuan tractor.

Reimenschneider followed us. He wore a starched gray uniform, with stiff chaps covering the front of his pants. His spurs jingled as he strode rigidly toward his horse. He mounted, and then rode slowly, circling our trailer while the other crews loaded. High riders, armed with long-range rifles, also circled the entire caravan.

When the trailers were loaded, and procession moved off slowly, carrying hundreds of inmates into the deep summer heat of the cotton fields. Already I eyed the water tank at the end of the trailer-train.

As we reached the fields, the trailers were disconnected one by one and we took up our positions at the end of what appeared to be endless rows of cotton.

Someone threw a large bag at me, with a strap to hang over my shoulder. I was still struggling with it when Reimenschneider yelled, "Catch in!"

The lead man bent his back to the work. His fingers skimmed across the cotton plants, plucking tufts of white fiber from among the green leaves, filling the hungry mouth of the bag slung over his shoulder. Others caught in behind him, each man staying just a few feet behind the man on his right.

Reimenschneider bellowed at me, "Pick cotton, boy!"

For more than three years I had barely seen the sun, let alone labored under it, and now I understood why breakfast was hearty.

The work was excruciating, but I learned quickly that it was vital to keep up with the others. If anyone fell behind the tail row, he was "stuck out," and, in prison vernacular, "had a problem."

As we worked, Reimenschneider rode alongside on horseback, barking out orders to his two inmate helpers, appropriately known as "strikers."

All across this vast Texas field, men labored under the morning sun that was already pushing the thermometer over one hundred degrees. Each field boss walked his horse around his own crew as Captain Shepard rode a circuit around the entire field. At the edges of the field, the high riders maintained vigilance.

Very quickly, I was stuck out, and Reimenschneider ordered his two strikers to help me catch up. They worked furiously with me for a few minutes, then glared at me and walked away.

Within minutes I was stuck out again. Once more the strikers were ordered to help, but their expressions told me that I was not making many friends this day. I worked frantically, grabbing at the fluffs of cotton, stuffing them into the bag and pumping my legs forward, not daring to stop to swat at the legions of sand fleas that bit at my forearms.

I must have had fifty pounds of cotton in my bag when we finally came to the end of the row. Captain Shepard supervised as we dumped our cotton into a large bin. "Hey, peckerwood!" he yelled at me, "too much green. Next time I don't want to see no green mixed in with the cotton."

We had a brief water break, gobbled salt tablets, and then started on a new line.

The morning assumed an aching rhythm. Through sheer effort I did a bit better, but still found it difficult to maintain the necessary pace.

Every so often someone dropped from the effects of the heat. The strikers hauled the victim's limp carcass over to the water trailer and threw him underneath. The moment he showed signs of life, he was ordered to resume his place on the line.

At lunchtime we rode the caravan of flatbed trailers back to the cell blocks and filed past the searcher's table. Reimenschneider accounted for each man and sent him off to lunch, but as I approached, he tapped me on the shoulder and commanded, "Catch the wall."

I stood in the hallway, with my back against concrete block, until he had finished his count and the rest of the crew was gone. The field boss strode up to me and put his face so close to mine that the stiff brim of his hat dug into my forehead. The One and Two Hole field officers flanked me.

"You were stuck out three, four times this mornin'!" Reimenschneider raged. "And I'm gonna let you know that you and I are gonna have problems if this continues."

In a quiet, respectful voice, I tried to explain. "Boss," I said, "you know where I've been. You know I haven't really been able to do anything, any kind of work. I never picked cotton before in my life, and I'm not used to being out in this heat."

Still, he glowered at me.

Finally I said, "Sir, look, it's going to take me time to build myself up. If you will allow me two weeks to get myself into shape, I'll make you one of the better workers you ever had."

He maintained his hostile stare, but I could see that he was thinking over my words. There were two simple considerations to his job: keep the men busy and pick that cotton. I could sense the wheels turning in his head as he attempted to figure out the proper strategy to use on a convicted cop killer. After a few moments, he relaxed his stare and let me go off to lunch, and I began to wonder if he was, in a relative sense, an okay guy.

At the end of the twelve-hour workday we stood on the back lot and stripped naked. With our dirty clothes in our arms, we marched past the searcher's table and straight to the shower room.

I was under one of the multitude of shower heads, lathering quickly, when my eye caught that of the man standing next to me. He was leering and rubbing his stiffened penis. I had to make an instant decision. As much as I wanted to avoid trouble, I reasoned that it would probably be better for me to pop this fellow in the jaw, right here and now, and thereby deliver a message to everyone else. My hand was curled into a fist when the man suddenly turned his attention back to his shower. I looked up to see Captain Shepard striding through the shower room in full uniform, his spurs jingling, his eyes glaring.

Each day, as we labored in the fields, we kept our ears tuned to the timbre of Reimenschneider's voice, for the field boss's disposition made a big difference in the tenor of the workday.

After more than a week, despite my best efforts, I was still stuck out frequently, drawing far too much attention, and I wondered how long the field boss's patience would hold. One morning I was laboring away furiously when I heard Reimenschneider say softly, "Adams, come here a minute."

I straightened my aching back and glanced up warily. In the

saddle, he towered above me. I approached slowly, for these horses were trained to bite if an inmate got too close. I stared questioningly up at the field boss, his stern face framed against the white-hot sky.

"Adams," he lectured, "let me give you a piece of advice. Anytime Cap'n Shepard is close to me, I'm yellin' at you people. But there's other times I'm not sayin' a word. Maybe I'm bullshittin' with one of the other bosses or whatever, but you ain't hearin' nothin' from me. The reason I'm not yellin' or screamin' is that Cap'n Shepard's clear down at the other end of the field. So, when you hear me screamin' and bitchin', you pick cotton as fast as you can. When you don't hear me, git your ass up ahead to the front of the row. Just drag your bag up there, don't worry 'bout the cotton you're leavin' behind. We'll be goin' over this field again. We'll git that cotton."

"Yes, sir," I said. I tried to measure his expression, but I could not penetrate through the shield of his sunglasses.

"Now pick cotton," he said.

"Yes, boss!"

That summer of 1980 was one of the worst in Texas history. Temperatures soared to 110 degrees day after day, and this brought frequent flares of temper. Fights among inmates were as common as the sand fleas that infested the endless rows of cotton. The field bosses viewed these altercations as a form of entertainment—convict cockfights. As long as neither combatant displayed a weapon, they could slug it out until quitting time and nobody seemed to care. But if you got yourself into a scrap, you had to keep flailing away, for as soon as you stopped, a striker would push you back onto the picking line.

Some feuds lasted for days, and these were the dangerous ones. You had to leave your fighting in the field, or you were asking for trouble. Scraps within the cell block, especially in the dayroom, often resulted in the brutal beating of both participants by the building tender and his lieutenants. It did not matter who started the fight, or who was on top when they came. They asked no questions and simply attacked both offenders, using clubs, chairlegs, and whatever else was handy. When they finished, they pitched their victims outside the run into the central hallway, where other tenders and turnkeys joined in the fun.

In October, we turned our attention to the peanut harvest. We had to pull the entire plant up by the roots, for that is where the peanuts grow. Then we had to shake the sandy dust off of the roots and set the plants at the side of the row to dry in the sun. It was a change of pace from picking cotton, but it brought us in contact with a new enemy.

Many years ago Texas imported fire ants to combat boll weevils. For TDC, this was a perfect solution, for the weevils attacked cotton, while the fire ants merely attacked men. One of their favorite nesting spots was just underneath the soil, and when we uprooted a peanut plant, we often uprooted a fire ant colony as well.

"Gettin' out of 'em here, boss!" an inmate would yell. There, in the midst of the field, the victim stripped naked, swatted the biting plague from his skin, and shook his clothes out violently. The scene was so common that no one paid any attention, until it was his turn.

After a day in the field with the fire ants, my hands were often swollen to nearly twice their normal size. It took about six hours for the effect to wear off. Each night, before I drifted into a coma-like sleep I muttered to myself, "Get used to it, Randall. Get used to it."

18

THE TIME

EARLY IN DECEMBER 1980, an event occurred which was to have a profound effect upon each of the 29,573 inmates of Texas's prisons. U.S. District Judge William Wayne Justice issued his ruling in *Ruiz v. Texas*.

Writing in dry, legalistic language, he condemned TDC from the top down. Wardens were so overworked, he said, that they were unaware of or unable to control even the most blatant human rights violations. He described the guards as men who "are usually overworked, lack effective managerial skills and have little understanding or appreciation of inmates' consitutional rights."

The building tenders, he said, "often brutalize their fellow prisoners, with the tacit approval or direction of civilian prison personnel."

His report concluded:

It is impossible for written opinion to convey the pernicious conditions and the pain and degradation which ordinary inmates suffer within TDC prison walls—the gruesome experiences of youthful first offenders forcibly raped; the cruel and justifiable fears of inmates, wondering when they will be called upon to defend the next violent assault; the sheer misery, the discomfort, the wholesale loss of privacy for prisoners housed with one, two or three others in a forty-five [square] foot cell or suffocatingly packed together in a crowded dormitory; the physical suffering and wretched psychological stress which must be endured by those sick or injured who cannot obtain adequate medical care; the sense of abject helplessness felt by inmates arbitrarily sent to solitary confinement or administrative segregation without proper opportunity to defend themselves or to argue their causes; the bitter frustration of inmates prevented from petitioning the courts and other governmental authorities for relief from perceived injustices. . . .

It is to these conditions that each inmate must wake every morning; it is with the painful knowledge of their existence that each inmate must try to sleep at night.

Judge Justice gave officials until April 1981 to come up with a plan for change. He wanted units broken down into smaller entities, which could be more easily supervised. He wanted no more than two prisoners housed in each cell. And he wanted the building tender system, which, he said, was already prohibited by state law, to come to an end.

District Judge Byron Matthews grumbled, "I've always felt that we've had one of the best, most humane, efficient and self-supporting prison systems in the world. People who think that a prison should be a country club and some people with bleeding hearts are going to always think that punishment should be merely taking candy away from the culprit."

Over the winter, my letters home resumed the droning quality that had characterized them during my death row years. If nothing happens, what can you write about? I always told Mom that I was doing well, that my spirits were good, that I was sure that *this* was the year when something was going to happen to my case. I always told her I loved her. What more was there to say?

Lethargy took hold of me, and refused to let go.

One noteworthy event did occur. I followed it closely in the newspapers and reported it to Mom.

Early in 1981, a young Texas man was charged with capital murder, alleged to be one of four men involved in the burglary of a home, during which the owner was shot to death. But he had an ace up his sleeve in the form of his father. Daddy was rich, and determined to secure the best possible defense attorney. His search led him to the Dallas district attorney's office, where he offered First Assistant District Attorney Doug Mulder a fee, up front, to resign his job and become a defense attorney. The fee was, according to various press reports, somewhere between $100,000 and $300,000.

Mulder had actually been prepared to prosecute the boy for capital murder, but he apparently found the offer intriguing. He had long been rumored as the natural successor to Henry Wade as district attorney, but Wade had clung to the job longer than anyone anticipated and showed no signs of tiring. In one of the quickest turnarounds in Dallas's legal history, Mulder accepted the offer, resigned from his sixty thousand dollar per year job with the district attorney's office, and, like a chameleon, instantly became a defense lawyer.

Eventually, the district attorney's office decided to drop the charges.

With that first notch carved into his new belt, Mulder's star rose quickly. Ensconced in a plush suite of offices high atop Dallas's Diamond Shamrock Building, he proved as efficient at defense as he had been at prosecution. "I didn't have any trouble moving from a prosecutor to the defense," he later told a reporter. "The whole thing is wanting to win."

Our springtime chore in the fields was to clear away the rubble from last year's crop, prior to planting. Armed with hoes, we hacked away, spooking an occasional herd of rattlesnakes. This provided good sport.

On frequent occasions a yell of "Got one here, boss!" broke through the normal madhouse sounds. The victor held up his trophy, the headless body of a rattler, and gathered expressions of appreciation from the white boys. The blacks all jumped back in horror. If it was a good skin, the benefits had a ripple effect. The field boss might pay the inmate an entire bag of coffee for it. He, in turn, could sell it to a craft shop inmate, and some tourist would eventually purchase it as a belt or wallet.

Arrowheads, hidden in the loose, sandy loam, were also profitable finds.

Judge Justice's April deadline came and went. Dissatisfied with the limited scope of a few modest changes instituted by TDC officials, the judge appointed attorney Vincent M. Nathan, a transplanted Texan who taught law at the University of Toledo in Ohio, as "Special Master" to monitor compliance with his orders.

The inmates knew that changes were coming, and tension ran high throughout the system. At the Ellis unit, the new warden, who had been on the job only eighteen days, was overpowered by an inmate trusty and drowned. The same inmate disarmed a guard and shot him to death.

The news of an assassination attempt on President Reagan also made everyone edgy. I was glad the president survived, but I knew that the incident was going to renew nationwide calls for law and order and make appellate courts more insensitive to the considerations of convicted felons.

For a time, newspapers were banned at Eastham.

I had been at Eastham for nearly a year, working in the fields, planting, cultivating, and picking cotton and peanuts, fighting off the sand fleas, fire ants, and rattlesnakes, before the Texas Court of Criminal Appeals ruled on my case. In May 1981 they agreed, by a vote of six to three, that I was entitled to a new trial on the issue of guilt or innocence, as well as punishment. They determined that the governor had acted in an arbitrary and illegal manner in commuting my sentence, and ordered Dallas County to retry me or set me free.

I was elated, and I wrote to Mom, "It's been a long time coming but I never doubted that it would. I knew the Lord was watching over us and that things would work out in time. Thank the church for their prayers."

I wrote directly to Judge Metcalfe at Criminal Court Number Two, asking when my new trial would be scheduled. He replied that so far he had only received a copy of the appellate court's opinion and could not schedule a retrial until he received the written mandate.

In the interim, the Dallas district attorney's office filed a motion for a rehearing before the appellate court and this threw a monkey wrench into everything. The timing, it seemed to me, was calculated, for the justices of the state court adjourned for summer vacation, and left me once more in legal limbo until the fall.

I had to remind myself that patience was a virtue. Dallas knew that it was fighting a losing battle. Henry Wade and his cohorts knew that they could never convict me a second time. They were just stalling, trying to drain me.

And so I was committed to another hot summer in the cotton fields.

During that summer, for unstated reasons, some of the members of the Court of Criminal Appeals experienced a change of heart concerning my case. On September 30, 1981, the court reversed its earlier ruling by a five to four vote, denying me a new trial.

"It was a letdown," I wrote to Mom, understating my disappointment. "I thought they would be fair and just . . . but then I think about it, and it is a Texas court, isn't it?"

It had been a long time since I had seen or even heard from my brother Ray. A *long* time. I tried to think back over the foggy years. The last time I had seen him was in the spring of 1979, the weekend that he had brought Mom and Marlene to visit, and had his truck stolen.

After that, I had no word. It was not unusual for Ray to move on to a new situation, to stay out of touch for a while, but I could usually count on hearing from him once in a while. I asked Mom, in a letter, if she had heard from him lately. She wrote back and said no, she had not. The rest of the family was concerned too. They had not wanted to bring up the subject, to give me something else to worry about, but Ray was, apparently, gone.

Where? Why?

I was called out one day late in 1981 to see a visitor, and was surprised to find my brother Ron waiting for me. He had driven from his home in Nashville.

He explained, "I got out of bed yesterday and decided I wanted to go for a drive, and next thing I knew, I was headed here."

It was good to see him, and I wondered if he had any word from Ray. No, he said, shaking his head, no one seemed to know where he was.

I thought back to the one brief conversation I had with Ray concerning his military service and now I wished I had spoken to him more about it. Had he dropped out of sight because of demons troubling him, or—my mind stopped short with the thought—had Texas lawmen once more taken what they termed "justice" into their own hands?

Ron told me that he had discovered a curious fact. He had learned from Ray's former employer that Ray had never bothered to pick up his last paycheck. This was not at all characteristic of Ray. Yes, he might decide to pack up and move, but he would not leave behind money that he had earned.

This information gnawed at me. There was no way to prove anything, but neither was there any way to stop my mind from racing, considering all the possibilities. What if Ray had been picked up for some minor infraction, and the police realized that he had a brother in Eastham for killing a cop, that he himself had been questioned under suspicion as a possible accessory? Would they find some way to take out their anger on Ray?

This was a paranoid thought, to be sure, but had I not earned the right to be paranoid? My naïveté had been left behind long ago in Dallas Criminal Court Number Two. I now believed that the authorities in Texas—some of them, at least—placed no limits on their behavior.

Ron returned for another visit in February, 1982, and this time he announced that he had quit his job in Nashville and moved to Huntsville, the hub of TDC. He had decided to settle here where he could be close to me. He was a skilled carpet installer and could always find work, even though the pay was not as good down south.

"Maybe I can help out," he said.

"Help out with what?" I asked.

"I dunno."

I explained my misgivings. Huntsville is a community that owes its existence to TDC. It is a town full of prison guards. Anything can happen if the brother of one of the inmates starts nosing around. I said, "Look, Ron, I'm grateful that you're here trying to help, but I don't think there's anything you can do. It's all up to the lawyers now."

He shrugged off my concern, and said that he would come to see me next month.

There was a decided grin on his face when he returned. In a quiet voice, he announced that he was dating a divorcée in Huntsville.

"So?" I asked.

"So, her father just happens to be on the parole board. I can put in a good word for you."

Once again paranoia took hold of me, and I lectured him on the facts of life in TDC. I could picture the building major sitting in his office with his boots up on his desk, digesting the information that Adams was suddenly getting frequent visits. From whom? He would check the records and see that the visitor was Ron, my brother. Then he would look at Ron's address and wonder, what the hell is he doing living in Huntsville? Are these two planning an escape or something?

In Texas, and particularly in Huntsville, it would be easy to make sure that he found himself in major league trouble.

"I don't want to see you in here with me," I said. "I think you ought to get the hell out of Dodge."

His face was pale now, and he nodded.

After the visit, he wasted no time in moving back to Nashville.

. . .

Eastham officials, in an attempt to respond to a federal court order to alleviate overcrowding, constructed a temporary tent city on the grounds. Each wooden-frame canvas-covered structure housed eight men. Everyone wanted the chance to live in the new facilities, where you could smell the fresh summer air at night, and even walk out and stare at the stars. The coveted new quarters were given over to the most trustworthy prisoners, who were promised fresh new living quarters by winter. As a convicted cop killer, I did not qualify.

One evening in November 1981, two building tenders in the tent city area of the southern yard amused themselves by harassing six Hispanic inmates. Some shoving ensued, and the six Hispanics fought back. The two building tenders fled for the safety of the main building.

Now, the 250 residents of the tent city were agitated. The first cold prewinter winds had hit, and the promised new cell blocks still had not materialized. They did not look forward to spending the winter in their tents.

The disturbance built. Some inmates set fire to their tents. Others piled mattresses on top of trash cans to form impromptu barricades. They danced around the flames in glee, feeling the illusion of freedom.

On L-Line, I was alone in my house, clad only in my underwear, reading a book and sipping a cup of coffee, when I heard a loud explosion. It sounded as if the entire window section had been blown off the E-Line dayroom, across the hall.

"Get these goddamn people in their houses!" screamed an authoritative but panicky voice.

Down the central hall, the cries of the building tenders reverberated:

"Get into your house!"

"Move your ass, move!"

Cell doors were cranked open. Men came stumbling in from the dayroom, cursing and screaming.

I threw on some clothes and tugged my boots onto my feet. Quickly I dropped my heating coil into a pail of water. Boiling water was the only weapon I could think of.

Then, after about five minutes of chaos and slamming doors, the cell blocks quieted. Like me, most of the other prisoners on line after line waited to see what would happen. Our ears told us that the trouble was outside, at the tents in the southern yard, and it did not surprise us.

We all knew that a dramatic and perhaps pivotal confrontation was taking place outside in the yard, between the tent city prisoners and the building tenders. Most of us adopted a quiet wait-and-see, keep-your-nose-clean attitude, but across the hall, a fat young fellow paced back and forth, venting anger at the building tenders. "You sons of bitches," he hollered down the line, "just wait till we get it on!"

Guards and building tenders assembled in the gymnasium, forming an attack force some two hundred strong. The guards were armed with three-foot-long clubs. The building tenders tied strips of white cloth about their foreheads to distinguish themselves from the rioters. As they armed themselves with trash can lids, pipes, clubs, and weight-lifting bars, they growled like animals on the hunt.

The attackers moved out, using their trash can lids to shield themselves from a barrage of rocks launched by the rioters. They crashed through the center of the barricades. Peering into a veil of smoke, they saw most of the rioters flee toward one corner of the yard and assume a posture of surrender.

Now the building tenders formed a gauntlet, what one of them called a "whupping line," stretching from the tent city all the way back to the door near the searcher's table. A lone building tender stepped out front, showing no fear, armed only with a bullhorn. He simply laid out the proposition: "All of you who's got nothin' to do with the riot, come inside. If you ain't inside within ten minutes, we know you're part of the riot and we're comin' out to get you."

There was an immediate pileup of men attempting to run through the whipping line. They came straggling through into the central hall, bruised, bleeding, whimpering. Some collapsed on the floor. Others limped toward the cell blocks.

Inside, several nervous hours passed. We tried to gauge the messages contained in the screams that emanated from the yard.

Very late that night, when the outside noise had subsided, Jimmy Joe's lieutenant Skinny Gates swaggered onto L-Line. He stopped directly across from me, in front of the fat boy's cell. "You need to get dressed," he said. I listened carefully to the timbre of his voice, to identify which personality he was at the moment. He was calm and controlled—Skinny at his most dangerous.

A timid, whiny voice responded from inside the cell, "Why?"

"Well, I b'lieve the building major wants to see you."

"What for?"

"Well, I b'lieve he's gotten wind of the fact that you were sayin' a few things here, 'bout some riots here, so he wants to question you."

As soon as he reached the end of L-Line, near the dayroom, a gang of building tenders jumped the poor fellow and beat him so severely that I feared for his life. I knew we had seen, and heard, the last of him. Whether they killed him, maimed him, or just broke a few bones, he would not be returning to our neighborhood.

The next morning as I walked the central corridor toward breakfast, I lost count of the men I saw who were patched up with bandages and splints, or merely limping. There was blood all over the floor and walls, particularly in the area by the searcher's table, near the door that led to the now-destroyed temporary tent barracks.

We were kept out of the fields and in our cell blocks for most of the next week, and it was not until we got back outside that I learned the extent of what had happened. A friend of mine from Three Hole told me about it as we rode out to the peanut fields.

He was an ex-Marine and a Vietnam vet. I stared at the huge knot that remained on his head one week after the riot, and heard him say, "You know, I was in the Tet offensive. I've been in lots of firefights. Here and there, I've seen my share of trouble, and I've been scared. But ain't nothin' ever scared me like looking down that whipping line. You *knew* that when you went through that line, you were gonna get an ass-whipping, and it was gonna be a bad one. But you also knew that if they had to come out and get you, you were probably dead. That's the worst decision I ever had to make."

In retrospect, he wished he had been quick-thinking enough to be the first man into the line, before the building tenders got limbered up. But he was caught in the midst of the mob, waiting his turn to squeeze through, and for many minutes he could see and hear the building tenders beating everyone unmercifully, with clubs and chains and whatever else was available. Finally, he stood at the head of the line. He took a deep breath, covered his eyes with his arms, and ran headlong into a hornet's nest. The next thing he knew, he woke up in the hospital.

"You know the old guy who rides the water wagon?" he asked.

I nodded.

"Look at the water wagon. He ain't there anymore. I heard that they found him hiding in one of the water tanks."

We never did see that man again.

"We got a new guy sitting in your house," Happy Eddie told me as I came in from the fields one day. "Let me know what you think of him."

The newcomer was asleep on *my* bunk, but he awoke as I entered the cell, and I pegged him immediately as a babbler. He was quite willing to spill out his story to a total stranger. I suspected that he would have problems in Eastham.

I fixed myself a cup of coffee, lit a cigarette, sat on the commode, and listened to the nonstop chatter.

He said he was thirty-one years old, which surprised me, for by his appearance I would have placed him about a decade younger. What he said next surprised me even more. He announced that he was fresh off of death row.

"No kidding?" I replied. "Think of that!"

He chattered on, explaining that he had been sentenced to death for the murder of a child. But, he said, he was now suffering a great injustice. Even though an appeals court had thrown out his death sentence, the governor, instead of allowing him to be retried, had simply commuted his sentence to life imprisonment.

"How did you win the appeal?" I asked.

He said that "this dude Adams" had won a Supreme Court decision based on the illegality of jury selection. That was the precedent that saved his own life. What's more, he explained, his lawyer said that the governor screwed "this dude" the same as him. But Adams was appealing and would probably win.

He had been talking for more than an hour before he asked about me. I told him that I had a life sentence and that I had been on the Ham for almost two years. I told him that my sentence had been overturned last May and then reinstated in October.

"Why?" he asked.

"Because the governor was playing politics with it."

He sighed and commiserated, "Boy, do I know how you feel."

"You don't know who you're talking to, do you?" I asked.

"No," he said.

"I'm Adams."

His mouth dropped open, but only for an instant. Soon it was in gear again, for he believed that we had been placed together by fate and he knew it was time to reveal his true identity to me. He lowered his voice until it was barely audible, then whispered, "I'm Jesus Christ."

I wrote to Mom about him, describing him as "very religious."

"Jesus" carried his Bible everywhere, even into the fields, and he spent every spare moment either at church or talking about it. Finally, I could stand no more of his self-righteousness, and I told him that I had difficulty accepting the fact that a punk who had murdered a child was really the savior of the world. He grew solemn and silent for the rest of the evening.

The next morning, something strange occurred. He woke up and announced that he did not feel like going to work.

"How're you going to manage that?" I asked.

He muttered, "The Lord works in mysterious ways."

Shortly before Captain Shepard called us into the fields, Happy Eddie came around and told "Jesus" that he was scheduled for some sort of testing today, and he had to stay home from the fields. As I trudged off to work, my cell mate grinned at me and winked conspiratorially.

One evening "Jesus" returned from the midweek church service a little later than usual. Huge tears welled in his eyes.

"What's wrong with you?" I asked.

"They got me," he sobbed, rubbing his backside. In the shower room he had been cornered and raped by two inmates who had been stalking him for weeks.

"Did you scream?"

"No," he said, "I was too scared."

"Did you fight?"

"No," he shook his head. "It happened too quick."

"Well," I snapped, "they obviously don't know who you are!"

After two long scorching summers in the fields, I was ready for a change. I had a friend who worked in the prison's garment factory, and he put in a good word for me with the shop manager, Major Bob Perkins. I started in the late spring of 1982, finding immediate relief from the Texas sun in the air conditioned workshop. Eventually I became the bookkeeper, working in a regular office, with a coffee pot and a radio. It was heated in the winter and air conditioned in the summer. The work was hectic whenever the periodic reports were due, but at other times it was very relaxed and Major Perkins allowed me time to read, write letters, work crossword puzzles, or just drink coffee and chat. I had the use of a typewriter that was handy for composing letters to Mom and the rest of my family. What's more, the job gave me a far greater degree of personal freedom within the compound.

Life stabilizes, even in the Ham.

The execution of my former neighbor and chess-playing buddy on death row, Henry Martinez Porter, was set for a Thursday in August 1982, but he was granted a last-minute reprieve. His latest appeal was based on the contention of improper jury selection, and the precedent cited by his attorneys was *Adams v. Texas*.

Death row, I knew, was populated by vicious men, most of them very guilty of their crimes, many of them little more than brutish animals. I did not know whether I wanted to see Texas execute any of them, but I did know that there were many men there who should never be allowed a chance to mingle with society. Henry was not one of them. He was guilty of his crimes, all right, but there was some good in Henry.

The man who finally gained the distinction of becoming the first American ever executed by lethal injection was Charlie Brooks, Jr. (who conversed daily with Aretha Franklin). Late on the night of December 7, a crowd of three hundred people gathered outside the

Walls unit in Huntsville. Some carried signs that blared: Kill Him In Vein. Inside, just after midnight, the state of Texas did just that.

Time passed, somehow. I looked ahead and the dismal days stretched to an endless horizon. I looked back and everything was a blur. For a while, I did not realize what it was doing to me.

At Eastham, the inmates themselves were a part of the food chain. Whatever we did not eat was sent out to the farm as slop for the hogs. It came back to us as fatty pork. Spend a few weeks here and you will forget what beef is.

Periodically, when the hog supply ran low, one of the field bosses took a crew of prisoners fishing in the river that runs between Eastham and the Ferguson unit. He stationed his men at the riverbank with nets, then ambled upstream and tossed a few sticks of dynamite into the water. Soon the nets were filled with dead fish. The crew brought them back to the kitchen and threw them, whole, into grinders. Out came a concoction of fish paste, complete with scales, eyeballs, and viscera, that the cooks fashioned into patties.

We knew immediately whenever fish patties were on the menu. If we did not hear the sound of the dynamite blast, we saw the prison population of wild scruffy cats triple in an hour's time.

It was lunchtime on one such day when I decided to bypass the chow line. I headed instead for the commissary and used a bit of scrip to purchase a pint of ice cream and a soda pop. I was lounging in the dayroom, eating my private lunch, leaning against the bars, ignoring the soap opera on the TV, chatting idly with an inmate trusty, when I heard someone coming down the stairway from the second tier. I glanced up to see that it was an older prisoner, the janitor for the line. Halfway down the stairs he seemed to lose his footing. He pitched down, face forward, and lay at the bottom of the stairs, his body twitching with convulsions.

The trusty picked up the phone and reported to the medical department, "Got one throwin' a fit in here." Then he turned his attention back to the soap opera.

I finished my ice cream.

Off to the side, the old inmate continued to convulse.

Randall, I said to myself, a few years ago you would have jumped over there and done what you could to help. Maybe you could not do much for the old fellow, but at least you would be there with him. Now, you simply consider it to be his problem, not yours. That is what TDC has taught you: don't get involved. I felt suddenly and deeply saddened.

Still, I did not go over to help the man.

To while away the passing years—to try to gain *something* from this time—I attempted to enroll in extension courses taught by professors from Lee College. Numerous bureaucratic hurdles were put in my way, but eventually I was able to begin working my way toward an associates degree.

In one of my assigned papers I wrote:

> I have lived in and survived the House of Sorrow (Death Row). Now I am faced with living the rest of my life in the House of Pain (Eastham). Few men who have spent any time within these walls are better men because of it. I like the man I used to be. I like the man I have become. But which is the *better* man? Maybe time will help me decide that question. For time is all I have left to me.

One day I received a letter from Mike Berry, and I did a double take over the date. August 7, 1983! How could that be? Where did the days and weeks and months go?

Berry was still at the Ellis unit, but he was off death row and in the general population. He said that his own fate was similar to mine. Apparently convinced that his death sentence would be overturned, the governor commuted his sentence to life also.

He wrote again on August 24 to tell me that he was working in the dental lab alongside Small Paul. He figured that, as more and more of the death row denizens found their sentences commuted to life, they too would wind up in the lab. Knowing that Texas would be reluctant to ever let them go, this would cut down on long-term training costs.

Despite the Supreme Court decisions, he reported that death row had a booming population. When I had arrived in 1979, only one line was full and they were opening a second line. Now four full lines were devoted to the condemned. Mike was convinced that Texas was going to clean them out soon with a spate of executions, and he predicted that Tommy Barefoot or the Candy Man would be next.

I did not know J.D. "Cowboy" Autry personally. His crime occurred on a Sunday night in April 1980 and by the time he arrived at death row, I was already at Eastham.

But I followed his case with interest. From what I had heard, he was both drunk and drugged when he had tried to walk out of a convenience store in Port Arthur with a six-pack of beer. When the clerk, Shirley Drouet, said, "That will be $2.70," he reportedly said, "Here's your $2.70," and shot the forty-three-year-old mother of five between the eyes. He also blazed away at witnesses, killing one, and severely injuring another.

Now Texas believed that it was his turn to pay. On a night in October 1983, Autry was taken to the death chamber and strapped to the gurney. An IV needle was inserted into a vein of his arm, dripping harmless glucose. Autry could only lay there, awaiting the moment when a technician would begin the flow of sodium thiopental, the first of three lethal chemicals.

The state awaited the go-ahead.

For a full hour Autry expected each moment to be his last. Finally, word arrived that he received a stay of execution. A small crowd of college students who had gathered outside received the news with jeers and boos. Nevertheless, the needle was removed and Autry was shipped back to death row.

He complained that his arms were sore.

I turned thirty-five years old on December 17, 1983, and calculated that I had spent 20 percent of my life locked up. A year or so in the Dallas jail. Three years on the Row. And now—I could not believe it—three years at the Ham.

Funny, I thought, it's easier to do death than life. On death row, with the issue of existence never far from consciousness, you maintain a sensitivity toward the passage of time. Not here. In the general

217

population, one miserable day is like the next. It takes effort to pay attention to a calendar, to remember the passage of weeks and months. Facing an unknown but extended period of years in the close company of human brutes, the senses dull, the soul stagnates.

It is so much easier that way.

Most people, no matter their station in life, retain some control over their own destinies. Not here. And that, I came to realize, is perhaps the single worst thing about prison.

There was nothing I could do to regain my freedom. I needed help, and I prayed that it would arrive.

1 9

THE ATTORNEY

EVER SINCE THE Court of Criminal Appeals had turned
down my application for a writ of habeas corpus in September 1981,
I waited for word from my court-appointed attorney, Mel Bruder,
as to what we would do next. An incredibly long and frustrating
period of silence ensued.

Finally, Mom and Mary packed Mary's boys into a car and drove
down to Huntsville for a visit with me.

"I'm sick of Dallas attorneys," I said to Mom. "We need a new
attorney, but let's stay the hell away from Dallas. You get an attorney who practices in Dallas, they know everything about him.
He was probably a D.A. at some point, working for Henry Wade.
Let's go to Houston or Austin, get somebody who's outside of that

clique in Dallas." We decided to try Randy Schaffer, the man previously recommended by Racehorse Haynes.

Mom and Mary drove to Houston, met with Schaffer, and liked him immediately. His assertive and energetic personality inspired confidence as he listened to their story and expressed his empathy with my situation. He agreed to come on board, to carry my case to federal court, for a fee of $7,500, plus expenses.

Mom thought it over. Each month she received a check for $348 as compensation for my late father's black lung disease, and she decided that she could earmark $300 of that for the attorney. Schaffer agreed to take a down payment of $300 and allow the family to pay $300 per month until the debt was satisfied.

Nancy's major worry was Mom's health. In the past, she knew, Mom had sacrificed her own blood pressure medication when she needed money for my legal fees. But she also knew that the price was cheap, if Schaffer could get something done.

In a way it was movement, and in a way it was not. I liked the tone of Schaffer's early letters to me, and I was confident that he would attack the case more vigorously than Bruder; on the other hand, he first had to familiarize himself with every facet. Under the rules of law, the federal courts would give us one and only one opportunity to file for a writ of habeas corpus. If we blew this chance, we would never have another. Schaffer had to make sure he did things right the first time.

We were delayed further when Bruder, instead of handing over his copies of my court records directly to Schaffer, simply returned them to the courts. Schaffer had to get them for himself from the state offices in Austin.

But as he probed, he realized that what had been conjecture back in 1977 was now fact. After my trial, officials in David Harris's home county had never revoked his parole, despite his confession to a burglary and armed robbery, nor had they bothered to prosecute him on those charges; clearly, he had been rewarded for his testimony against me.

We now possessed a wealth of evidence with which we could cast doubt on Harris's character. As White had warned everyone in the courtroom, if Harris was allowed to get away with his scam of blaming Officer Wood's murder on me, he was sure to cause innocent people further pain and suffering. Here is what Schaffer learned about Harris:

After my trial, he had joined the U.S. Army. During the Christmas season of 1977, while home in Vidor on holiday leave, he broke into a trailer and attempted to rape the woman inside. When she declined to press charges, Harris returned to military duty. Subsequently, while stationed in West Germany, he burglarized house trailers belonging to Hildegard Steupenrauk and Robert Schaffer and assaulted his commanding officer. In October 1978, a court-martial sentenced him to serve eight months at a military prison in Fort Leavenworth, Kansas.

Upon his release from Leavenworth, near the end of June 1979, Harris stole a car in Kansas and drove to California, where he committed additional robberies and burglaries and kidnapped a hitchhiker at gunpoint. In November of that year, he and two accomplices broke into an electronics store in California, unknowingly tripping a silent alarm. When police surprised them on the scene, Harris drew a gun, aimed it directly at one of the officers, and pulled the trigger. The gun misfired. At his subsequent trial in February 1980, Harris tried to blame the burglary on one of his accomplices; nevertheless he was sentenced to six and one-half years in a California state prison. Harris had spent the past seven years proving Dennis White's crime spree theory!

In sum, if the Dallas County district attorney's office wanted to bring David Harris back to the witness stand to accuse me once more, Schaffer would be more than happy to conduct the cross-examination.

Furthermore, simply by reading newspaper accounts subsequent to Officer Wood's murder, Schaffer discovered a key point that Dennis White and Mel Bruder had missed. Shortly after the murder, a newspaper reported that Police Officer Teresa Turko had been hypnotized in an effort to enhance her recollection of the events surrounding the crime. In his brief, Schaffer argued that many jurisdictions do not permit the testimony of a witness who has been hypnotized, because that testimony is likely to be tainted. Where such testimony is allowed, courts require strict procedural safeguards. But White had never noticed the newspaper account, and had never been told about it. Therefore, White could not use the information to cast doubt on Turko's ability to recall the facts.

With reluctance, Schaffer decided that he had to launch an attack upon a fellow attorney. He composed a brief charging that White's defense "fell below the minimum standards acceptable by the federal and state constitutions." He based much of this on opinions previously expressed by the Texas Court of Criminal Appeals, which chastised White for failing to preserve evidence of the court's errors in the trial record, failing to lodge a specific objection that the excluded evidence demonstrated that Harris had a motive for testifying against me, and failing to lodge a timely request with the district attorney's office for Emily Miller's prior statement.

Schaffer added the contentions that White should have offered a standard request for disclosure concerning whether any of the state's witnesses had been hypnotized prior to trial, and he should have objected to the testimony of Detective J.W. Johnson, who asserted that I had told him that I returned to the motel after 1:00 A.M. on the night of the murder. The admission of this testimony concerning an uncorroborated oral statement of a defendant in custody was in violation of Article 38.22 of the Texas Code of Criminal Procedure and, said Schaffer, if White had interrupted with the mildest objection, Judge Metcalfe would surely have excluded it from the evidence.

Upon the first appearance of the three surprise rebuttal witnesses on Friday afternoon, Schaffer declared, White should have requested an immediate continuance of the trial. Had he done so, the witnesses would not have been excused, thus assuring their presence in the courtroom on Monday. His failure to do so left him in the dark when it came time for cross-examination. A continuance would have given him, we knew now, ample evidence and opportunity to impeach the testimony of all three.

The new evidence and the new arguments were refreshing, but anything in the judicial arena is a double-edged sword. We could raise our old points in federal court, since state courts had already ruled on them. But if we wanted to introduce new evidence, we had to start at square one, back in Judge Metcalfe's court, and make our way once more along the meandering path of the court system.

We held little hope that Metcalfe or any Texas judge would grant me a new trial, but we had no choice. Until the state courts denied us, the federal courts would not consider our new evidence.

On February 3, 1984 (as I was suffering from a bout of flu during a major epidemic that hit Eastham), Schaffer filed our application in Criminal Court Number Two of Dallas County, Texas, contending that I was illegally restrained of my liberty.

Schaffer's appellate brief was a thing of beauty to me. As I awaited action by the courts, I found it excruciatingly difficult to cool my heels in Eastham. On February 18 I wrote to Mom:

> I have thought and prayed over this and believe me it is the only thing I can do. I didn't start any of this and I can't let it go. I have to have the conviction removed—the only way to do that is to appeal it until the courts overturn it! Texas would like nothing more than for me to accept this and ride it out and that is something I can't do! Mom, Texas has ruined *our* name and *our* lives . . . and no matter what happens later (whether I wait for parole or fight them in court) they have branded me a killer, which is bad, but saying I'm a cop killer is something I cannot let go. I must fight them . . .
>
> I don't want to hurt or scare you, but I'll fight Dallas until they either kill me or admit the things they have done . . .
>
> Mom, you may be afraid of H. Wade, but believe me he is also afraid of us and if we can keep him from doing this to someone else it will be enough— how many has he done this way and got away with it?

Searching for some way to help mold my own destiny, I sent copies of Schaffer's brief to numerous individuals and organizations in an attempt to interest them in my case. My local congressman in Ohio,

Chalmers P. Wylie, was sympathetic, but there was little he could do.

I wrote to the ACLU and the NAACP, both of which had expressed interest in my case when it was a death penalty appeal. I wrote to an organization called HOPE (Help Our Prisoners Exist).

I tried the media, writing detailed letters to ABC's "20/20" and CBS's "Sixty Minutes." I wrote to the legal departments at Playboy Enterprises and Larry Flint Publications, trying to interest them in writing an article about Texas's version of justice.

I busied myself with work and was thankful that it was a busy time at the garment factory. One day at the factory I hosted a tour of inspectors sent out by Judge Justice to inspect conditions at Eastham, which they characterized as their "headache."

Three evenings a week I lifted weights to get my flabby body back into shape.

On a bleak night in March 1984, Texas had another crack at Cowboy Autry. The lethal chemicals began to flow at 12:26 A.M. For a full ten minutes Autry was conscious enough to converse with his girlfriend. At 12:36 A.M., his body shook, then stiffened, and his dreary twenty-nine years were over.

All along, Autry had maintained that he had not committed the murder for which he was condemned. Without really knowing the facts of the case, I could not form an opinion but I was quite willing to believe that Texas did not care all that much whether or not he was guilty, so long as it got to kill someone.

On the final day of March, Texas added Ronald Clark "Candy Man" O'Bryan to its growing list of official victims.

In Dallas County Criminal Court Number Two, Judge Metcalfe, without granting a hearing, denied my application for a writ of habeas corpus and bumped us up to the next step, the Texas Court of Criminal Appeals.

After he filed my application with the higher court, Schaffer reported to me that there was concern in the Dallas County district attorney's office. Henry Wade's boys were trying desperately to avoid an evidentiary hearing that would allow us to develop our new lines of argument. Rather, the state's attorneys were attempting to get the court of criminal appeals to base its decision entirely upon the transcripts of the original trial, thus sandbagging our effort to introduce new evidence, to debate fresh issues.

Whether or not the court granted us an evidentiary hearing was now the critical question.

20

THE PAROLE

IN JUNE 1984, I had an initial interview with a fact finder for the parole board. We spoke for about a half hour and he said that everything about my record looked good, except for the nature of the crime. He was certain that the parole board would deny me the first couple of times, but believed that by my third hearing, if I kept my prison record clean, I would have a good chance for parole. If he was correct, release could come as early as eighteen months from now. That was encouraging, but I believed that the courts would free me earlier than that.

Six months later I was still at the Ham, awaiting word from the slow-moving Court of Criminal Appeals.

. . .

One day I encountered Captain Shepard sitting on the back slab, his head in his hands.

"How ya doin' Cap'n?" I asked.

"I'm gittin' tired of this place," he said.

"What's wrong?"

"Things've changed."

Indeed, TDC officials faced a number of sticky problems. One of them was Judge Justice's order to phase out the old building tender system. They could not simply demote the building tenders and then place them in amid the general population—for that was a death sentence. Some were moved to the Diagnostics Unit in Huntsville, where they worked in the laundry. Life was relatively easy—we heard that they could even order out for pizza. Others were paroled.

This latter strategy did not work too well. The Texas streets were filled with ex-cons ready and willing to settle past-due accounts. New inmates spread the reports that numerous building tenders were tracked down on the outside and executed, many of the jobs contracted for by the "Mexican Mafia." Skinny Gates, the afternoon tender from L-Line was one of their victims in Houston.

With the building tenders gone, Eastham desperately needed an influx of new guards, but the labor supply was limited. It was through the prison newspaper, the *Echo,* that we learned the solution to the dilemma. TDC was now hiring female guards.

The women were first assigned to clerical jobs, but they gradually worked their way onto the cell blocks. It was an obvious prescription for trouble, and some of the older officers exploited the tension. Sometimes, when a new female officer was working with an older male officer, the veteran would keep his eyes out for an inmate, perhaps some dude whom he knew was hung down to *there,* and order him to submit to a strip search. At other times, the old guard might find a convicted pervert who would be more than happy to expose himself to the female officer.

Before long, it was routine for the women officers to patrol, even in our showers. It was an indignity that I felt was unnecessary.

An environmental and safety study conducted by a health consultant concluded that TDC was infested with rats and plagued with faulty plumbing. Even the newest facilities failed to meet minimum requirements.

Governor Mark White criticized the study as a call for "Cadillac prisons." What TDC needed, he said, was not millions of dollars for renovation, but soap and water.

One TDC official commented, "It's going to take a hell of a lot more than soap and water to fix the problems."

In 1984, a total of twenty-five TDC inmates were stabbed to death. Another four hundred were injured. Some claimed that this represented only an increase in reporting, not an increase in occurrences. Others blamed it on the fact that less violent convicts were increasingly placed in alternative programs, such as work release, and that the remaining populace tended to be more violent.

A survey conducted by the *Echo* reported that 44 percent of TDC inmates said that they had been involved in a violent incident within the confines of the prison system. Sixty-four percent believed that the rate of violence was increasing.

Walking the halls of Eastham those days, I felt as if I was standing on an atomic bomb. The building tender system, with all its faults, seemed better—and safer—than this craziness.

Feeling the pressure, TDC paroled 600 men in a single week and another 400 the following week. The word was out that a total of 12,000 would be freed in this first wave to comply with Judge Justice's orders against overcrowding. I doubted that I would be included in this group, but I could hope.

On December 21, 1984, parole board member Winona Miles wrote a memorandum concerning my case:

> Mr. Adams is a first offender with a criminal history limited to an arrest for driving while intoxicated. His social history would indicate a rather stable individual who had completed high school, completed a vocational course and enlisted and honorably discharged from the U.S. Army with subsequent stable employment upon his discharge.
>
> The inmate lists his parents as his residence on his

parole plan. He seems committed to returning to Ohio and has several offers of employment from that geographic area.

He has been at Eastham since the commutation of the death sentence and has been able to maintain a discipline-free record.

Mr. Adams is an impressive, articulate man who seemed quite sincere during the interview. He stated his case without histrionics and those trappings of manipulative persuasion that generally accompany these interviews. He was informed that due to the nature of the crime itself, parole will not be recommended.

That very same month, David Harris was paroled from California's Soledad state prison. By a special arrangement, he was allowed to return to his hometown of Vidor, Texas.

21

THE PRODUCER

IN LATE MARCH 1985, Major Perkins, my boss at the garment factory, informed me, "Somebody wants to see you."

I knew that no one from my family was in town. Perhaps it's Schaffer, I thought.

In the visiting room I was confronted by a stranger, who identified himself as Errol Morris, a filmmaker who was interested in the story of Dr. James P. Grigson, alias Dr. Death. Some time earlier he had seen a "20/20" segment about Grigson, and he was intrigued. By now, the psychiatrist had attracted a great deal of national attention.

In the spring of 1981, the U.S. Supreme Court had ruled on the case of *Estelle v. Smith*. By a vote of nine to zero they voided the death sentence of Ernest Benjamin Smith on the grounds that his constitutional rights were violated by Dr. Grigson's penalty-phase testimony. The Court ruled that Grigson had violated Smith's right to remain silent by not warning him that anything he said during the psychiatric interview might be used against him in court. He had not warned me either.

The press reported that the *Smith* case, along with mine, would "break the back" of Texas's death row.

But it did not stop Grigson. He simply changed his tactics, claiming the ability to declare a defendant to be a sociopath without ever bothering to interview him. He had used this tactic in the trial of Thomas Barefoot, with whom I had discussed religion on death row. The prosecutor, Bell County District Attorney Cappy Eads, had asked Grigson "hypothetical" questions, the details of which mimicked what the jury already knew about the defendant. The conclusion of Grigson's testimony was that the person described in the hypothetical situation was, hypothetically, a sociopath who would kill again.

When the Supreme Court considered the case of *Barefoot v. Estelle* late in 1983, the American Psychiatric Association filed a brief with the court, arguing that psychiatrists are unable to predict the future conduct of anyone.

In the end the Supreme Court ruled that such hypothetical testimony was, indeed, admissible during the punishment phase of a trial, paving the way for the state of Texas to execute Thomas Barefoot.

Morris was fascinated with the entire subject of psychiatric testimony, and he had landed a modest grant to produce a Public Broadcasting Service documentary concerning the use of court-appointed psychiatrists to evaluate death penalty candidates. One of his goals was to show that, contrary to Grigson's usual testimony, former death row inmates can still become productive members of society.

Texas authorities, proud of their image as a tough law-and-order state and probably unaware of the thrust of Morris's proposed documentary, were eager to cooperate and had provided him with a list of inmates against whom Grigson had testified. In all, Morris planned to interview more than twenty inmates here at the Eastham unit, as well as the Ellis, Darrington, and Coffield units. I happened to be one of them.

For a time, Morris and I spoke in general terms about my case. I answered his questions with guarded honesty, for I really had no idea who he was, nor who had sent him. When he left, I believed that my brief fling with the media was over.

But he returned two weeks later, on Thursday, April 11, to inform me that he had narrowed the focus of his research to three or four cases. Mine was one of them.

I was skeptical. Why should I cooperate with this fellow? On the other hand, I asked myself, what did I have to lose? Here I was, stuck in the Ham with a life sentence even though the U.S. Supreme Court had decreed that the selection of my jury was unconstitutional. Schaffer was doing what he could on the legal front, but what I could use was another independent thinker who would dig into my case, and I liked the fact that Morris said he was an investigator by trade.

"I'll do your documentary," I agreed, "under certain conditions." I spelled out my terms: first, he was to contact my lawyer and get his approval; I needed to make absolutely sure that my cooperation with Morris would not harm my chances, either for parole or a favorable ruling by an appellate court. Second, he was to contact my mother, so that she would know what was going on. I told Morris that if he fulfilled these two preconditions, I would open my life to him completely. He could ask me anything he wished, and I would answer with total truth. Then I added my third condition. "As you look into my case," I said, "anything you find, good or bad, I want to know about it, and I want my lawyer to know about it."

He agreed. Immediately I wrote to my mother and to Schaffer, to apprise them of the situation. I said to Mom, "I feel that there are things that should be said and I feel that this could be a good way of saying them."

On April 17, 1985, Morris met with David Harris at a bar in Vidor, in the hopes of persuading him to grant a filmed interview. During the course of the conversation, Harris found himself caught up in his memories of the events of November 27 and 28, 1976. At one point he said that he "will never forget that look in the policeman's eyes."

It was then that Morris knew with certainty who had killed Officer Robert Wood.

Harris must have noticed the flash of recognition. As Morris was leaving, Harris offered him a piece of advice: "You really need to be careful about driving out here," he cautioned.

One morning soon thereafter, Major Perkins pulled me away from my desk at the garment factory. "Come on Adams," he said, "The warden wants to see you." There was a look of genuine concern on my boss's face. "Have you been in trouble lately?" he asked.

"No, sir," I replied. "I've always kept my nose clean."

"Let me know what happens," Major Perkins said, as he left me at the searcher's table.

Fifteen minutes later, I stood before Warden Myers. He glanced at a sheet of paper that he held in his hand, then tossed it in my direction, asking, "Adams, what the hell is this shit?"

It was a letter to the warden from Errol Morris, stating that he would be arriving the very next day with a full film crew. He wanted the warden to provide space for the interview, and he wanted my time reserved for the entire day.

The warden's initial reaction to these requests was to level a scowl at me.

"This guy was here several weeks ago," I explained. "You allowed him in, sir, remember? He's doing a documentary on the state's psychiatrists."

Through tight lips the warden informed me that he would authorize the filming. I knew that he hated to allow prisoners access to the media because it disrupted daily operations, but I could see in his expression that he had received word from someone higher up that he was supposed to cooperate.

Late that night, after I attended a college class, I received my mail. Two letters were waiting for me and they left me apprehensive. In response to my note, Schaffer wrote to tell me that he had not been contacted by a film producer named Errol Morris and knew absolutely nothing about the man. The second letter was from Mom, who said that this Morris fellow had not contacted her either. She warned me that she had a bad feeling about this development.

I muttered to myself, "What the hell is going on? What is this guy trying to pull?"

That night brought only fitful sleep as a fierce argument raged inside my head. I was tired of doing what everyone else told me to do, tired of keeping a low profile, tired of submitting to the system like a docile lamb. Where had it gotten me? I was thirty-six years old and facing an indefinite future in the Ham. So was it not about time that I took charge of this joke that was called my life?

At 8:30 A.M. May 23, an aging, gray-haired guard escorted me into forbidden territory, the long, narrow visitors' side of the lounge, where a crew of about fifteen people were busy setting up lights, cameras, and microphones. Morris walked over, smiled, and extended his hand. He was tall and slim, and carried himself with a sense of sophistication that bordered on artiness. This crew, he boasted, had been flown in from New York and California, just to spend the day with me.

"We need to talk," I said in a very serious tone.

Before Morris could respond, the guard ordered me to sit down on one side of the room and wait quietly until the film crew was ready for me.

As I replied to the guard I suddenly found my voice imbued with a sense of authority that seemed to arise from the distant past. "Look," I said, "the warden has authorized these people to be in here and the warden has authorized me to be in here, so *you* go sit down. I have got to talk to this man. Errol, get over here!"

To my surprise, everyone obeyed. The guard stumbled over to the side of the room and took a seat. Morris leaned forward to listen to whatever it was I had to say. I reminded him, "Before you left last time, I asked you to do two things for me."

"Oh, yeah, yeah," he said, "I contacted your attorney and he's fired up about this, and your mom is really happy about it too."

I had ammunition with me. I waved Mom's letter in his face. "I got this last night," I said. "She says you never contacted her."

Morris protested that there must have been some kind of missed communication. "I was late," he apologized, "but I did contact your mother, just a day or two ago."

"Well, how am I supposed to know that?" I asked. He had no answer, and I continued, "We have another problem. I also told you to contact my attorney, and you didn't do that."

"Yes I did."

I whipped out the letter from Randy Schaffer and displayed it.

He groaned, "Oooooh. I contacted Mel Bruder."

"Mel Bruder is not my attorney, Errol, and he hasn't been for a long time."

Morris held up his hands in supplication. "I'll tell you what I'll do," he suggested. "I'll run out here to the warden's office and call Schaffer right now."

"How would I know who the hell you called?" I asked. It was too little, too late, as far as I was concerned. I shared Mom's apprehension about opening my life to this stranger. I made my decision out loud: "I'm not doing this interview." I called over to the guard in the corner, "Boss, do me a favor, get me out of here."

Morris's face gave way to a panicked expression. He was apologetic and apoplectic at the same time. He ordered the guard to stay put, promising that we would work out our misunderstanding.

The poor old prison guard had probably spent forty years working for TDC, and must have thought he had seen everything. Certainly he had seen beatings and murders. He had survived riots. Beneath his gray hairline he probably dreamed of an approaching retirement. But now, in the twilight of his career, he found himself *ordered around* not only by a prisoner, but by some hotshot visiting film producer. It was too much for him to comprehend. He simply sat in his chair and shook his head as Morris and I railed at each other for at least ten more minutes.

Finally, the face of another guard appeared on the prisoners' side of the room. He opened the sliding window and passed a slip of paper to me, along with the terse command, "Sign this."

It was a standard media release form, protecting TDC from any legal ramifications resulting from the interview.

"I'm not signing it," I said.

"You've got to sign it," the guard insisted.

"I don't have to do a damn thing," I shot back. There, again, was that new forceful voice coming out of my mouth. I added, "I'm not signing *anything!*"

"Well, then I've got to take this up with the building major," he said.

"I wish to God you would. I've been trying to get this damn boss to get me out of here. I want to terminate this interview."

Within ten minutes the warden arrived, flanked by two tough-looking assistant wardens, a building major, and a handful of men from Eastham's elite riot control team. They busted through the back door and stormed in.

I muttered under my breath, "I am in a world of trouble."

"Adams," the warden demanded, "what in the hell is going on here?"

I tried to keep my voice calm and reasonable, detailing the story as quickly as possible. I showed the warden the two letters I had received the previous day, and concluded, "I want to terminate the interview."

"You do?"

"Yes, sir. I am not talking to this man."

That was good enough for the warden. He turned to the building major and told him to escort me to the main hallway and back to my cell block. "Mr. Adams is free for the day," he said.

He reserved his wrath for Morris. As I left the visiting room I heard him say to the producer, "You've got ten minutes to get all this equipment and all these damn people off my goddamn property or I am going to have you in a cell on the south end." He summoned his best East Texas drawl and commanded, "Now git!"

Behind me, I could hear the sounds of furious activity. Morris was "gitting."

In the early morning hours of July 9, the state of Texas executed Henry Martinez Porter, my former neighbor on death row.

His last words were: "I want people to know that they called me a cold-blooded murderer, and I shot a man who shot me first. I didn't tie anyone down on a stretcher and put poison into his veins from behind a locked door. I call this and I call your society a bunch of cold-blooded murderers."

. . .

The flap with Morris turned out to be a matter of timing and crossed signals. His letter to Mom and her letter to me had crossed in the mail; he had, indeed, written to her, and the tone of his letter convinced her that he was intellectually honest. Furthermore, he contacted Schaffer and convinced him that his credentials were in order.

The interview was rescheduled for Tuesday, July 16, and, this time, Schaffer was present to guard my interests. I signed the TDC release, and I signed another release for Morris, granting him permission to use my image, voice, and name in his documentary on Dr. Death.

The cameras began to roll and we spoke for three and one-half hours.

At about the same time, another promising media contact developed. I fell into a discussion with another inmate about the book *Blood Will Tell,* the story of the T. Cullen Davis murder acquittal. I had read and enjoyed the book, and decided to contact the writer, Gary Cartwright, to see if he might be interested in the story of my case.

Cartwright, who was an editor of *Texas Monthly* magazine, had worked closely with Racehorse Haynes on the Davis book. I wrote to him immediately.

In another letter to Mom I reported that my attitude toward publicity had changed. If the courts insisted on dragging their feet, we would see what the press could do. "I will not let this publicity go by," I wrote, "and I will use it to force some sort of change in this case."

22

THE DEMON SEED

AT 2:40 A.M. on September 1, 1985, David Harris, armed with a .38 caliber pistol that he had stolen in a burglary earlier in the evening, entered an unlocked apartment at 6550 Lexington Drive in Beaumont, Texas. A hall light that had been left on illuminated the scene as Harris made his way through the apartment. He opened a bedroom door, surprising the sleeping tenant, Mark Walter Mays, a thirty-year-old car dealership finance manager, and his twenty-six-year-old girlfriend, Roxanne Lockard. Both were naked. At gunpoint, Harris forced Mays into a bathroom and then told Lockard to throw on her robe and come outside with him to his pickup truck.

Lockard was already inside the truck and Harris was walking toward the driver's door when he heard a noise, felt something on the right side of his neck, and realized that he had been shot.

Mays had broken free from the bathroom and come after Harris with a 9 millimeter pistol.

Harris ducked down behind the door of his truck, pulled his pistol, rose to view his pursuer and felt another shot strike him in the shoulder. Harris fired back, and Mays fell to his hands and knees.

As Lockard raced away to safety, Harris ran around the front of the pickup and approached his victim, firing at least one fatal shot at point-blank range before he fled.

Four days later, Vidor police arrested Harris after a break-in at the local Texas Pride Gunshop. Chief Sam Kittrell questioned him about the source of his wounds, investigated, and turned him over to Beaumont authorities. Subsequently, the local district attorney indicted Harris for murder committed during the course of another felony—a capital offense.

Harris dictated a confession to Kittrell and Detective Pat O'Quinn of the Beaumont police department. He admitted shooting Mays, but complained that it was the victim's fault. If the man had kept quiet and not tried to save his girlfriend, he would still be alive.

When I heard about all this, I recalled Dennis White's prophetic words during his closing statement at my trial: "David Harris is the demon seed if I have ever seen it. If we don't get him this time he will kill again."

23

THE FILES

THE TEXAS LEGISLATURE and the state courts spit in the face of Judge Justice's orders to alleviate overcrowding by enacting and exploiting a new sentencing law whereby an inmate convicted of an aggravated felony (which generally meant that he brandished a deadly weapon) had to serve at least one third of his sentence before he could even be considered for parole. Many of these men arrived at the Ham slapped with sixty-year sentences and the realization that they had little or nothing to gain from good behavior. They were placed under the supervision of an army of young, untrained, inexperienced guards, many of them now women, who were under severe new rules to avoid violence against inmates. The natural result was that more and more prisoners took matters into their own hands. Gang wars erupted; eight inmates were murdered in as many days.

In response, TDC officials ordered a crackdown. Throughout the system, some seventeen thousand inmates were locked into their houses and kept there for up to two weeks until guards could complete comprehensive shakedowns. At Eastham, nearly six hundred men, more than 25 percent of the population, were found with contraband and were ordered into isolation cells. The entire south end was locked down, but it did not affect those of us in the dormitories on the north end.

All of this turmoil was reflected in several entries in my journal:

September 9, 1985, Monday. I heard today that 26 people have died in TDC this year. At this time 13 farms are locked down because of these killings. It seems a Mexican Gang War has started. Are they acting? No, I believe they are for real. Some of the people hurt should not have been. The public may have the right to put us away from them. But do we not have the right *not* to be harmed? Not everyone here has hurt someone, but they are forced into this place and a lot of them must turn mean just to maintain. Why have you, Mr. Public, not watched the watch dogs?

September 12, 1985, Thursday. Now they want us to be "good little inmates" and act as if nothing has happened. "Go to work, get a haircut, shave, tuck your shirttail in, stay behind the green line in the hall." Why should they care about the killings now? They didn't care when the building tenders were killing . . . Don't they know that some of these "Good little inmates" will one day get out and walk the streets with them? I do not like to walk the halls of a prison with a lot of these people.

September 14, 1985, Saturday. So much for lock downs. Yesterday at the Coffield Unit (three) more Toy Soldiers fell, hurry, we only have 4 months to

go! The count is 30 and holding in this TDC's most
killing year. Why so many? Maybe because they have
to report the killings now. Four years ago, they didn't
have to report the killings the inmate guards got
away with. "It's getting Curiouser and Curiouser,
cried Alice!"

I had no intention of troubling my family with this news, but my
sister Nancy heard a report about the trouble in TDC and wrote
me a worried letter. I tried to quell the family's fears, informing
them that I was not on one of the locked down units and that the
major inconvenience to me was that my college classes were canceled
for two weeks. I hoped that they could not read my personal fear
between the lines.

During the course of his research, Errol Morris asked to see the
district attorney's files on all of the Dr. Death cases, but it was my
file that he particularly wanted to study. As far as the unsuspecting
Henry Wade was concerned, *The State of Texas v. Randall Dale
Adams* was old and all but forgotten business. He had planned a
three-day weekend fishing trip, and he saw no reason to change his
plans. He granted Morris unrestricted access to his files during his
absence.

Morris made good use of the opportunity.

In my original trial, there was much confusion over the time that
David Harris and I had left the drive-in movie. Harris testified that
we were still at the drive-in movie at midnight. He said that his
memory was clear on that point because he had gone to the conces-
sion stand to buy popcorn at that time. I said that we had left around
9:30 P.M. Now Morris unearthed an old report from State Investigator Jeff Shaw, whom Mulder sent to the drive-in on March 29,
1977, to check the details of the movie times. Shaw's written report
made fascinating reading:

November 27, Saturday evening the 183 Drive-In
in Irving, Texas, was showing a double feature; *The*

Swinging Cheerleaders and *The Student Body*. Show times were: *The Student Body* started at 7:00 P.M., ran to 8:25 P.M. *The Swinging Cheerleaders* started at 8:40 P.M., ran to 10:14 P.M. *The Student Body* started at 10:24 P.M., ran to 11:45 P.M. No other showings that night.

Confusion about the movie times was further indicated in Mulder's handwritten pretrial notes concerning the various points of testimony he planned to elicit. Concerning the movie times, he originally noted, "Last feature was still in progress when they left close to midnight." But underneath, he added in parentheses, "Actually, the last feature was over at 11:45 P.M., so they must have left around 11:30 P.M." It was easy to conjecture that he penned the comment after he received Shaw's report.

Yet at the trial, with Shaw's report sequestered in his files and illegally withheld from the defense (because, Mulder would later explain, he believed it to be inaccurate), Mulder attempted to get the theater managers to admit on cross-examination that *The Swinging Cheerleaders* had run a second time, ending after midnight, presenting the jury with a description of events that corroborated Harris's testimony.

Another important discovery was a copy of a telephone bill. We knew that, during the trial, the district attorney's office had ensconced Emily and Robert Miller at the Adolphus Hotel, and we also knew that by Monday, May 2, when they were mysteriously unavailable to respond to Dennis White's subpoenas, they had moved to the Alamo Plaza Hotel. We still wondered whether Mulder had known their whereabouts, but we had never been able to prove that he did. However, here in the district attorney's all-but-forgotten files was a bill for 135 phone calls made by the Millers from the Alamo Plaza Hotel between April 30 and May 2.

The bad news was that we were unable to get any of this new evidence into the record. On October 9, 1985, the court of criminal appeals, basing its decision solely on the trial transcript and without granting an evidentiary hearing, denied relief on my application for a writ of habeas corpus.

After receiving the notice from the court, I waited for a week to see what Schaffer would suggest next. When I did not hear from him, I wrote and asked. To my surprise and frustration, he replied that my letter was his first notice of the denial. The court had not even bothered to notify him!

The good news was that the way was now clear for us to take the case to the feds. Schaffer's next step would be to file the application in the U.S. District Court for the Northern District of Texas, Dallas Division, and I prayed that the federal response would be more congenial.

We had new evidence. We needed to have that evidentiary hearing!

On October 17, 1985, Morris and his crew filmed an interview with Emily Miller. During the interview, she made the astonishing admission, contrary to her courtroom testimony, that she had picked out the *wrong* suspect from the police lineup.

On the following day, Morris and his film crew caught up with Michael Randell. Perhaps the fact that he had a few drinks under his belt loosened his tongue. For whatever reason, he told Morris why he had lied at my trial about playing basketball until 10:00 P.M. in a gymnasium that had actually closed at 5:00 P.M. Now divorced, Randell admitted that on the night of the murder he was driving a woman named Debbie home from the Plush Pub in Fort Worth. "My wife would kill me," he said. "She would have tore my head off if she'd knowed that night I was out with another woman. I was trying to get her—the other woman—home."

Morris also interviewed Doug Mulder, but the prosecutor-turned-defense lawyer refused to sign a release, so Morris could not use any of the footage.

Morris was due to visit me to discuss the progress of his film and to get me to sign releases authorizing him to obtain information concerning my polygraph examination and my medical records. A few days before he arrived, I was summoned to Eastham's main office and cross-examined by a unit warden, an assistant warden, two officers in charge of security, and two members of the special security team. They wanted to know, in no uncertain terms, what the hell a New York film producer was doing coming to visit me yet again. Obviously they were concerned that Morris was probing TDC, in light of the ongoing problems with the *Ruiz* lawsuit.

I tried to assure them that the producer was simply interested in my case and that he was not going to be asking me about conditions within TDC, but I was not sure they believed me.

When Morris showed up on November 14, he was told that I had been placed in administrative security detention and, therefore, our visiting time would be limited to fifteen minutes. We spoke only briefly, I signed the necessary papers and then, suddenly, a guard informed us that time was up.

Morris asked quickly, "Why have you been placed in security detention?"

"I haven't," I replied, confused.

The guard demanded that I leave the visiting room immediately.

Morris was angry, and he located a phone in the lobby of the visiting area and called the warden's office to find out what was going on. Whoever he spoke to claimed that there had been some kind of mix-up and, ten minutes later, we were allowed to resume our visit for a full hour.

The incident placed us both on our guard. What kind of game was TDC playing with us?

At the end of 1985, the inmate newspaper, the *Echo,* reported that the official TDC murder count for 1985 was 27, and an additional 622 inmates survived knife wounds. All told, during 1984 and 1985 there were a reported eighty thousand incidents of violence within TDC; it was a trend that seemed to be growing.

In an attempt to gain control of Eastham, TDC sent its best man. George Waldron, Eastham's fourth new warden in the past five years, came in and at least brought some cosmetic changes with him. He had the cells repainted and broken windows repaired. He reopened the library and saw to it that the kitchen was brought up to sanitary standards.

. . .

At his trial for the capital murder of Mark Mays in Beaumont, David Harris admitted, "It's my fault. I offer my condolences to his family." On the witness stand, Harris began to sob.

But he contended that circumstances mitigated his guilt. Yes, he said, he had broken into the apartment and abducted Mays's girl-friend at gunpoint. But he only fired his gun after Mays had shot first. Harris said that he was defending his own life and only fired at Mays from a distance.

A pathologist from the Harris County medical examiner's office contradicted that testimony, declaring that the two fatal shots, which destroyed Mays's aorta and right lung, were fired from a distance of no more than two feet.

On April 19, 1986, the jury found Harris guilty of capital murder. It took them only twenty more minutes to decide to sentence him to death.

Morris attended that trial as an observer, and then came to visit me once more on May 1, to apprise me of the latest developments, and there were many.

During this visit, Morris asked if I would allow him to talk to Melvin Bruder, my first appellate attorney, about my case and, of course, I agreed.

Following up on this, Morris traveled to Dallas and met with Bruder. Morris liked the lawyer, and he took it upon himself to ask if Bruder would be willing to get back into the case. Bruder indicated that he would, at no cost to my family.

At the garment factory, the state decided to replace inmate book-keepers with free-world CPAs, so I moved to a job at the mainte-nance department. My task was to dispatch repair crews to various parts of the prison, as needed. The new responsibilities would assist me in applying for an elevation in my status, from third-class to second-class trusty.

In my new position I got the chance to meet an interesting fellow by the name of Tommy Ray Kneeland, whose job was to take care of electrical and telephone line repairs. Tommy Ray was serving two life terms *plus* 550 years for murders in Winkler and Tarrant Counties. Back in 1970, he kidnapped a twenty-seven-year-old housewife and left her body in a shallow grave alongside a highway. Two years later he slit the throats of a seventeen-year-old girl and a fifteen-year-old boy. The girl was raped before she died.

Despite the viciousness of his crimes and the length of his sentences, Tommy Ray had it pretty good at Eastham. He lived in a small shack *outside* the compound, complete with a color television, refrigerator, and a prison tractor for transportation. He had a ring full of keys to every lock in Eastham and, if he craved a midnight snack, all he had to do was let himself into the kitchen, grab some hamburger, trot on home, and cook it. Or he could drive his tractor over to a nearby general store, load up on groceries, and charge them to his account. Once a month or so, whenever his wife came for a weekend visit in the shack, she paid the bill.

Tommy Ray was visible proof that, in Texas, it's not what you've done, but who you know that counts.

Schaffer wrote me a very disturbing letter on August 18, 1986. He advised me, during the course of my discussions with Errol Morris, not to seem too vengeful in my comments about Dallas and its criminal justice system. He noted that if we succeeded in being granted a new trial, that trial would take place in Dallas, unless the district attorney's office decided to dismiss the case, or I sought to plea bargain.

A month later, I received another disturbing letter from Schaffer. He felt rejected because of Errol Morris's attempts to get Mel Bruder involved in the case once more, this time as an unpaid cocounsel. He warned me that the maxim, "too many cooks spoil the broth," applies to the courtroom as well as the kitchen.

I wrote back immediately, expressing the hope that Schaffer and Bruder could work together toward the common goal of securing my freedom.

I wanted action, and I told Schaffer so:

> I for one am tired of being patient or passive. Ten
> years of my life have been taken from me. My youth

fled from me long ago thanks to Dallas County. I
want some answers as to why. My family has gone
through a great deal of heartache. Not to mention
the financial burden this has placed upon them. I
feel that they deserve those answers also.

Then I addressed what to me was the most disturbing issue, Schaffer's remark in his previous letter that, if I was granted a new trial,
I might opt to plea bargain. Frustration poured out of me as I wrote
back:

I would like to know what the *hell* you meant by
that? Dallas County tried to murder me with and
without the backing of the state . . . I feel that you
do not understand that I must talk about Dallas.
How could I not talk about them if someone will
listen? I will talk about the things done to my family
and to myself while I was held in Dallas. I have
many questions that need to be answered . . . I do
not believe you understand our goal. I will accept
nothing less than answers to those questions. I will
get them if it takes the rest of my life . . .

Schaffer responded a few weeks later, agreeing to have Bruder assist.
He informed me that Federal Magistrate John B. Tolle had scheduled an evidentiary hearing for December 4, 1986, and he noted:

This will probably be our only real opportunity to
develop the record in an effort to prove the allegations made in the application . . . If Mr. Morris has
any information which is relevant to our allegations,
now is the time for him to make it available. It will
do little good if it comes out for the first time on
television a year from now.

While I was, of course, very pleased that we were finally going to
get our evidentiary hearing, I found myself nervous about the location. I received a court order to have me transferred to the Dallas

County jail on November 20, in order to be present for the hearing. I knew the inner workings of that system very well, and I asked Schaffer, Bruder, and Morris to see what they could do about assuring my safety.

Only two weeks prior to the federal evidentiary hearing, Morris agreed to abide by his earlier promise and provide Schaffer with the evidence of his discoveries. They set a meeting, in Morris's New York office.

Schaffer flew in at his own expense and became further rankled when he realized that the meeting was intended to be more of a taping session than a conference between allies. Nevertheless, Schaffer obtained the new evidence.

Next, my attorney wrote to David Harris on death row, asking if he would be willing to cooperate with us during the hearing. Schaffer did not expect Harris to own up to the murder of Officer Wood, but he hoped that Harris would testify concerning any deal that may have been struck among him, the Dallas County district attorney's office and prosecutors in his hometown of Vidor. Was he told that he would not be prosecuted for burglary and armed robbery, and that his probation would not be revoked, if he testified against me in Dallas?

To our surprise, Harris replied that he had "decided to assist" us. Schaffer set a meeting with him at the Ellis unit on October 22 to discuss the details.

Prior to the evidentiary hearing, I was transported back to Dallas and housed in a cell at the Lew Sterett Justice Center. One day Morris appeared for an unannounced visit, and he brought news that was both amazing and exhilarating. During the course of his research, he explained, he had changed his focus. He had at least temporarily scrapped his plans for a documentary about Dr. Death. Now, he was planning to do his entire film about my case.

"I want to know if you will give me a two-year option on the rights to your story," he said. Through a slot in the visitor's cage, he slid two copies of a short contract and asked me to sign them.

My mind buzzed. A decade ago I had received a severe lesson on the problems of signing legal papers without an attorney's opinion.

But Morris was here, and he wanted me to sign now. Even if I had the luxury of time, it would be difficult to run this one past Schaffer, I realized. He and Morris were feuding.

Morris was insistent, and I finally decided, what did I have to lose? No one else was screaming for the rights to my life story.

When I told him that I would sign, he immediately called in a notary public, who had been waiting outside. She witnessed my signature. Morris gave me a copy but I made him promise to send one home to Mom because I knew I would have to destroy my copy.

I stared at the piece of paper that I clutched in my hands and felt something close to panic. I knew that if the district attorney's office got wind of the fact that I was negotiating with a filmmaker, they would use that information against me in the press. Here in Dallas, they had me in their clutches. *Anything* could happen in this jail and I resented being put in this position.

The moment I returned to my cell, I tore my copy of the contract into minuscule bits and flushed it down the toilet.

24

THE EVIDENTIARY HEARING

TWO OFFICERS FROM the Dallas County sheriff's office, a man and a woman, escorted me to the evidentiary hearing. The woman was particularly hostile toward me, swearing and spewing venom, making no secret of the fact that she wished Texas had executed me.

The hearing began at 11:30 A.M. on December 4 in the court of the U.S. Magistrate, Northern District of Texas, Dallas Division. There was no jury involved, and the atmosphere was much more relaxed than my previous court appearances. Nevertheless, I was in handcuffs and leg shackles. Mom and my sisters were on hand, and we all knew that we were on the verge of winning, finally.

Schaffer played a clever card. One of the witnesses he subpoenaed was Harry Green, general counsel of the Texas Board of Pardons and Paroles. On the surface, he simply wanted Green to present the court with copies of the correspondence that had prompted the governor to commute my sentence. Beneath the surface, he hoped that Green, hearing the evidence, would report to his associates on the dubious nature of the case against me. If the federal judge did not see fit to overturn my conviction, perhaps, at least, the parole board would set me free.

Gary Cartwright was there, too, researching his article on my case for *Texas Monthly*. He planned a lengthy interview with me during the time I was housed at the Lew Sterret Justice Center.

All three of the principal attorneys who had represented me over the years were present, Schaffer as my attorney-of-record, Bruder as volunteer cocounsel, and White, who would testify as a witness to the numerous high jinks conducted by the prosecution. Following my trial, White was so disillusioned that he had never again accepted a criminal case, and now he had given up his law practice altogether. Today, he presides over his own investment company.

Because we were in federal court, we were fighting the state more so than the county. Texas had its own big gun on hand in the person of William C. Zapalac, Assistant Attorney General. Assistant District Attorney Henry J. Voegtle was there to represent the Dallas district attorney's office in its attempt to deny us access to the files it had previously opened to Morris.

"Before we start," said Magistrate John B. Tolle, "let me get something on the record. Mr. Bruder knows this. I've discussed this with him, but I want to get this on the record. At the time this case was tried, I was an assistant district attorney of Dallas County, as I had been for a number of years. I was not assigned to this case. I had nothing to do with the prosecution of this case. In fact, at that time I was not even in the criminal prosecution section. But I want that known. If anybody has any objection, I want you to state it now, if you have any objection to me hearing this matter."

Schaffer replied, "Your Honor, please, from our standpoint, we have no objection as long as the court feels that you have no problem being objective about it."

"I have no problem that I'm aware of," Magistrate Tolle declared.

Schaffer was directed to open his case. He began by requesting that my handcuffs and leg shackles be removed, but Magistrate

Tolle, noting that there was no jury present to be influenced, declared that he would allow the state to do what it thought necessary for security.

So I remained in chains as the attorneys quibbled over Schaffer's motion that the district attorney's office turn over all of its records concerning my case, as well as those of the old long-ago dismissed robbery charge against Ricki Lynn Aguilar, Emily Miller's daughter. The Aguilar records were gone, Voegtle said, destroyed in a flood four years ago. The files on my case were available, but he argued against turning them over, claiming that they were protected under provisions of the Texas Open Records Act as well as attorney-client privilege and, furthermore, they were a work product of the state, to which we were not entitled.

Schaffer countered that all of these points were moot because, he said, "Henry Wade has been cooperating with an independent film producer from New York City, who's making a movie about this case. Henry Wade has been filmed by this producer, and has in fact turned over a copy of the entire district attorney's file in this matter." If Henry Wade was willing to give the materials to a filmmaker, he should also be quite willing to turn them over to a court of law.

Voegtle commented, "I have not been made aware of this." Zapalac said that this was news to him too.

To clarify the situation, Schaffer called Morris to the stand, who testified that Wade had, indeed, "volunteered to give me access to the file." He said that the file was quite voluminous, consisting of several boxes of trial transcripts, exhibits introduced into evidence, attorneys' notes, records of the Dallas police department and background material on witnesses.

Hearing this, Magistrate Tolle ruled in our favor.

Now, David Harris took the stand, but before testimony began, Magistrate Tolle delivered a lecture. He warned Harris, "In Texas, there is no limitation on a prosecution for . . . murder. There is no period of years which runs which will not render you able to be prosecuted, like there is in most cases. So there is still a possibility that anything you say may be used against you." He explained the full scope of Harris's rights to him, and then had him sworn as a witness.

Schaffer took Harris back in his memory to December 20, 1976, when he was being questioned by Vidor Police Officer Sam Kittrell on the subject of the murder of Officer Robert Wood. Schaffer asked, "Did you ask Officer Kittrell during that interview what would happen to you if you didn't do it, yourself, but if you knew who did?"

"Yes, I did," Harris answered.

"Did Officer Kittrell tell you that that would depend on the extent of your cooperation with law enforcement authorities in identifying that person and testifying at trial?"

"Basically, that's what he told me. Words to that effect."

Schaffer asked, "Obviously, you didn't want to be charged with capital murder of a police officer, did you?"

"Correct."

"You did not want to be certified for prosecution as an adult on the . . . armed robbery you had committed after you returned to Vidor? Did you?"

"That's correct."

"You did not want your juvenile probation revoked for the burglary you had already committed, and didn't want to be sent to the youth council for any period of time?"

"That's true," Harris said.

"All right," Schaffer said, getting to the core of the issue. "Did you make a determination in view of those potential problems you had to cooperate with the authorities and to implicate Randall Dale Adams in the shooting of Officer Wood?"

"Yes." Harris said that he spent a total of about three hours with Dallas prosecutors, going over his testimony prior to my trial.

"What, if anything, were you told about the charges pending against you in Orange County in terms of what was going to happen to that?" Schaffer asked.

"The prosecutor that was in charge of the case told me not to worry about that and that it would be taken care of or something to that effect."

Schaffer showed Harris portions of the transcript from my original trial, and took him through a long series of testimony wherein Mulder had asked him to tell Judge Metcalfe whether anyone in Dallas district attorney's office, the Dallas police department or the Orange County district attorney's office had offered any deals or promises in exchange for his testimony. Harris's answer, back then, was "no."

"Now," Schaffer asked, "those . . . questions I've just gone over with you, were your answers at that time true or false?"

"They were false," Harris admitted.

Schaffer asked, "Were your criminal problems in Orange County over with and done as soon as you testified against Mr. Adams?"

"Yes, they were."

On cross-examination, Zapalac asked a question hesitantly, "Mr. Harris, are you saying that you did not testify truthfully at the trial of Mr. Adams?"

After Magistrate Tolle reminded Harris of his rights, the witness answered, "Let me just say, not totally."

When Harris was excused from the witness stand, Magistrate Tolle checked the time. He was nearly ready to call for a lunch break, and he asked, concerning Schaffer's next witness, "You got a real short one?"

Schaffer could not resist. He replied, "I think Officer Turko's about five feet, but . . ."

I joined in the laughter that swept through the room.

"That was not what I had in mind," Tolle interrupted, missing the humor. "I mean like a five-minute witness, I'm talking about." Recapturing his dignity, the magistrate called for a lunch recess.

After lunch, Police Officer Teresa Turko was called to the stand. By now, she was an eleven-year veteran, assigned to the identification division.

Schaffer went over her oral and written statements describing the murder. Her earliest accounts had never been presented for the jury's consideration. He asked, "in any of these documents, did you indicate at all, that the driver of the car had bushy hair?"

"No, it's not in here," Turko admitted.

Schaffer drew out her recollections of a session with a hypnotist brought in from California, about two days following the murder. The episode took place in a motel room, "somewhere off Northwest Highway," she recalled.

"Do you remember who was present at the hypnotic session?" Schaffer asked.

"Two strange men and myself," Turko replied. She agreed that, prior to hypnosis, she did not remember that the suspect had bushy hair.

"Just out of nothing but idle curiosity," Schaffer drawled, "when is it that it dawned on you that the driver of the car . . . had bushy hair?"

"I don't remember."

Schaffer called his next witness, Dale Holt, currently Chief of Police in Ennis, Texas. In November 1976, Holt was an internal affairs investigator for the Dallas police department. He recalled that in the days following the murder of Officer Wood, Turko's account of where she was positioned at the time of the murder was severely questioned by senior investigators and by Chief Byrd himself. Turko claimed that she followed procedures, emerging from the patrol car to take her backup position at the right rear fender of the stopped car. Another witness claimed that she had remained inside the cruiser until after Officer Wood was shot. If that was true, then what little information Turko had been able to supply was even more dubious. Ultimately the police department returned her to duty, suggesting that they believed her account.

Schaffer asked if a tape recording had been made to document Turko's hypnosis session.

"No, sir. I don't know that for a fact," Holt replied.

"We've been through the entire district attorney's file," Schaffer noted, "and there is no tape recording, there is no transcript, there's not even a note reflecting about the hypnotic session. Do you have any idea where we could find such documents?"

Holt admitted, "Sir . . . I tried to get a copy of this investigation and I was unable to do so."

"Was it your assessment of the situation that the superiors in the police department were putting a tremendous amount of pressure on Officer Turko at the time of this investigation to remember details about the driver and the incident?"

"That's correct."

"In many respects, almost treated her like she had been the criminal?"

Holt said, "We were uneasy about, about some of the things that

were being—or how she was being treated, let me put it that
way. . . . I never was comfortable and still not today about the way
she was treated, personally."

"State your name, please," Schaffer requested of his next witness.

"Emily Blocker."

Her last name was different, and her hair was now platinum
blond instead of ebony, but she was the same eyewitness who had
identified me in court on May 2, 1977, as the killer of Officer Wood.
And she was just as cantankerous.

Calling her by her former name, Schaffer asked, "Ms. Miller,
what is your present address?"

"Dallas."

"I understand. Your street address?"

"I don't care to give it."

Schaffer pressed on, reviewing her testimony at my trial. Very
quickly, she repeated the assertion that she had been working for
Fas-Gas that night, even though company records showed that she
had been terminated two weeks earlier, and she repeated her identification of me as the driver of the murder car.

But when Schaffer showed her the written statement that she had
given to the police on December 3, five days after the murder, she
said that she did not remember it.

"Is that your signature on the statement?" Schaffer asked.

"Yeah, that's my signature."

"Is that your handwriting?"

"Yes, it's my handwriting."

"Was your name Emily Elizabeth Miller?"

"It was."

"At the time you were a white female, age thirty-six?"

"Yeah," the witness said, "I don't think I've changed."

Magistrate Tolle intervened and said, "Well, yeah, you got ten
years older like I did."

Schaffer sought to bring things back on track. He asked, "You
do know the difference between white, black, and Mexican, don't
you?"

"Well, yeah, I'd be pretty stupid if I didn't."

My attorney took Mrs. Miller through the statement line by line, until he reached the point where she identified the driver as "either a Mexican or a light-skinned black man." He asked, "That excludes the possibility that the driver of the car was a white man?"

"It was dark," Mrs. Miller replied. "Who knows?"

Turning to a different subject, Schaffer asked, "Now, you were called to the police department the day after Mr. Adams was arrested, to view a lineup, were you not?"

"That's right," she replied.

"You and your husband both went and viewed the lineup. Correct?"

"That's right."

"And isn't it true that in the lineup, you identified someone other than Randall Dale Adams?"

"Yeah . . . I picked a guy out that had an Afro, just like the guy did the night."

"But it wasn't Mr. Adams."

Mrs. Miller rambled on, and none of us could quite believe what we heard next: "Okay. And I turned to the police officer, and I, well, whoever took me in there, I don't remember, but he said—I said, which one is it and he showed me who he was at that time, and I would have picked him out first, but he . . ."

Flabbergasted, Magistrate Tolle interrupted. "Wait a minute. Wait a minute. You asked the officer who it was? Who the guilty person was?"

"Uh-huh," Mrs. Miller replied. "I sure did."

"And the officer told you?"

"The officer, well whoever was in the room told me, yes. After I'd picked one, yes."

Schaffer asked for clarification, "Then so in other words, when you came and testified before the jury at trial, having picked the wrong guy in a lineup, a police officer had told you who the right guy really was?"

"Well, sure," Mrs. Miller said. "But I had seen pictures before then, so that wasn't no big deal."

"And then at the course of the trial you told the jury that he was the one you saw driving the car? Correct?"

"Well, I'd still swear he was the one I seen."

Schaffer commented, "I'm sure you would, Ms. Miller."

Then he moved on to the subject of Mrs. Miller's daughter, Ricki Lynn Aguilar. He asked, "You knew that she . . . had been charged with sticking up a Jack-in-the-Box, somewhere in Dallas?"

"I—yeah, I knew about it," she admitted.

"Can you tell me when you discussed your daughter's robbery charge with Doug Mulder?"

"I didn't."

"Ever?"

"Oh," Mrs. Miller said, "he knew about my daughter . . ."

"How do you know that Doug Mulder knew about your daughter's robbery charges?"

"Because I knew that he knew about it."

"How did you know he knew?"

"Well, that's personal," Mrs. Miller asserted.

"No, it isn't, ma'am," Schaffer snapped. "Not in a court of law."

Magistrate Tolle directed her to answer.

Mrs. Miller replied that she had hired a lawyer for her daughter, John Danish, and that he had spoken to the district attorney's office about the case, but she asserted that there was no deal to dismiss the charges against her daughter in return for her testimony against me.

The lawyer and the witness bantered back and forth for some time, occasionally growing very agitated. On numerous points, particularly concerning her whereabouts on the critical morning of May 2, 1977, Mrs. Miller simply claimed that she could not remember.

Assistant District Attorney Winfield Scott took the stand, and recalled that it was Mulder who brought to his attention the fact that Mrs. Miller's daughter was a defendant in a robbery case under his authority. His memory on dates and details was sketchy, and the files had been lost, so Schaffer called his attention to a *Dallas Times-Herald* story reporting that it was May 9, 1977, less than a week after my conviction, that Mulder came into his office to ask about his plans concerning the Ricki Lynn Aguilar case, and it was the following day when those charges were dismissed. Scott claimed that Mulder "did not in any way tell me that I had to do this." He added, "Mr. Wade always made it clear to us to do what our conscience dictates."

Schaffer asked, "Did you kind of get the secret wink, and hand shake, or something?"

Scott stood his ground. "No," he said. "I'm probably one of the few people in the district attorney's office who has, without reservation, stood up to Mr. Mulder on a number of occasions."

Using the transcript of my trial to refresh Scott's recollections, Schaffer portrayed the curious lapse in Mulder's memory, wherein the prosecutor had simply "forgotten" to provide the defense with Mrs. Miller's written statement to the police. He asked Scott to comment.

"I can only speak for myself," Scott demurred. "I cannot speak for Mr. Mulder whom I understand is in Wisconsin right now trying a murder case or something."

Schaffer noted sarcastically, "Maybe he's in Belleville, Illinois."

Scott was excused. Before the next witness was called, Magistrate Tolle asked Schaffer whether or not he was finished with David Harris. Did bailiffs need to keep him on hand, or could he be sent on his way back to death row? Schaffer replied that he might need to call Harris as a rebuttal witness, in the event that Mulder testified.

Tolle asked, "Are you going to call Mulder as a witness?"

Zapalac interjected, "Mr. Mulder is not going to be testifying. He's not available. He is in Wisconsin in the middle of a trial."

"All right," Tolle commented.

It is not all right! I thought. I've waited ten years for this day in court. The prosecutor in my case had quit the district attorney's office in January 1981 and now was one of Dallas's richest and most successful defense attorneys. I'm cooling my heels in the Ham while, from what I had heard, Mulder flew to Scotland on occasion just to play golf. It was most definitely *not* all right that my chief tormentor was unavailable for these proceedings.

Schaffer declared that he was ready and willing to return to court whenever Mulder became available. Tolle took note of that, and ordered him to finish the day's business.

Thirty-nine-year-old Michael Randell now testified. Schaffer had him read a transcript of his filmed interview with Errol Morris, in which he claimed to have something akin to a photographic memory. During that interview, Randell explained the reason for his perjury at my trial: he had been on his way home from the Plush Pub with a woman named Debbie, and he did not want his wife to find out.

Randell recalled that, before filming the interview, Morris had taken him "over to Boone's and we had a few drinks." But now that he was sober and on the witness stand, Randell's tune changed.

Schaffer asked, "You lied under oath at Randall Adams's trial, didn't you?"

"I don't remember," Randell said.

"You the kind of guy that would lie under oath, Mr. Randell?"

"I don't—that's your own assumption."

"I'm asking you. Are you the kind of guy that would lie under oath?"

"I don't have no reason to lie, sir."

"Then who's Debbie?"

"I don't remember."

"Where's the Plush Pub?"

"It don't exist anymore."

Time after time Randell responded to Schaffer's questions with a shrug and the comment, "I don't remember." Finally, Schaffer asked sarcastically, "You're not claiming to have any brain damage to prevent you from remembering things, are you?"

"I'm supposed to go over to have a checkup tomorrow," Randell said.

"So you might be brain damaged, huh?"

"I might be."

"Who you supposed to see tomorrow for your checkup?"

Randell replied, "I don't remember."

When Schaffer had finished, Magistrate Tolle asked, "May he be excused?"

"Forever, as far as I'm concerned," Schaffer grumbled.

Schaffer called his final witness of the day, Dennis White, and asked, "Since the Randall Adams trial, have you tried any other cases?"

"I've not tried any major cases. I've not tried a felony case since," White said.

"Did this case basically put you out of the criminal business, so to speak?"

"I became so disillusioned with the way that the criminal justice system was handled as a result of this case, I did not have a jury trial in a criminal case after this."

"So it's been almost ten years and you've not gone back for more?"

"That's correct."

"Did you get a lifetime full in this case?"

"I certainly think so," White said sadly.

With the disclaimer that he was not attempting to pick on White, Schaffer took him through a litany of his efforts at the trial, covering the series of frustrating events that prevented him from getting vital testimony before the jury. As the repartee continued, White's face developed an expression of resolve. He knew that the moment had arrived when he could help to bring about true justice in this case. Schaffer, too, was unable to conceal his contempt for the manner in which the state had convicted me.

At one point, Schaffer asked, "Did you feel, as the lawyer present at the time of trial, that Officer Turko was generally a more credible witness than Emily Miller, Robert Miller, and Michael Randell?"

"Very much so," White replied. "She was a police officer and they were flakes."

When Schaffer commented that such a remark might be "unfair to flakes," Magistrate Tolle intervened and told them to get on with the testimony.

"These other people," Schaffer said, "even if you believed everything they say, were on the other side of the highway, and various places down the road and didn't even see the shooting. Correct?"

White spoke with passion: "Every night of my life since this . . . I've tried to observe people in oncoming vehicles as I drive down the street. I haven't been able to successfully observe anybody's face in an oncoming vehicle in the succeeding ten years, and I don't think it's possible."

Turning to the subject of Emily Miller's early statement to the police, Schaffer asked, "All during the trial, during the state's case in chief, as Mr. Mulder would pass every witness for cross-examination, would he also tender to you prior statements of the witness?"

"He did."

"Did he lure you into thinking that if he had a prior statement, you were getting it when you started your cross?"

"I felt he was complying with the motion."

"Did you see . . . how he was sandbagging you?"

White answered, "I do now."

This was a painful ordeal for both attorneys. Schaffer did not wish to portray White as incompetent, but rather as a victim of the machinations of the prosecution. White, for his part, was willing to do whatever he could to achieve simple justice.

Schaffer asked, "Were you surprised by the testimony of the rebuttal witnesses, Emily Miller, Robert Miller, and Michael Randell?"

"Totally," White conceded. "I had no knowledge of their existence."

"You were a trusting soul at the time, I guess."

"Yes."

White explained that his first real ammunition to attack the rebuttal witnesses came when he received a phone call from Elba Jean Carr, a former coworker of the Millers. It was this call that suggested to him that Mrs. Miller may have made a previous statement identifying the killer as a Mexican or light-skinned black man. That was why he had requested, on Monday, to see Mrs. Miller's statement. When he finally read it, he realized immediately that it was powerful evidence to impeach her courtroom testimony. He tried valiantly to get it before the jury, but Judge Metcalfe would not allow it. He tried to recall Mrs. Miller to the stand, but Mulder advised the court that she had left town. "I later saw her on television," White recalled, "being interviewed from the Alamo Plaza Motel."

"Is that when you realized that she had not gone back to Illinois, but was in fact still in Dallas?"

"That's correct." White detailed his actions in the ensuing days: "I filed a motion for a new trial. I filed a grievance against Mr. Mulder. I went to the FBI. I did a lot of things because I realized this had been totally mishandled by Mr. Mulder."

"Didn't do any good, did it?" Schaffer asked.

"Nothing did any good," White admitted.

Schaffer entered a pile of new evidence into the record, including uncut videotapes of Morris's interviews with Robert and Emily

Miller and Michael Randell. Then he had one final issue to discuss.

"If Your Honor please," he began, "I'm a little confused about Mr. Mulder's whereabouts. Mr. Zapalac told me earlier this morning that he had spoken to Mr. Mulder on the phone, that Mr. Mulder was in his office waiting for a phone call to decide whether or not to come over. Then I hear from Mr. Scott he's in Wisconsin. So I'm confused as to whether he's in Dallas, Wisconsin, Belleville, Illinois, or where."

Zapalac explained that there was a miscommunication between himself and Schaffer. "I said I had talked with Mr. Mulder," he detailed. "I had asked him if he would be available in case I needed to call him today. He said he would try to be. I called his office this morning and was informed that he is in trial in Wisconsin. This was a surprise to me."

Magistrate Tolle noted that if Zapalac wished to call Mulder as a witness, he could continue the hearing at a later date. Zapalac agreed, for he had decided that it was important to put Mulder on the stand to defend his actions as the prosecutor of my case.

On the way back to my jail cell, the woman escort officer who had, just this morning, been ready to spit in my face, expressed a change of heart. She had listened carefully to the long day of testimony and left me with a simple, quiet, "Good luck."

On the following day, Morris met with David Harris in the visiting room of the Dallas County jail, to film an interview. Harris was in a pensive mood, and now that he was under a death sentence of his own, he seemed ready to atone for past mistakes.

As luck would have it, Morris's camera equipment broke down during the most crucial part of the interview. Using a backup tape recorder, he captured this conversation:

Morris: "Is Randall Adams an innocent man?"

Harris: "I'm sure he is."

Morris: "How can you be sure?"

Harris: "Because I'm the one that knows."

25

THE PROSECUTOR

I SAW HIM immediately, sitting alone in the jury box.

To reach my seat at the defense table, I had to shuffle directly past him. He glanced up in surprise. His eyes shot briefly toward my cuffed wrists and shackled feet. Then he looked me in the eye and smiled wryly, but he said nothing.

Moving slowly, so as not to alarm my guards, I leaned over until I was about two feet away from his face. "How you doin', Doug?" I asked.

"Oh, pretty good," he drawled. "How're you doin'?"

"Could be better, could be better," I allowed. "I hear you're doin' pretty good."

"Could be better," he echoed.

"Yeah. But it could be a whole lot worse, couldn't it, Doug?"

The grin left his face, and remained absent throughout the remainder of the day.

Magistrate Tolle convened the hearing at 1:30 P.M. on January 9, 1987, and Assistant Attorney General William Zapalac called the former first assistant district attorney to the stand.

This was the man who, shortly after he entered private practice, was quoted by the *Dallas Morning News:* "I like the thought of public service, and I really enjoy doing something that I felt I did better than anybody had ever done before and better than anybody is going to do it again." Now, he had to justify that boast as it pertained to my trial.

Mulder assured the court that he had never made any deal with David Harris in return for the boy's testimony against me. As for Emily Miller, he recalled, "She positively identified him in a photo lineup, I believe." He denied making any deal regarding the charges pending against Mrs. Miller's daughter.

Zapalac's questions were brief. Within minutes, he turned Mulder over for cross-examination.

Schaffer asked Mulder why he was so sure that David Harris told the truth at my trial.

"I was distrustful of David Harris," Mulder conceded, "and that's why I went to the lengths that I did to establish his truthfulness."

Schaffer now confronted Mulder with his statements to Errol Morris, many years after the fact. On film Mulder had said, "I tell you, that kid was a sociopath himself. He later went into the Navy and I don't know what—whatever happened to him. He's probably doing time someplace right now."

Now, Mulder tried to soften his words, pointing out that it may have been his opinion that Harris was a sociopath, but "I'm not a psychiatrist, perhaps not qualified to make that diagnosis."

As he probed, Schaffer pointed out that Mulder's characterization of Harris as a sociopath was made to Morris *before* Harris killed a Beaumont man. It was based, Mulder admitted, on what he knew of Harris's criminal record back in 1976—based on the same criminal record that he fought so hard and successfully to keep away from the jury.

Schaffer asked, "Can you tell us as we sit here now, why it was you didn't want the jury to know about the cases pending against David Harris in Orange County?"

Mulder admitted, "Well, I think it would have impeached his credibility." He further admitted that now that he was a defense lawyer ("one of the brethren," as Schaffer put it), he himself would argue as vigorously as possible to get such evidence before the jury.

Schaffer discussed the requirements of the Brady motion, wherein Judge Metcalfe ordered Mulder to turn over to the defense any evidence that might help my case. He showed Mulder a copy of Emily Miller's December 3, 1976, written statement to the police and asked if he saw anything in it that might have been helpful to the defense.

"I don't," Mulder said.

"All right," Schaffer asked, "What color was Mr. Adams at the time of the trial?"

"He's white."

"In Ms. Miller's statement, what color does she say the driver of the car was?"

"She says that back at that time, he was either a light-skinned black or a Mexican, complexion-wise, and that he had an Afro."

Schaffer asked, "Now, what you're telling this court as you sit here today is that a witness who is looking across a highway at night as she's driving by and catches a glimpse of the driver in another car on the opposite side of the road and tells the police five days later that the driver . . . was either Mexican or a light-skinned black man and then comes to trial and identifies a white man as the driver—you don't think that statement constitutes Brady material?"

Mulder said no, still claiming that Mrs. Miller's statement did not contradict her testimony.

If Mulder had not provided the statement ahead of time, Schaffer asked, why, then, had he not turned it over to the defense immediately following Mrs. Miller's testimony? Mulder admitted that he should have and would have, but, since White had not reminded him by asking for any such statements, it had slipped his mind.

Schaffer asked "You mean to say that the number one prosecutor in the Dallas district attorney's office has such a short memory that you've got a statement setting right in front of you and you can't remember after fifteen years of experience to pick it up and hand it to the defense lawyer?"

Mulder explained, "He forgot to ask for them and I forgot to give them to him. It's as simple as that." He went on to contend that, in any event, the statement was consistent with my appearance at the time, when I had a large, bushy hair style and a suntan from working outdoors. "His hair is quite a bit different from the way it is right now."

"Ten years of prison in death row will do that to you," Schaffer commented. "Won't it?"

"I wouldn't know."

At last, I thought, he told the truth about something.

Schaffer turned to the subject of Emily Miller's whereabouts on Monday, May 2, 1977. Mulder said he was aware that she had moved out of the Adolphus Hotel but unaware that she had checked into the Alamo Plaza. "And we didn't pay her expenses there," he asserted.

Schaffer produced the bill for 135 telephone calls made by the Millers during their stay at the Alamo Plaza, and Mulder admitted that a note on the bill was in his handwriting. Still, he denied that the state had paid those expenses.

Schaffer noted that Emily Miller claimed that she told Mulder that she was at the Alamo Plaza.

"I don't care what she says she told me," Mulder retorted. "She didn't tell me she was in the Alamo Plaza. I assumed she was going up to Belleville."

Schaffer asked why the district attorney's file did not contain any record of Emily Miller viewing a lineup of suspects.

"There weren't any lineup sheets," Mulder replied. "Jackie Johnson took a photo spread to Emily Miller's house on Ewing and she picked Adams out of that photo spread. . . . I don't think they ever saw a live lineup of Adams."

After Schaffer reviewed the trial record with Mulder, the witness remembered that Emily Miller had testified, outside the presence of the jury, that she had, indeed, picked Adams out of a lineup. Then Schaffer asked a hypothetical question: "If she had picked out someone other than Adams in a lineup and a police officer had told her she had gotten the wrong guy and pointed out Adams, would you agree that it would have been improper on the part of the officer?"

"No question," Mulder agreed.

Mulder squirmed a bit as the lengthy cross-examination continued, noting to Magistrate Tolle that he had a 3:30 P.M. appointment to view a videotape of a will.

Schaffer said he had only a little more territory to cover. He wanted to talk about the role that Mulder played in the governor's decision to commute my sentence from death to life imprisonment. He commented, "I noticed from the newspaper clippings at the time, that when the case was first reversed by the Supreme Court, apparently you and Mr. Wade were quoted as vowing a retrial and again seeking the death penalty. Would you generally agree with that?"

"I suspect he was probably quoted on it rather than me," Mulder replied, and I thought I detected a hint of bitterness in his voice. His ex-boss was a master at stealing the limelight, grabbing the headlines.

Schaffer wanted to know why Wade, after promising publicly to retry me, had recommended the commutation to the governor?

Mulder replied that he did not know.

After Mulder was excused, Schaffer had a brief chance to argue the merits of our case. He touched upon each of them briefly, citing strong evidence developed during the two days of hearings. When he reached the final issue, there was sadness in his voice. This was the contention that I had received inadequate representation by counsel.

"When I first got into this case and read this record," Schaffer recalled, "I had one view of Mr. White. After listening to his testimony, quite frankly, I had another view. . . . I think his biggest failure, and it may not even be a legal failure, it's probably a failure of the heart and not the mind, is that he deeply believed in the innocence of his client. He thought everyone else could see it and he trusted his friend. And the things that got him into trouble in this case . . . are really errors made by a decent man who was trying to do a good job, who got run over by a train he never saw coming. . . . If the blame has to fall in this case, it should not fall on his shoulders."

I couldn't have said it better myself.

Now the issue rested with Magistrate Tolle, and we knew that it would take more time to resolve this. Attorneys from both sides would submit written briefs. The magistrate would study them, probably at his leisure, and only then issue his decision.

Mulder headed off to his appointment. Later this afternoon, or perhaps tomorrow, I knew that he would return to his penthouse office.

"Mr. Adams," Magistrate Tolle declared, "can now go back to TDC." He looked at me directly and added, "I know, you may not want to go back, but I got to send you back down there."

26

THE BLUNDER

I WAS TRANSFERRED FROM the Dallas County jail back
to the Diagnostics Unit in Huntsville. The hearings in Dallas had
cost me a semester of college studies, but that was a small price to
pay, for now I was certain that I could finish my degree on the
outside, and soon!

During a reclassification interview with a psychiatrist, the man
informed me that I would be returned to Eastham, the bottom of
the TDC barrel.

"Thank you," I said.

He regarded me as if I was crazy.

"I've lived there for seven years," I explained. "That's where I'm
comfortable. I have a good job, friends who look out for me, and

I get along well with the staff. So why would I want to change that?"

As I contemplated the bus ride back to the Ham, I made several resolutions. I was going to cut way back on my smoking, and I was going to get my body into shape. I had let myself go a bit slack, and when I walked out of TDC as a free and vindicated man, I wanted to present a good appearance.

My new house was R-Line, 2-Row, 12-Cell.

The state filed its reply brief only weeks following the second evidentiary hearing. Mel Bruder offered to write our response, and Schaffer agreed. Since Bruder was now voluntering his time on the case, his work would save my family a great deal of money.

The two men discussed strategy. The new evidence elicited from Emily Miller—that she had picked out the wrong man in the lineup—had to be handled very carefully. Since it was a new point, we had never before had the opportunity to raise it as a basis of appeal in state court. If we tried to capitalize on it now, the federal court might rightly rule that we had to begin again in the state courts. The consequences of such a disaster were clear. Schaffer had first filed our application for a writ of habeas corpus in February 1984 and it had now taken three years to reach the federal courts. Starting the appeals process all over again would keep me in Eastham for at least another three years.

The proper way to handle the lineup fiasco, Schaffer stressed to Bruder, was not to use it as additional new evidence pointing to my innocence, but to wedge it in sideways, simply as more proof that the suppression of Emily Miller's written statement did, indeed, constitute harmful error.

I waited, at first patiently, for Bruder to complete his task, but weeks dragged into months. I wrote to Bruder, but received no response.

Meanwhile, in late April, the May issue of *Texas Monthly* appeared in print, featuring Gary Cartwright's story concerning my case. On balance he treated me fairly, and presented a strong argument for my innocence. It rankled me a bit to read his description of me as "slow-witted" and lacking in charm, but I theorized that he was trying to show my naïveté when I confronted the Texas courts in 1977. I wrote to my sister Nancy, "And who is to say that at that time I was not what he said. It was not a time to be charming and being stupid of the law as I was, you could call me slow-witted because of it."

I came up for parole once more. On April 24, 1987, Schaffer wrote an eloquent appeal to the Texas Board of Pardons and Paroles. In his letter he included a copy of Cartwright's article and he begged the board members to read it carefully. He wrote:

> It should illustrate beyond dispute not only that Mr. Adams is innocent of the offense for which he is presently confined, but also that he was convicted in a trial which was shockingly unfair. I recognize that the Board has no authority to parole an inmate based on the unfairness of his trial. Indeed, that is the reason that we are presently in federal court. On the other hand, the Board should have a moral, if not legal, obligation to parole an inmate who has already served ten years for an offense which he did not commit, especially when the evidence developed in the federal hearing (and summarized in the article) so overwhelmingly demonstrates his innocence.

Schaffer wrote Bruder and tried to reach him by phone, but he, too, could not seem to ferret out any information. In frustration, Schaffer wrote to me on April 20:

> I have worked too hard and too long on your lawsuit to see it jeopardized by the omissions of another lawyer. My attitude at the present is that it would not benefit your lawsuit to have the responsibilities divided among different counsel. I would suggest that you pick a horse and ride it.
> I felt that at the conclusion of the evidentiary hearing, we had an excellent chance of obtaining a new

trial. If we do not, the reason is because the State's brief persuaded the judge and we filed no response, you will have only one person to blame.

Six months passed after the conclusion of our evidentiary hearings before Magistrate Tolle, and still Bruder had not produced his promised response to the state's posthearing brief.

I wrote home:

> Mom, please don't worry about me getting discouraged. Yes, I want this to end and I want to go home. But until that time I must stay here. Until that time we must wait. But that time will come (soon I hope) but it is coming and I can and will hold on until then. I will not let Texas discourage me and I hope you believe that. I hate this place. But I will make the most of my time here. So please do not worry about that. Just try and think of it as if I was away at school. (smile)

Mom and Mary came down to see me late in July and Warden Waldron allowed us a contact visit. For the first time in eleven years we had the opportunity to touch. There was no glass window or wire mesh or bars between us. With tears in her eyes, Mom hugged me with such force that I thought she might strangle me then and there, and thus save the state of Texas a whole lot of trouble.

I decided to ride the Schaffer horse. I wrote to Bruder and informed him that he was off the case, and I instructed Schaffer to prepare the brief that Bruder had promised to submit. Schaffer had begun work on that when he received a copy of a memorandum of law after it had already been submitted to the court. It was filed under the names of both Bruder *and* Schaffer, but it was written solely by Bruder and signed only by him.

Dated July 23, 1987, it argued a number of issues, and the very first point it raised was this:

Emily Miller testified at the evidentiary hearing held in this matter that shortly after Adams' arrest she viewed a line-up conducted by the Dallas police. At the line-up—which included Adams—Emily Miller identified someone other than Adams. Immediately after viewing the line-up and outside of the line-up room, Miller inquired of a police officer if she had selected the right man and was informed that she had not. Miller was told by an officer which of the persons in the line-up was Adams and that he was the primary suspect in the murder of Officer Wood.

Although the Dallas District Attorney's office was in possession of all line-up documentation of all other persons who attended the same line-up referred to above, no documentation concerning Emily Miller's viewing of the line-up was found among the district attorney's records.

Incredibly, Bruder had made the very mistake that Schaffer had warned against! Not only did he raise the new issue in his brief, he highlighted it, opening the door for Magistrate Tolle to throw the case out of federal court. And Bruder *knew* that this was likely to delay a decision—and keep me locked away in Eastham—for several more years!

The state seized the opportunity. On August 12, it filed a motion before Magistrate Tolle to dismiss my appeal, because Bruder's memorandum had raised a new issue that properly belonged before a state court.

Schaffer now had to dissociate Bruder from the case and scramble to stay in federal court. On August 21, he filed his response to the state's motion to dismiss, pointing out that he, not Bruder, was the counsel of record. Bruder's memorandum, Schaffer said, was written without the knowledge or consent of the plaintiff or his attorney. Therefore, he said, ". . . it should be disregarded by the court."

Instead, Schaffer argued, this new information concerning the lineup fiasco was simply additional evidence to show that, if the defense had been apprised of everything the state knew about Emily

Miller, it could have planted severe doubt in the jury's mind concerning the truth of her testimony. It was simply ammunition to show that the trial court's errors were not, indeed, harmless.

Schaffer was angered and frustrated with Bruder, but he was also reaching the limits of his patience with the Texas authorities. His brief showed signs of deep emotion:

> There is a philosophical observation to be made in all of this, even if it does not impact directly on the results 'of this proceeding. Has respondent forgotten the tenets of article 2.01 of the Texas Code of Criminal Procedure, which provides, in pertinent part, "It shall be the primary duty of all prosecuting attorneys . . . not to convict, but to see that justice is done."

Schaffer argued that I was convicted by a system that "laid to waste this fundamental principle of our law." He pointed out that I had now been imprisoned for eleven years, and raged:

> . . . it smacks of something less than bravado for respondent's counsel to suggest seriously that this court dismiss the petition and compel petitioner to return to state court, especially in view of the evidence developed in this court.
>
> Certainly, experienced counsel well knows what this would mean as a practical matter . . . a return to state court would not only be futile, but also a gross waste of time . . .
>
> Petitioner is more than willing to throw down the gauntlet at this time. If justice is to be done, it must be done now.

Schaffer sent me a copy of Bruder's memorandum, the state's motion for dismissal and his own response, plus a personal letter explaining the legal bind that Bruder had put us in. "You had better hope and pray," he wrote, "that the court accepts my position. Otherwise,

you had better get real comfortable in your present surroundings."
He concluded, "Keep your fingers crossed."

My response to Schaffer, written on August 25, revealed that I had finally come to grips with the decision presented to me by the interest that Errol Morris had shown in my case:

> I will begin to broadcast my case as long and loud as I can. With whatever voice I have available. I refuse to stand by and allow the State to do this again without protesting their actions. This will not be done for my sake only. I feel that there are many others that need to know the truth of the things done to me in that trial in Dallas eleven years ago. The Wood family must know that the Dallas D.A. allowed the killer of their son to "make deals" in order for them to get their conviction placed upon me. I think the Dallas Police Department may like to know that their lives are on the line so that a prosecutor can further his "win-loss" record. The families of the young woman and the man that was killed in Beaumont, Texas, by Harris have the right to know that because of those deals Harris was allowed to do to their loved ones what he did. With the right voice I believe that WE can reach these people and will be able to broadcast this story. I will do whatever I must do to reach them.

Over time I developed a friendship with one of the newer guards, George Black, who was intriguingly different from the other employees I had encountered in TDC. If you played straight with him, he actually seemed to regard you as an important human being. My curiosity was piqued.

One day my boss at the maintenance department instructed me to deliver a batch of paperwork to the warden's office. On my way, I encountered Black at a searcher's table. On an impulse, I said, "Mr. Black, can I ask you something?"

"Sure," he replied.

"What are you doing here?"

"Oh, man," he said. He waved a hand in the air, shook his head, and said, "Tryin' to keep track of all you guys."

"No, Mr. Black, I mean, what are you doing *here*?"

He finally caught my drift and explained that things were tough in Texas. He was forced to take this job with TDC in order to feed his family. I felt a sense of empathy. Neither of us wanted to be here.

That feeling deepened in September, when the state granted parole to Tommy Ray Kneeland, even though he was serving two life terms plus 550 years for a vicious string of kidnappings, rapes, and murders. Kneeland moved from his shack outside the walls of Eastham, turned in his keys and his tractor, and went home to his wife. I could see the questions in Black's eye: why did they let Tommy Ray go and why are they keeping Randall here?

Over the course of the next month I was presented with a difficult set of options, arising from Bruder's error. Schaffer explained them to me clearly.

First, I could refuse to let the courts duck the issue of Emily Miller's misidentification at the lineup. If I stood fast on this point, Magistrate Tolle indicated that he would grant the state's motion to dismiss my appeal, and we would be back in the Texas courts, facing at least another three years of legal wrangling.

The second option was to waive the issue for the purposes of this present proceeding. If we won, if Magistrate Tolle granted me a new trial on the basis of everything else that we had presented, the issue would be moot. If we lost in Tolle's court, we could still appeal his decision higher up, to the fifth circuit and then to the U.S. Supreme Court, if necessary, but in neither case would we be allowed to include the lineup evidence in our argument. If we won either of those appeals, fine. If we lost them, we could return to state court and begin again, raising the issue of the lineup snafu. But it would end in Texas; we would have waived our right—forever—to address that new issue in the federal courts.

Schaffer favored the second option, but he demurred to me. It was my life and, quite clearly, my call. Magistrate Tolle said that he would hold off on issuing his decision until I had made mine.

I swallowed my misgivings and, late in October, I sent a letter to Schaffer informing him that I was ready to go with the second option. I instructed him to formally notify Tolle to disregard Bruder's opinion, but as I scrawled my name on the necessary papers in front of the prison notary public, I found myself musing once again on the same issues that had beset me during the original trial:

I was brought up to believe that the U.S. judicial system is concerned with right and wrong, with good and evil, with truth and falsehood . . .

With justice.

But once more the process had devolved into an exercise in judicial nitpicking.

I turned thirty-nine years old in December, and the birthday left me feeling morose. Life seemed to be passing evermore rapidly.

Two other milestones occurred that month. I finished college courses in literature, business law, and math, completing the requirements for my associates degree. In May I would graduate!

But it appeared likely that the commencement ceremony would be right here in TDC, for just in time for another set of holidays, the Board of Pardons and Paroles once again denied my parole.

27

THE FILM

IN MARCH 18, 1988, Errol Morris previewed his new film, *The Thin Blue Line*, in the Aidikoff screening room at the San Francisco Film Festival, where fifteen hundred motion picture industry employees viewed it. The title was taken from Mulder's closing argument during the penalty phase of my trial, in which he declared that the police force is a thin blue line standing between law and anarchy. The 106-minute film attempted to cover the major issues of my case in a quasidocumentary form, jumping back and forth between interviews with the principal, and recreations of events. Morris was clever in his presentation; the film never blatantly proclaimed my innocence or David Harris's guilt; rather, it more or less purposely confused the viewer in the beginning and then inexorably unraveled the web of lies and half-truths, allowing the viewer to draw his or her own conclusions. It was flawed, but compelling; a low-budget, high impact, true-life drama. Morris had scrapped his plans to run it merely as a PBS special; now he sought to have it distributed nationally.

Paul Mowry tried to secure the distribution rights for Orion Pictures, but he was outbid by Miramax Productions. Nevertheless, Mowry was so moved by my plight that he wanted to do something to help. He set up an organization known as "Free Randall Adams," and wrote to me, describing his approach:

> The first stage of our plan is to hold information evenings. We'll invite friends, relatives, work associates, friends of friends, etc., in small-ish groups and then present the evidence and have paper, pens, even stamps and envelopes on hand so that everyone can get a letter or two off right then.
>
> The second and probably most effective step will be alerting major news media . . . We are committed to seeing this through and will not stop our efforts until you are out.

Morris sent me a copy of the first review of the movie, in *Variety*. It declared:

> It doesn't seem to have been Morris' original intent to prove either of the men's guilt or innocence, but the weight of all the evidence provided heavily suggests that justice was not done.
>
> In a shocking final scene, Harris, now on death row for a later murder, as much as confesses to Morris on audiotape that Adams is innocent after all. While such a conversation is inadmissible in court, the film makes such a strong case for Adams that the viewer cannot help feeling a new trial would be in order.

Mom's world was beginning to spin. She flew from Columbus to Dallas and found herself to be a celebrity of sorts. She was in Texas for two reasons.

The first event occurred on April 30, when *The Thin Blue Line* received its first public screening at the USA Film Festival. Mom attended the premiere along with Morris, and then was treated to a fancy dinner.

Schaffer first saw the movie at the Dallas Film Festival in May, and reported to me that Morris did a good job, although he made a few notable errors of fact. For example, he allowed retired Detective Gus Rose to state erroneously that my brother Ray had not testified at the trial. But on balance, Schaffer said, the presentation was fair. And fair was all that I could ask.

Schaffer wrote to me, "If we could have tried your case to the audience in attendance at the film in Dallas, you would have been acquitted on the spot." He planned to obtain a copy of the film and send it to the parole board, and he expressed the hope that I would have the opportunity to view the film soon, "preferably at the theatre of your choice."

Following the premiere, Mom remained in Texas, meeting with Schaffer to discuss the latest issues in the case. They both hoped that the success of the premiere would persuade Magistrate Tolle to rule in our favor, and to do so quickly.

On the evening of Wednesday, May 11, Mom was at the Ellis unit, when I arrived there, via TDC transportation, for a commencement service. That night I graduated from Lee College with an Associate of Arts degree. During the same ceremony, Mike Berry received a Bachelor of Science degree in Psychology from Sam Houston State University.

In a bizarre sense of the word, I was the first member of my family to have the "opportunity" to get a college education. I held the diploma in my hand and thought, here, at last, is something good, something tangible, that has come out of all these years in TDC. They can never take this away from me.

After the ceremonies, a two-hour reception was held in a prison courtyard, with coffee, tea, and cake. For a second time, we were allowed to touch. Mom looked good as she hugged me. The tears in her eyes were very becoming.

28

THE MAGISTRATE

MORE THAN A full year after the second session of our evidentiary hearing, after weighing the written opinions and rebuttals of both sides, Magistrate Tolle rendered his judgment on May 13, 1988, two days after my graduation.

On the question of whether or not David Harris had struck a deal with the prosecution in return for his testimony, the magistrate chose to believe Mulder, rather than Harris, and he chose to disregard the circumstantial evidence showing that, indeed, Harris was never prosecuted for serious felonies in Vidor. He ruled that there had been no deal.

On the question of Emily Miller's first statement to the police, Magistrate Tolle concluded from the evidence that, since she was only one of four witnesses who identified me as the driver of the car, the introduction of the statement before the jury would have made no difference in the ultimate verdict. If this was error, therefore, it was harmless.

Despite the curious timing of the dismissal of robbery charges against Emily Miller's daughter, he chose to believe Assistant District Attorney Winfield Scott's assertion that he was unaware of the relationship between the state's witness in my case and the defendant in the robbery case; he again concluded that there was no deal.

He dodged the question of the legality of the governor's commutation of my sentence from death to life, declaring that this was an issue of state law, inappropriate for his federal courtroom.

Finally, he made it clear that he was unimpressed with the media's attempt to usurp the powers of the court. He wrote:

> At the evidentiary hearing, petitioner presented, as evidence, video tapes of statements made by Emily Miller, R.L. Miller, and Michael Randell in connection with a movie being made by Mr. Errol Mark Morris of New York City. Much could be said about those video tape interviews, but nothing that would have any bearing on the matter before this Court. It is sufficient to note that nothing said by those persons in those unsworn statements would constitute evidence sufficient for a federal habeas court to vacate the conviction in this case. And even though petitioner has waived any claim for relief concerning any alleged event which took place at a line-up as testified to by Emily Blocker (formerly Miller), I believe that such testimony is not credible in any event . . .
>
> I recommend that all relief requested be denied.

This was crushing! How could any reasonable person have considered the weight of all our evidence and then dismissed it so completely?

Three days after the magistrate released his decision Dennis White reported a disturbing possibility to Schaffer. In the one and one-half years since White's testimony at the evidentiary hearing, a memory had gnawed at him, and the specifics had finally surfaced in his mind. He could not be sure that his suspicion was grounded in fact, but he advised Schaffer to check it out.

Schaffer wrote me a cryptic message, declaring that he had "learned a fact of major significance. Rather than reveal it in this letter, I will do so when I file the written objections. You will be shocked when you hear it."

That same day, Schaffer sent an agent to the Federal Records Center in Fort Worth, Texas, to review the dusty court papers pertaining to *Randall Dale Adams v. Douglas Mulder and Henry Wade*, the civil suit filed by White and Edith James one week after my trial, way back on May 11, 1977. The investigator discovered that, two days after that civil suit was filed, a Dallas County assistant district attorney countered with a motion on behalf of Mulder and Wade to dismiss the lawsuit, and he submitted a more comprehensive brief eleven days later. In both documents, he argued that district attorneys were statutorily exempt from any liabilities arising from the performance of their duties. These briefs were upheld by the court and, indeed, the case was thrown out. But we already knew that.

What almost no one knew, and what White vaguely remembered, was the name of the assistant district attorney who prepared those briefs and concluded that my allegations had "no basis in fact." It was none other than John B. Tolle, now a magistrate in U.S. District Court, who had proclaimed at the beginning of our evidentiary hearing, "I was not assigned to this case. I had nothing to do with the prosecution of this case."

Schaffer wasted no time in feeding this information to David Jackson of the *Dallas Morning News*. Jackson reported on the apparent conflict of interest, and his story quoted Magistrate Tolle's explanation that, years ago, he represented the Dallas district attorney's office in nearly all federal civil rights cases, and therefore did not remember his work on the Adams case. "It was such a routine thing, it didn't make an impression on me," he declared.

Miramax Productions began to distribute *The Thin Blue Line* nationally. It played in small "art" theaters around the country to enthusiastic reviews and irate audiences. The *New Yorker* wrote:

> In showing us the lies, the fears, the social pressures, the cultural influences, the unwarranted assumptions, the ulterior motives, the stubborness, and the plain confusion that combined to produce the case against Randall Adams, Morris . . . seems to be investigating not just this squalid murder but the very nature of untruth. It's hard to think of another movie (let alone another documentary) that has such a richly developed sense of the *texture* of falsehood, that picks out so many of the strands that, woven together, blind us.

I was ecstatic that the public was now paying attention to my plight. But the grim reality was that a film could not free me; only my attorney and a Texas court could do that.

Acting on his own, Paul Mowry of Orion Pictures, along with his friend Joey Silverton, put the "Free Randall Adams Campaign" into full gear. As patrons left the theater, volunteers handed out copies of a blue flyer headlined: You Can Help Free Randall Adams. The flyer summarized the important facts brought out in the film and noted, "Randall Adams enters his eleventh year of incarceration while waiting for the justice he has never known." It urged moviegoers to write in protest, and provided them with the addresses of Texas Governor William P. Clements, Jr., State Attorney General Jim Mattox, Dallas District Attorney John Vance (who had replaced the now-retired Henry Wade), and Harry Green, General Counsel of the Texas Board of Pardons and Paroles.

Tens of thousands of letters poured into the offices of these men, and one of the most eloquent was this:

Perhaps you cannot comprehend the agony of my soul. When Randall was on death row, when today, or tomorrow, or tomorrow's tomorrow would be his final day.

My life savings are gone, I am sixty-five years old and money from my pension is still going toward the bringing to light the innocence of my son . . .

My daughters and I have spent our monies and vacation time in visiting Randall these eleven years. At the time the crime took place, Randall was twenty-eight years old, and will be forty years old in December. What youth he had is forever gone.

Yet the encouragement to my heart is that he never became embittered, and in all his letters to me, he has encouraged me and supported me.

He is a son I am most proud of.

On July 10, Martin Yant of my hometown newspaper, the *Columbus Dispatch*, wrote an analysis of my case, based upon his study of the film. It was the first notice that many of my old friends had of my plight.

Yant included an interesting point. He noted that Ohio State University criminologist C. Ronald Huff estimates that six thousand Americans are wrongfully convicted every year. "And one of them," Yant concluded, "might be Randall Adams."

I could no longer walk the halls of Eastham without being recognized. Friends yelled out greetings to me and strangers accosted me, wanting to talk about the injustices of *their* cases. For a man who had spent more than a decade trying to avoid attention here, it was unsettling.

One day about three in the afternoon, I was summoned from the maintenance department for an interview with a reporter from ABC news, who was preparing a story on the furor caused by *The Thin Blue Line*. I went through what was now a familiar routine, signing the required releases, and preparing myself mentally as the camera crew set up its equipment.

An assistant warden approached me, his face set into a scowl. "Adams, what the hell is going on?" he snapped.

"I'm getting ready to talk to these people here," I explained.

"Well, I think I need to tell you, we're getting a little tired of all this attention."

"Well, sir," I said, "I don't know what to tell you, I was under the impression that Warden Waldron didn't have any big argument with these interviews."

"We're getting a little tired of it," the assistant warden repeated, "and if I was you, I would get wise." With that, he stormed out of the room.

A week later I was interviewed by a reporter from *Time*, and on the following day a photographer arrived from Houston to take the shots that would accompany the article. He was ordered to set up shop in the parole room.

The photographer was checking lighting conditions when a captain arrived and instructed my escort officer, "You make sure there are no pictures taken outside this room here. They can take all the pictures they want, but only in this room."

The captain left and another building major arrived to stand watch with my guard. The photographer snapped a few rolls of film in the parole room, but he complained about the lighting conditions, and asked the building major if we could take some shots in the hallway.

"I don't see why not," the major responded.

I was standing adjacent to a hallway window, responding to the photographer's directions, when I heard the captain's voice bellow, "Stop! Stop!" He called for assistance and had me hustled back into the parole room. Then he yelled at the photographer, "You get your ass up front! The assistant warden wants to see you."

I sat in the parole room for about an hour before the photographer returned, shaken. "These people are trying to take my film away from me," he moaned. The assistant warden had threatened to lock him up if he did not relinquish his film. And now, he said, the man wanted to see me.

"I told you last week you were going to get yourself into a world of trouble doing all this media stuff," the assistant warden raged. I told you to take pictures only in that room and then I find you're out by the window . . ."

I tried to explain that the building major had given his permission for the change in location.

The man was not interested in details. He declared simply, "I want that film."

"Warden," I said, "That's his film. If he doesn't want to give it to you, I can't make him. I will ask him very politely to give you the film, but if he won't do it, I can't make him do it."

"I'm going to have that film, Adams."

An escort of guards took me back to the parole room and the waiting photographer. "You're right," I told him, "he does want that film."

"Well, I'm not going to give it to him," the photographer said with resolve.

"That's your prerogative."

"Let me ask you something," the photographer said, "If I tell them to go to hell and leave right now, are you in any trouble?"

"If I am in trouble, whether or not you give him that film makes no difference."

He thought about that a minute and then said he wanted to see the assistant warden once more. Again I was left alone in the parole room for about an hour before he returned with a progress report. He had telephoned his editors in New York and explained the situation. During a conference call among the photographer, the assistant warden, *Time*'s editors, and its legal department, a compromise was reached. If the assistant warden would allow additional photos to be taken in the parole room, *Time* would make every effort to use them. If, however, the hallway pictures were superior, they would use the hallway pictures.

The photographer told me that one editor had added the statement, "We want you to know that we will be in touch with Mr. Adams in the future. If there are any repercussions over this, we will have *you* locked up!"

When the story ran in *Time*, it utilized photos taken in the hallway, where the lighting was better.

. . .

I discussed my case with reporters for CBS News and the *New York Times*. The *Times* reporter, Peter Applebome, said that Doug Mulder had refused to speak with him and that retired Detective Gus Rose had cussed him out and hung up.

Fox Television Network's brand-new show, "The Reporters," picked up on the publicity surrounding the film, and decided to produce its own feature. Fox reporter Steve Dunleavy interviewed me on August 8, and said he was going to try to get an interview with David Harris.

Schaffer labored long and hard on his response to Magistrate Tolle's decision and finally fired off a devastating paperwork barrage. In a brief filed in the magistrate's very own court, he asserted that Tolle:

> . . . not only represented Mr. Mulder in petition-
> er's civil rights lawsuit emanting from his conviction
> and death sentence, but took an aggressive posture
> in contesting the merits of petitioner's allegations.
> Magistrate Tolle asserted, in essence, that petitioner
> had committed the murder . . .

Schaffer argued that Tolle's contention that he had simply forgotten all of this when he declared that he "was not assigned to this case" and would have "no problem" being objective, was irrelevant. It simply meant that the "integrity of his findings, conclusions, and recommendation is destroyed by his prior representation of Mr. Mulder."

Schaffer dissected how this prior, hidden involvement may have affected the magistrate's consideration of our appeal. He was required to make numerous determinations as to the credibility of various witnesses, and he invariably decided those issues in Mulder's favor.

For example, Harris declared at the evidentiary hearing that he understood that his criminal problems would be "taken care of" if he testified against me. Mulder later denied this, and Tolle chose to believe his old crony, rather than a death row inmate. Nonetheless, Schaffer argued:

> . . . the proof is in the pudding. Even though Harris is a two-time ex-convict and is presently on Death Row, his testimony on this point undoubtedly has the ring of truth. He confessed to these first degree felonies committed while he was on probation, yet the charges were dismissed and his probation was never revoked after he testified against petitioner. There is no other legitimate conclusion that can be reached by reasonable minds other than that Harris had the understanding with the State to which he testified.

In another instance, Schaffer said, Tolle accepted Mulder's testimony that he simply forgot to give the defense Emily Miller's statement in a timely fashion. Schaffer complained:

> It is strange indeed that this "brilliant" prosecutor who "always got his man," and was trusted to prosecute the most heinous of offenses—the murder of a police officer—would have such an exceptional memory lapse in the midst of perhaps his most publicized trial. And, it is even more regrettable that his memory lapse related to a written statement in which his key rebuttal witness just happened to describe a person of a race different than petitioner. Of course, we now know that magistrate had already personally decided in 1977 that Mr. Mulder's version of the events was credible.
>
> The magistrate totally missed the boat in his purported harm analysis . . . The issue is not simply whether Miller saw Harris or petitioner driving the car. It is possible that she did not see anyone. At the time she came forward with her "information," the reward for information leading to the arrest and conviction of the suspect had surpassed $20,000.00. Had

the jury learned that Miller had described the driver as a light-skinned black man or a Mexican, the jury could reasonably have concluded that she did not even get a good look at the driver . . .

What Schaffer found most disconcerting in Tolle's behavior on this point, was that he obviously placed his seal of approval on Mulder's actions. At the evidentiary hearing, Mulder "explained away" the discrepancy between Mrs. Miller's written statement and her court testimony, contending that it would not have made any difference to the jury and was, therefore, harmless error. Tolle agreed, whereas, Schaffer wrote angrily, the defendant "had the right to have the jury make that determination."

Tolle had chosen to excuse the prosecution's failure to reveal the hypnosis attempt upon Police Officer Teresa Turko. Schaffer quoted a news story in the December 15, 1976, *Dallas Times-Herald*, which stated, "Turko . . . underwent hypnosis in an attempt to recall further details of the shooting. . . ." Then he argued, "Although defense counsel apparently never read this article, it is highly doubtful that it also avoided the attention of the district attorney's office."

Schaffer's appeal grew eloquent as he addressed the issue of Mulder withholding the information that Emily Miller's daughter had been charged with robbery, and that this may have influenced her to testify against me:

Surely it must have some impact on this court to observe that after petitioner was sentenced to death, the aggravated robbery and burglary charges pending against David Harris were dismissed and his juvenile probation was not revoked, while simultaneously, the robbery charge against Emily Miller's daughter was dismissed. Petitioner's jury was not even aware that these charges existed. These post-trial dismissals constitute either one of life's great coincidences or demonstrate circumstantially that there were "understandings" between the District Attorney's office and Miller and Harris regarding the disposition of these pending charges. Although the evidence is circumstantial, as Thoreau once observed, sometimes circumstantial evidence can be quite strong, "like a trout in the milk."

Clearly, it was for the jury to determine whether Emily Miller was biased in favor of the State as a result of the robbery charge pending against her daughter in the same court. This court should seriously question how Miller's pretrial description in her written statement of the driver being black or Mexican, coupled with her identification of someone other than petitioner in a police line-up, at trial was magically transformed into a positive identification of petitioner as the driver combined with false testimony that she also identified him in the line-up. It has often been said that justice is blind, but there is no excuse for it also being deaf and dumb.

My battling attorney was not yet through. He wanted to know why Tolle was so willing to refute his contention that I had not received adequate counsel during my trial. Why had Dennis White not kept a file of newspaper clippings, and thus been made aware that Officer Turko had been subjected to hypnosis? Why had he lamely accepted as a *fait accompli* Mulder's contention that the three surprise rebuttal witnesses had left town? At the very least, he should have filed a motion for continuance, so that we could get them back. "Of course," Schaffer pointed out with sarcasm, "since the Millers were really at the Alamo Plaza Motel in Dallas, their attendance in court could have been secured in a matter of minutes." And why had White not objected to Detective Johnson's testimony that I had told him I arrived back at my motel about 1:00 A.M. that night? Clearly it was an inadmissible oral statement.

Magistrate Tolle withered in the face of Schaffer's fusillade. On August 17, he withdrew his findings and disqualified himself from the case. U.S. District Judge Joe Fish indicated that he planned to reassign the case to a new magistrate in Fort Worth. Tolle's failure to disqualify himself from the case eighteen months earlier meant that we would have to start our federal writ application from scratch.

But an important event had occurred in Dallas recently, prompting Schaffer to suggest that we forget about the feds and return to Dallas Criminal Court Number Two to begin a new habeas corpus proceeding, wherein we could use with full force all of the new evidence we had developed, including our knowledge of Emily Miller's mistake in picking out the wrong suspect during the lineup.

The new development was this: Judge Donald Metcalfe was no longer on the bench. Schaffer advised me by letter:

> I understand that his replacement, Larry Baraka, is fair and impartial . . . I believe that he will provide us a full and fair hearing on the new allegations. In addition, I believe that we can get through the state system fairly quickly. If we succeed, you receive a new trial. If we fail, you are still back in federal court within about six months, in no worse a position than you are at present.

Schaffer's plan was to approach D.A. John Vance with the accumulation of our evidence and ask him to actually join us in seeking a pardon. If Vance declined this opportunity to right a wrong committed by his predecessor, Schaffer would then file a new writ application with Judge Baraka.

29

THE HEAT

I WAS CALLED TO the warden's office on August 16.
Warden Waldron waved a letter in front of me and demanded impatiently, "Adams, I want to know what the hell is going on."

I studied the letter. It was a request for an interview by a film crew from the "Geraldo" show. "Well sir," I answered finally, "the next time you have about three hours, I'll try to run it all down for you."

His gaze was direct. "The coffee pot is right there," he said, pointing. "Help yourself. Pull up a chair. If you've got cigarettes, light 'em up."

For the next several hours, someone within the Texas criminal justice system finally gave me a hearing, approaching the subject with as few preconceptions as possible. The warden, by the necessities of his job, was oriented toward assuming the guilt of the men he held in his grip. But he was not blind to reason.

When I finished the account of my interrogation, my trial, and subsequent developments, Warden Waldron sat quietly for many minutes. I studied his expression, looking for signs.

Finally he said, "Regarding all these interviews, Adams, I'm going to allow you to do them. With whomever. Whatever you need to do, you go ahead and do it. Just don't break any rules."

"Thank you, sir," I replied, "I really appreciate it."

I wondered if I should attempt to shake his hand, and I could see the same question in his eyes. Then he said, with a suddenly stern timbre in his voice but a hint of sarcasm, "Get your ass outta here, boy."

I received a letter from a woman named Faith Quintano of Dallas, Texas. She explained that she and her boyfriend had gone to see *The Thin Blue Line*, and that it had convinced her of my innocence. She wanted me to know that she had signed a petition asking the governor to set me free. It was similar to thousands of other letters that I received, except for the fact that her boyfriend was none other than Robert L. Miller, ex-husband of Emily Miller.

I wrote to my family on August 21:

> Things are beginning to happen. People are start-
> ing to ask questions. Dallas is beginning to see the
> light. I ask that you not worry overmuch for me . . .
> this is something that has to happen. We have no
> more control over it—not that it would change even
> if we did. This must be done because of your faith,
> your trust, your *love*. It must also be done in the
> memory of Officer Wood. I hope and pray that the
> Wood family is a strong one. Mom, please have
> everyone pray for them at this time and to remember
> them alongside the prayers being said for us. Both

families need them at this time. They must be strong. As we must.

By now, David Harris realized that his earlier talks with Morris and a few other reporters had landed him in hot water, and he refused further interviews, including the request from Steve Dunleavy of Fox Television.

Tom Horan, a production assistant at Fox, wrote Harris a carefully worded letter, urging him to speak. The truth could only help, he argued, so why not tell it?

Harris accepted the reasoning, and acquiesced to the interview. Dunleavy and a taping crew made their way to the Ellis unit and spoke with Harris for several hours.

The tapes of those interviews were handed over to Lisa Raby, senior videotape editor for "The Reporters." It was her job to sift through the rambling conversation and piece together a coherent story. Murders, rapes, and atrocities of all kinds were frequent visitors to Lisa's cutting room floor—after all, they were the stuff of news—and she sometimes wondered if she had grown jaded. But when she came upon a five-minute segment of the Harris interview, she was both horrified and amazed.

Then she set to work on the tapes of Dunleavy's interview with me, and she found it inconceivable that I could commit so violent an act as murder. "If Hitchcock were alive, he'd love this story!" she exclaimed to a coworker. "It's the wrong man theme come to life." She decided: "I'm going to write Randall Adams a letter."

On September 1, Schaffer sent Dallas District Attorney John Vance a copy of the new application for a writ of habeas corpus that he was prepared to file in Criminal Court Number Two, and offered him the chance to demonstrate that he was ready to make a clean break with Henry Wade's old regime. He wrote beautiful, impassioned words:

> The reason for this letter is to request that you personally review the allegations contained in this application, and if persuaded that any of them have

merit, that you join me in seeking a pardon for Mr. Adams . . .

Although we have never met, I am familiar with your reputation as a trial and appellate judge. I have heard that you do not countenance unfairness in any form and that you called the legal issues as you saw them, without favor to either litigant. If you review these materials and conclude in good conscience that Mr. Adams' trial was fair and that your office can defend Mr. Mulder's conduct, I will respect that decision and proceed to file the application. On the other hand, if you believe, as I do, that it would be inappropriate for your office to defend a conviction obtained in this manner by a former administration, I hope that you will join me in requesting a pardon. After 12 years, Mr. Adams should be freed from an unjust conviction and this litigation should end . . .

In the long run, your decision may speak volumes regarding your administration's position on the type of conduct and tactics which are permissible in the prosecution of a criminal case in Dallas County.

As we waited for word from Vance, I finally had the opportunity to see *The Thin Blue Line*. George Black brought a VCR into the maintenance department, along with a tape of the film. It was difficult to watch myself in the picture, along with the other people whose lives had been entwined with mine for a dozen years, but it was good to see the truth come out. I wrote to Morris and to the people at Miramax, thanking them for their hard work.

I also saw myself on "Geraldo." Mom was there in the studio; I thought she looked nervous, but very beautiful. It was amazing to me the paths that lives can take. We were rather average people from Columbus, Ohio; now we were plastered all over the media.

In mid-September, shortly after "The Reporters" ran its story concerning my case, I received a letter from the show's videotape editor. She said:

My name is Lisa Raby, and I work for Fox Television in New York City. . . . I had the privilege of working with Steve Dunleavy on your story. . . . I am the person whose job it was to put all the pictures and sound together, and for an entire week, I lived with images and feelings that were rare for my professional experience.

What I wish to tell you, Mr. Adams, is that . . . your story and your life touched me deeply, and you are still in my thoughts often. . . . I understand that you might be able to use the David Harris interview with Steve Dunleavy as part of your grounds for a new trial. . . .

What I admire about *you* is your *lack* of anger and lack of bitterness over what has been thrust upon you. What I admire and respect about you is your integrity in the face of such ugliness, your ability to remain human in what I suppose is a rather inhuman situation. I'm happy for you, Mr. Adams, that you've not let twelve years of unfairness and blatant wrong turn you into a man full of anger and revenge. Instead you've emerged a man of conscience, a man who cares, a man who knows and lives by the truth, and a man who, as you stated to Steve, is willing to wait another twelve years for the truth to come out, not only for you but for Robert Wood's family and friends. . . . To state it simply, I am on your side and a lifelong fan. . . . I would like to say now that if there is anything that I or anyone else at Fox can do to help you, please just ask, and we'll certainly do all we can. I'm not the only one who's rooting for you.

Yours is a story I shall never forget, Mr. Adams. I don't ever want to. You taught me something about what a person can be, despite the fact that just about everything and everyone is conspiring against him.

Please keep up the good work, and don't *ever, ever* let them get you down. . . .

The letter was remarkable. I reread it many times and thought about how to respond.

I did not want to do anything that would jeopardize my friendship with George Black; I did not want to ask him to do something that could cost him his job. But this was important. If I utilized the regular prison-mail channels, two or three weeks might pass before I could get my hands on those tapes.

At work, I showed Black Lisa's letter. He was as impressed as I, and he, too, saw the need for speed. He copied her phone number and promised to call her that evening with my message: "Yes, please send the tapes, and tell her that a letter from me is on the way."

He reported to me the following day that he had contacted Lisa and that she would expedite shipment of the tapes.

Lisa and I began a quiet correspondence.

Vance considered Schaffer's eloquent plea and rejected it, stating publicly that he believed I was as guilty as Oswald.

Wasting no time, Schaffer filed the application for a writ of habeas corpus.

Lisa Raby asked Fox Television's legal department for clearance, but even before it was granted (and at the risk of losing her job), she copied the David Harris interview and expressed tapes to Schaffer and Black.

The evening that the tape arrived at his home, Black and his wife watched it in amazement, and the very next day he brought it out to Eastham, along with his VCR. He sat me down at my desk in the maintenance department, and we watched it together.

Perhaps Harris was in a pensive mood. Perhaps he realized that he had little left to lose. Perhaps he was dazzled by the notoriety he had so suddenly achieved. Perhaps he was simply tired of the whole affair. Whatever the reason, he spoke more candidly during that interview than ever before—or since.

At the reporter's urging, Harris discussed the night of November 27, 1976. "We went to the movies," he said, "but we left around let's say eleven, somewhere around there. Anyhow, we was going to see if I could stay at their apartment or whatever this kitchenette they were staying at. Randall Adams went in . . . said he was going to ask his brother if it was all right if I stayed there and he never came back out. I stayed out there about five minutes and it was a real cold night that night. It got cold fast, so I started the car. . . . Figured he wasn't coming back out . . . I left and that was probably before twelve midnight."

Dunleavy asked, "Officer Wood was shot around?"

"Twelve-fifteen, twelve-twenty, I don't know," Harris said. He added, "So that tells you there that Adams wasn't in the car."

"Well, Randall Adams has been on death row for shooting Officer Wood. Should he have been there?"

"No, he shouldn't."

"An innocent man went onto death row?"

"That's right."

"How did that happen?"

"The system," Harris replied. "The system doesn't so much care about justice as they do about convictions, you know, vengeance, retribution, whatever they can get, and at that time that's all they wanted because, you know, I started telling my story, because in this manner, you know, he was the one, and you know, they're believing it, you know. I'm kind of a kid, you know, I don't know what I'm doing, you know."

Dunleavy asked about Michael Randell and the Millers: "So, those witnesses were either mistaken or they're lying?"

"That's correct."

"You want your conscience clear?"

"Well, I want to do the right thing."

"You want Randall Adams free?"

"Right."

"And he had nothing to do with the shooting of the police officer?"

"That's right," Harris said. "Nothing whatsoever."

But if Adams did not kill Officer Wood, Dunleavy asked, then who did?

Harris answered, "I can't say . . . You can draw your conclusions. I mean, all the inferences are there, you know, but I'm not going to sit here and tell you that I did it."

"Why is that?"

"Why should I? I don't think there's a statute of limitations on murder."

Dunleavy persisted: "I'm drawing an inference right now that you shot the police officer."

"Uh-uh."

"Incorrect inference?"

"I can't say if it's incorrect."

"If you know Randall Adams isn't guilty, I mean you know that for sure?"

"No doubt about it."

"No doubt about it. There's only two people in 1976 who were aware that a death or injury was about to happen. That was a police officer and David Harris. Is that correct?"

"That's right."

"And then a gun went off. You were the only person who knows for sure who shot the officer?"

"I'm the only one. Anybody who says that they saw—they were driving down the street and saw that guy from thirty yards away at night going thirty-five, forty miles an hour, please, no way. We got common sense, let's use it."

"How did the shooting go down?"

"Just happened."

"Just happened? You had your lights off?"

"Just the parking lights on, I believe, and that's the reason the car was pulled over."

"What was going through your mind at the time? Fear?"

"Fear."

"Panic?"

Harris nodded.

"You were in that car?"

"I was in the car."

"Officer Wood was to your side?"

"He approached the car, yeah."

"And then within thirty seconds he was dead?"

"I suppose, yes."

Dunleavy asked, "Wouldn't you like to do just one incredibly noble thing in your life, one, and make sure Randall Adams could live, and live like a human being for the rest of his life?"

"Well, to be honest with you, I don't think they would let him go, regardless of what I say, because they are going to say it's a recanted testimony, they had other witnesses, and they had this and they had that. They won't even give the man a new trial even though they know he deserves it. What makes you think they're going to let him go?"

Dunleavy's answer was "this thing called television, enormously powerful, seen by millions . . . if you said on television right now, what I know to be the truth and you know to be the truth and the authorities know to be the truth, you would go to your maker a much more peaceful man, and you would release Randall Adams [from] this terrible nightmare . . ."

Harris responded, "I've sat here and told you the man is innocent, what more do you want?"

Dunleavy waited for more, but Harris remained silent. Finally the interviewer declared, "Someone shot Officer Wood."

"No doubt about it. It didn't happen by itself."

"And you know who shot Officer Wood?"

After a five-second pause, Harris said, "Yes."

"You are the only one who knows?"

"That's right."

Did you shoot Officer Wood?"

Harris was silent for a full ten seconds, but he maintained eye contact. Finally he said, "I was the only one in the car."

"Did you have a gun in your hands?"

"Sure I did."

"Did that gun go off?"

"Five times."

"Was your finger on the trigger?"

"Yes it was."

"Did you see Officer Wood fall down?"

"Yes, I did."

Dunleavy pressed for the full, final admission. He said: "You shot Officer Wood!" It was a statement of fact, not a question.

On the screen, Harris's and Dunleavy's eyes locked. An interminable ten silent seconds followed before Harris abruptly averted his gaze. He glanced around, suddenly seeming to remember that a camera was on him, that a microphone was recording every word.

He straightened his shoulders and took a deep heavy breath, but he said nothing.

Say it! the camera pleaded.

"Whewwww!" Harris expelled his breath and shook his head slowly from side to side.

Twenty additional seconds—a very long time on television—passed in silence. Harris kept his head down, his eyes averted.

As the head of the writ section of the Dallas district attorney's office, Leslie McFarlane's responsibility was to evaluate the merits of all writs relayed to her by the head of the appellate section. At first, she regarded our new application for a writ of habeas corpus with a detached professional demeanor. She saw no new issues in the application, and felt that Judge Baraka would dismiss it in short order.

But her interest was piqued and she began to wade through the mountains of paperwork generated by the original trial, the federal writ of habeas corpus, and, most particularly, the evidentiary hearing conducted by Magistrate Tolle. The more she read, the more she found herself disturbed. She came to the conclusion that, whether or not this Randall Dale Adams fellow was guilty of the crime, it seemed clear that he had not received a fair trial. She determined that she had to do something about this case, and she decided to go directly to the man who would decide the issue.

Tall, dapper, thirty-nine-year-old Larry W. Baraka was the first black—and undoubtedly the first Muslim—ever elected as a district judge in Dallas County. Although he was relatively new on the bench, he was known as a man who refused to kowtow to the Dallas "good ol' boys" legal establishment. In Arabic, his surname means "blessed."

"This may well cost me my job," McFarlane announced as she began a private conference with Judge Baraka. Only once before had she recommended a full-blown evidentiary hearing on a writ application, but she did so now. Baraka listened carefully to the details and agreed. The hearing was set for November 30, 1988.

McFarlane made a clear decision: she would *not* view *The Thin*

Blue Line prior to the hearing. She wanted the chance to evaluate the witnesses from a fresh perspective.

On September 29, Ann Harris of Beaumont, Texas, wrote a letter to Schaffer, noting that it was "very hard" for her to do. She detailed that when her son David began talking to reporters, she and her husband responded with "total disbelief," and she wrote to her son, requesting an explanation. She was shocked at his reply, and sent it along to Schaffer because she knew that she "had to help" me.

Having read this, Schaffer turned his attention to the enclosed copy of a letter from David Harris, which began with the salutation: "Dear Mom." Harris admitted that he had not done "the right thing" when he should have. Now, he said, clearing me was something he had to do, because I was innocent. This, he told his mother, "is the truth."

As a sixteen year old, he said, he did not comprehend the wrong he had done to me. But now, he said, he could not bear the guilt.

Schaffer immediately sent copies of the letters to me, to Leslie McFarlane of the Dallas district attorney's office, to Texas Assistant Attorney General William Zapalac, and to Harry Green of the Texas Board of Pardons and Paroles. He also sent Green an uncut version of Dunleavy's interview with Harris. Later, he found out that Harris's mother had also sent the incriminating letter to the parole board.

Schaffer forwarded to me a copy of a letter from Bennett L. Gershman, Professor of Law at Pace University in White Plains, New York. The letter offered Schaffer some legal ammunition on the subjects of hypnosis-enhanced testimony and prosecutorial misconduct, and suggested that Texas was a "wretched place" for a criminal defense attorney to practice law.

The Sunday *Dallas Times-Herald*, on October 23, ran a comprehensive story about my case, written by staff reporter David Pasztor. He had researched the case thoroughly, studying the voluminous court records, and interviewing the principals.

Mulder defended his conduct to the newspaper. He agreed that

Harris was "a no-good SOB and I knew that going in." But, he said, "I took what I had and did the best I could with it." On the point of whether or not he should have turned over to the defense the investigator's report stating that the drive-in theater closed at 11:30 P.M. that night, he said that he believed the report was incorrect and he did not feel that the movie times were an important factor in the trial.

When the newspaper asked Dennis White for his opinion of Mulder's actions, White responded, "Totally reprehensible. He should not be a member of the Bar."

White told the reporter why he had given up the practice of law:

> If you're trying to be ethical, and you feel that the people you're up against are not ethical, then you can't give your clients a fair shake. You have to be unethical to deal in an unethical system. I couldn't in good conscience continue in a system like that.

I was quoted in the article, too, and I directed my comments to the former assistant district attorney of Dallas County:

> Doug Mulder is a very dangerous man. Maybe he can convince himself that he was doing it for the public good. But that isn't saying much for me, for my mother, for Teresa Turko and, most important, for Robert Wood and his family . . .
> I don't hate Harris . . . he was a sixteen-year-old kid that was scared. Doug Mulder gave him the keys to the city and let him run loose.

As an appellate attorney, the courtroom was not Leslie McFarlane's milieu. In previous cases her boss, District Attorney John Vance, had always assigned a more experienced trial lawyer to take over the courtroom duties. But as the hearing date approached, McFarlane was left in charge, and no help was offered. A sense of isolation began to hover over her, as though she was being hung out to dry.

"This is some weird shit going down," John Cruezot said to her on the phone a few days prior to the hearing. He was a friend and fellow assistant district attorney, assigned to work directly out of Judge Baraka's office. "You need some help going into that courtroom," he declared. He volunteered to assist.

On October 28, Schaffer journeyed to the Ellis unit to meet with Harris. The death row inmate was agitated because his mother had sent Schaffer a copy of his letter, which he had intended to be confidential, and now said he had severed ties with his mother.

Nevertheless, Harris promised Schaffer that at my upcoming evidentiary hearing before Judge Baraka, he would testify that I was innocent and was not in the car at the time of the shooting. That was as far as he would go, he said, because he would not incriminate himself and thereby jeopardize his prospects in the event that his own death sentence was overturned. He indicated that he would exercise his Fifth Amendment right against self-incrimination if asked questions relating to the circumstances surrounding the actual shooting.

Schaffer felt that he could probably get Harris to acknowledge, under oath, that he told the truth during the Dunleavy interview. "All things considered," he wrote to me on October 31, "I believe that his testimony will benefit your cause. Of course, you never know what a death row inmate will say when he actually takes the stand."

As he scrambled to prepare for the hearing, Schaffer found himself increasingly agitated by the actions of the publicity agents for *The Thin Blue Line*. They phoned him for frequent updates, which he was reluctant to provide, lest he alert the Dallas district attorney's office to the details of his case. When he declined to provide specific information to the film publicists, Morris himself called and pumped for news.

What new facts Morris did obtain seemed to find their way to Dallas reporters and one of them, in particular, appeared to be a conduit to Mulder.

The final blow, as far as Schaffer was concerned, came when several Dallas attorneys called him to report that Morris had contacted them to see if they were willing to take over my case. To

Schaffer, it was obvious that Morris, having directed the movie, now wanted to direct the court proceedings.

Schaffer also reported some secondhand information to me. According to *Dallas Times-Herald* reporter David Pasztor, Assistant District Attorney Leslie McFarlane was "having sleepless nights" about my case.

"I am turning the heat on," Schaffer concluded. "We will smoke the truth out of them yet."

30

THE CHAIN BUS

SURROUNDED BY GUARDS, I was ushered onto the chain bus, at the Eastham unit, for the first leg of the convoluted trip back to Dallas for my hearing before Judge Baraka. With a few other inmates who had their own business in court, I climbed aboard. Guards placed us into seats one by one and secured our handcuffs to the central chain that ran the length of the vehicle.

The driver ground the ancient bus into gear and set off on the Texas country roads. We stopped at the Coffield unit, where additional prisoners boarded and were linked to the chain. We stopped at the Ferguson unit, where we took on a few hapless teenage inmates, whose appearance drew appreciative leers from some of the passengers.

Again we headed off, down a dusty lane. Someone wailed, "I gotta take a piss," and the rest of us groaned.

"Shut up," a guard said. "He's gotta take a piss, he's gotta take a piss."

We all rose and moved toward the rear of the bus, stretching the chain so that it would reach to the bathroom, and we stood in the aisle until the man was finished with his business. It was a long ride to Dallas, and we knew that we would find ourselves standing more often than sitting.

Eventually the chain bus pulled up at the back slab of the Ellis unit. There, a man wearing prison-issue civvies was placed aboard. He was a death row inmate and, therefore, subject to special security procedures. Securely trussed in leg shackles and handcuffs lashed to a belt loop, he did not have to be clipped to the central chain. He sat by himself in a front seat, under the direct scrutiny of the guard.

Finally we hit the open road. The chain bus picked up speed, and the inmates settled into their own private worlds. Several of them nodded off. A few babbled gibberish. A few more conversed quietly. I kept my eyes on the man in the front seat.

Several times we had to rise and assemble in the aisle as someone relieved himself. Whenever we sat back down, my gaze reverted to the death row prisoner.

After a time, he said to the guard, "Boss, gotta take a piss."

"Mmmph," the guard replied.

The man assumed that this was permission, and he rose, shuffling along in the slow mincing pace dictated by leg shackles.

As he neared my seat our eyes met. He stopped cold.

"How you doin,' David?" I asked softly.

He whispered, "Hey, man, you know I can't do this. I can't go in there man, and take the stand and say, what the hell . . ."

"David," I interrupted, "it don't make a damn bit of difference. You do whatever it is you have to do. You already took thirteen years from me. I'm gonna prove what I can in that courtroom tomorrow. You just do whatever you need to do."

31

THE LISTENER

MOM WAS THERE, bless her heart. She would not have missed this for the world.

Even as the governor was receiving petitions bearing the signatures of about one and a half million Americans, asking him to free me, Judge Baraka convened court on Wednesday, November 30, 1988. Baraka ruled his courtroom in a somewhat informal individualistic style, and before the proceedings began, he warned the lawyers to keep their questions relevant, because if he grew bored, he had difficulty paying attention.

Schaffer began slowly, taking his first witness, David Harris, through the sequence of events surrounding the murder of Officer Wood. Then he asked, "Was your motive in implicating Randall

Adams and testifying against him to get yourself out of the criminal charges pending against you in Vidor?"

"Yes," Harris said, "for that reason and to save myself, you know, from being charged also."

"With capital murder?"

"Right."

Schaffer asked Harris to explain to Judge Baraka how he came to understand that the pending charges in Vidor would be dropped in return for his testimony.

Harris detailed, "The district attorney, Mr. Mulder, stated to me at one or two points in our meetings . . . the questions he was going to ask and whatever he anticipated that the defense was going to ask. And he told me at one of those meetings or discussions not to worry about the charges pending against me, that they would be taken care of—something to that effect, you know . . . you scratch my back, I'll scratch yours."

The possibility of a deal was, of course, something that the defense would inquire about on cross-examination, and Schaffer asked if Mulder had coached Harris on how to answer such questions.

Harris replied, "He told me if I was asked, which he was pretty sure that I would be, whether or not there was any kind of agreement or anything of that nature, to answer 'no,' which I did."

"And was that testimony false?"

"That's correct."

Schaffer then filled the record with evidence showing that, no matter how hotly Mulder protested that there was no deal, all charges against Harris concerning his spate of felonies were dropped. "Did Mulder keep his word to you?" he asked.

"Yes, he did," Harris answered.

One by one, Schaffer had Harris recount the crimes he had committed in subsequent years: burglary, armed robbery, kidnapping, and ultimately murder. For the record, he elicited the fact that Harris was currently on death row, awaiting execution for the murder of Mark Walter Mays. Then he changed subjects abruptly, asking, "Mr. Harris, I want to ask you, did Randall Adams kill Robert Wood?"

"No, he did not," Harris finally said in open court, under oath.

"Randall Adams knew nothing about this offense. He was not even in the car at the time that it occurred."

When Schaffer asked what really happened that night, Harris said that he could not go into the subject. Schaffer then introduced into evidence a tape of the interview that Harris had given to Steve Dunleavy of Fox Television. He had a television set and a VCR brought into the courtroom, and played the dramatic videotape.

Afterward, the courtroom was hushed and Schaffer paused to heighten the drama. Finally he asked, "Mr. Harris, do you stand by the statements that you made in the videotape interview with Mr. Dunleavy?"

"Yes," Harris said simply.

"Mr. Harris," Schaffer said, "I think it is a fair question to ask you why at this point in time you are changing your testimony from what you said at trial regarding Randall Adams having committed the offense."

"Well, twelve years ago, I was a kid, you know, and I'm not a kid anymore, and you know, I realize that I've been responsible for a great injustice. And I felt like it's my responsibility to step forward, to be a man, to admit my part in it. And that's why I'm trying to correct an injustice."

Judge Baraka wanted to be clear. "Maybe I'm missing something, Mr. Harris," he said. "From all I've heard from the video, sounds like you said you did it. Let me hear you tell me. You're in the car by yourself . . . when the officer drove up?"

"Yes, sir."

"The gun is in your right hand, correct?"

"Yes, sir."

"And it goes off."

"Yes, sir."

"And you say five times?"

"Yes, sir."

"Again, Mr. Dale Adams is not there present?"

"Correct."

"And you're the only person in the car?"

"Yes, sir."

Baraka exclaimed, "Man, what is he saying? He's saying he did it."

"He's not coming out and saying it," McFarlane commented.

"He says he's the only one in the car. What conclusion can I come to?" Baraka asked. "So he is in effect telling me he did it. That's how the court would find the facts to reach a conclusion."

Schaffer called a series of witnesses who, by now, were familiar to all of us, with the notable exception of Judge Baraka. His face expressed intense interest as he learned that Police Officer Teresa Turko's initial statements indicated that there was only one person in the car, that the windows were too dirty for her to provide much of a description, and that she had never mentioned that the suspect had bushy hair until she testified in court, after she had been hyp- notized.

When he realized that the jury had never learned of Emily Miller's statement describing the killer as a black or Mexican, Judge Baraka exclaimed, "This was suppressed?" He showed further surprise when he heard the story of the lineup fiasco.

As in the earlier evidentiary hearing before Magistrate Tolle, Schaffer found that pulling information out of Emily Miller Blocker was like extracting impacted wisdom teeth. When he raised the subject of her daughter, Ricki Lynn Aguilar, Mrs. Miller snapped, "She's not on trial."

Judge Baraka lectured, "Ma'am, listen. Help me out. You're here under oath to testify, you will respond to any questions asked of you. I don't want to get nasty here today. I will lock you up if you don't. Now, if you don't mind going to jail, I don't mind sending you. I'll be glad to do it. Do you understand what I'm saying to you?"

"Yes," Mrs. Miller said.

Schaffer drew from her the fact that her daughter's robbery charge was dropped five days after I received the death sentence. Then he moved on to the subject of *The Thin Blue Line* and her comments as recorded on film.

Mrs. Miller moaned, "Everybody has tried to make an ass out of me, and I'm just tired of the whole thing."

Judge Baraka said, "I understand."

Schaffer gave the witness an out, a chance to withdraw from the story that she told a dozen years earlier. He said, "Don't you believe, Mrs. Blocker, in all fairness that in your identification of the driver of that car under circumstances where you view his face for less than two seconds across three lanes of traffic in the dead of night could be mistaken? In all fairness, could you have made a mistake?"

"Not on the hair part and stuff, no," she replied. "I seen it, if I seen it. I seen it if they had a gun to my head, I'd say I seen it. You know, I don't blame you for trying to get the man off, but if I seen it, I seen it."

"You don't think you're capable of making that mistake in identifying somebody else?"

"Not with this bushy hair and what I seen, no."

Schaffer requested, "Then just tell me one final thing. If you can't make a mistake on identification, how did you pick the wrong man out of a lineup?"

McFarlane objected that Schaffer was putting words into the witness's mouth, and Judge Baraka sustained. Mrs. Miller did not have to answer.

Schaffer called Assistant District Attorney Winfield Scott to the stand, to elicit testimony concerning the dismissal of charges against Emily Miller's daughter. The examination turned into a discussion of various procedures and witnesses at the trial. At one point Scott said, "I know I was convinced that your client was guilty as sin as soon as Teresa Turko finished testifying."

I tried not to show a reaction to this, but the realization struck me with force: after all that's come down during a dozen years, after Harris has confessed to the killing, after Emily Miller's testimony has been repeatedly destroyed, some of these people *still* think I'm guilty! Then, I wondered, what do they intend to do about it?

That question was answered at the very end of Scott's testimony, when he declared, "I stand ready to prosecute him again."

Dennis White was a subdued witness. In response to a series of questions by Schaffer, he admitted, "In retrospect, my trusting Mr. Mulder to abide by the Brady motion and provide various statements . . . was foolish. But at the time, I thought he was going to abide by the rulings of the court."

Schaffer asked, "You deeply believed in your client's innocence during the trial, did you not?"

"Yes, I did," White said. "I still do."

Regarding key pieces of evidence that Mulder failed to turn over to the defense in a timely fashion, Schaffer asked White if he thought they would have affected my case.

"I think he would have definitely been acquitted," White asserted.

Here in Criminal District Court Number Two, White now had an opportunity to view a piece of paper that he should have seen a dozen years earlier. It was investigator Jeff Shaw's report on the movie screening times at the drive-in, documenting that the theater closed well before midnight. Schaffer asked, "Do you feel that in cross-examining the movie managers in such a way as to suggest that there was a later showing, that Mr. Mulder was trying to portray to the jury an impression of the facts that was . . . belied by the document he had?"

"That's true," White said.

"Do you think a nice guy like Doug Mulder would do something like that?"

White replied softly, "I can't answer a question like that."

At another point in his testimony, White did have a chance to speak to that issue. Schaffer asked, "Don't you think it's a terrible mistake for a lawyer in a trial of a lawsuit to trust his opposing counsel?"

"Well, apparently it was," White admitted. "And if that's the way you try cases, that's why I'm not trying cases. I would like to think that if I'm going to be a defense attorney and obey the law that the state . . . would also obey the law rather than try to kill an innocent man."

Outside the courtroom, ex-First Assistant District Attorney Douglas Mulder quipped to the press that he had not seen *The Thin Blue Line*, but he was disappointed that Morris did not sign Robert Redford to play his part.

On direct examination by McFarlane, Mulder stuck to his guns, repeating his old tired story. Finally, he launched a tirade, much as he had done at the very beginning of my trial: "We had both Adams and Harris examined by the psychiatrist. Dr. James Grigson examined both of them and reported back to us that Adams was a primary sociopath and that he felt Harris was being truthful when he accused Adams of being the triggerman. . . . Of course, there were the polygraphs . . ."

"Excuse me," Schaffer said. "Judge, this is just a rambling sermon."

"I don't know what the point is," Judge Baraka agreed. "The polygraph isn't worth anything."

Schaffer began his cross-examination with a wry comment: "Well, I guess today you've returned to the scene of one of your greatest triumphs, haven't you, Mr. Mulder?" He turned, pointed at me, and shouted at Mulder, "You see Mr. Adams over here, the man who's in shackles like a wild animal? . . . If you had your way, he'd be dead today, wouldn't he?"

Mulder maintained his cool. He replied, "I think that was the appropriate sentence in this case, yes, sir."

Schaffer worked Mulder over on the subject of Emily Miller's pretrial statement, and why he had not turned it over to White in a timely fashion. One of Mulder's reasons was that the statement was not helpful to the defense. "I think it's clear from the statement that she gave that she was not describing David Harris," he said.

"I think it's clear she's not describing Randall Adams," Schaffer retorted. "But that's a jury question, isn't it? It's up to the jury to decide who she was describing, isn't it?"

"It's certainly not up to you or me," Mulder conceded. Still, he argued, there were no discrepancies between Mrs. Miller's statement and her trial testimony.

Schaffer showed him Defense Exhibit 34, and gave him time to study it. It was a graphic comparison of the testimony given by Emily Miller at my original trial, contrasted with what she told police in her earlier written statement, the one the jury was never allowed to see:

TRIAL TESTIMONY (4-29-77)	WRITTEN STATEMENT (12-3-76)
Told Robert to slow down so I could see who was in the car stopped by the police	No mention
I recognized Officer Wood because he had taken my daughter home before	No mention. Refers only to "one officer" walking up to the car
Identifies Adams, a white man, as the driver	Driver was "either a Mexican or a very light-skinned black man"
Identifies Adams, who had a large moustache	No mention of moustache
Heard a noise and told Robert, "Well, that policeman probably got shot."	"We passed the cars and I did not know about the shooting until the next day."
Returned to scene later and saw police and ambulance	No mention of returning
Identifies Adams as driver	No mention she could identify driver

Mulder studied this and pronounced, "I don't think there's a conflict."

Again Schaffer resorted to silence, allowing the discrepancy between Mulder's words and the document to speak for itself.

· · ·

"May it please the court," he said, "I guess I can tell you initially that after twelve years, it has been a pleasure to finally get a full and fair hearing in this case. . . . That's all we ever asked is for somebody who really cares to listen." He tackled, one by one, the thirteen points we raised in the application.

The first was our formal request for the judge to rule on my guilt or innocence. In a sense this was a moot point, for in a habeas corpus hearing, as he pointed out, "Innocence is not a basis for . . . relief."

Here was another one of those procedural quirks in the justice system. Under the rules of law, a judge or appellate court could overturn my conviction on a matter of procedural irregularities, but not on the basis of right or wrong. It seemed to me to be the definitive statement that a courtroom is not a search for truth but is, instead, a simple game played out by the members of the club, who often seem to lose sight of the consequences of their deeds.

Despite this, Schaffer detailed why a ruling of innocence would help us out. First, it would strengthen our case to have the Texas Board of Pardon and Paroles lobby the governor to issue a full pardon. In addition, it would counter the state's continuing contention that, if there was error in my trial, it was harmless.

Many long years ago, the court of criminal appeals ruled that Mulder should have supplied us with Emily Miller's previous written statement, but discounted the error because White had failed to ask for it in a timely fashion. Schaffer pointed out that Mulder was under a standing court order to provide those statements, whether or not they were requested. He moaned, "Dennis White is a trusting soul. . . . He trusted Doug Mulder to follow court orders. Have we come so far that the defense can't trust the prosecution to play fair, and must continually be there saying, 'obey court orders, obey court orders'?"

Regarding the fiasco of Mrs. Miller and the lineup, Schaffer said, "I don't see any way around that for the state. She lied, and her lie precluded Dennis White from getting to the truth about the lineup."

Schaffer was incensed that the original jury was kept in the dark concerning any possible deals the witnesses may have made with the prosecution. "Maybe I came from another place and another time," he said facetiously, "but doesn't it seem a little bit strange all the good stuff that happened to the witnesses in this case after this man was sentenced to death? I mean, really now. Multiple first degree felony charges against David Harris going away, a robbery charge against . . . Emily Miller's daughter. . . . And do you believe in your heart of hearts that Emily Miller knew she was helping the state hang a man in a capital murder; and that she wasn't going to say a word to Doug Mulder about her daughter's case at this time?"

Finally, Schaffer addressed a subject upon which, he admitted, he had mixed emotions: his contention that I had been inadequately represented by counsel. "I hate to see relief be granted at the expense of Mr. White," he said, "when the truth of it is it ought to be granted at the expense of Mr. Mulder, because this case is really a prosecutorial misconduct case." But Schaffer noted that he was forced to raise this issue because of past rulings by appellate courts, which said that some of our issues could not be addressed because White had not lodged the proper objections at the proper times. Schaffer only partially agreed with this. But if that is how the state wanted to play it, he said, then it added to the contention that my lawyer had done an insufficient job. "He lost his objectivity because of his belief in his client's innocence," Schaffer conjectured. "He stopped functioning as a lawyer . . . because he felt the jury would see through everything."

Schaffer said, "Let me give you a couple of closing observations . . ." and I leaned forward in anticipation. As I sat there for my day in court, I heard words fashioned of brilliance, garnished with passion, and I knew that finally—a dozen years late—I had the right attorney.

"You know, what this is really all about," Schaffer told Judge Baraka, "is the district attorney's not wanting to take responsibility for a bad prosecution from a former administration of people who are no longer here. And I don't blame these folks. I know it wasn't their decision. But they should have done the right thing at some point, and they should have come forward and said . . . this isn't the way to prosecute people in Dallas County. This isn't fair. I wonder, do we lose our humanity in representing our clients to the point where we can stand up and tell the court he wasn't harmed; it was okay; we had the right man so what if we didn't give him the evidence . . . it's okay; the jury convicted him; the Court of Criminal Appeals confirmed it. What the heck."

Instead of doing the right thing, Schaffer said, the present administration of the district attorney's office decided to hand the ball back to Criminal District Court Number Two, forcing Judge Baraka to make a decision that would then be affirmed or overruled by the court of criminal appeals. "When you boil all this other stuff away," Schaffer said, "what this is all about is your courage and your character, and your sense of justice and your conscience. They don't have to have one." He added that nobody who has "seen all the evidence in the last three days could ever believe that this man had the fair trial that the law entitled him to. Nobody could ever believe it in their heart of hearts. And they just want somebody to blame when he's given a new trial. They don't want to take the responsibility; they don't want to put it on Doug Mulder; they want to try to blame somebody else. So they'll try to blame it on Errol Morris who, if he hadn't gone out to make a movie and had Henry Wade give him the file, we never would have known any of this. How about that? Wouldn't have known any of it. This man could have been executed, and we never would have known about a single one of these documents suppressed. They'll give their file to a moviemaker, because they think they're going to be in the movie and be famous, but they wouldn't give it to a defense lawyer so a man can have a fair trial."

Schaffer spelled out the choices to the judge. "You can tell the Dallas district attorney's office there are no rules; do whatever you want to do, and if you get away with it . . . no court is going to step in and do anything about it; and you can tell the rest of the country, that's the way we do it down here in Texas, that's the way we do it in Dallas. . . . Or you can have the courage that I know you have and you can say uh-uh, we don't try people like this; we don't convict them like this; and if we do, at some point even if it's twelve years later, we stand up and say we made a mistake, and we're going to do it again and give him a fair shot. And that's all we're asking—one fair trial before a jury. I don't really think that's too much to ask after twelve years. There is no decision that any man of conscience and integrity could make after hearing all of this evidence other than Randall Adams is entitled to a new trial on at least ten of the issues raised in this writ. I tell you the evidence permits it, the law requires it, and by God, *justice demands it!*"

If ever there was a task that called for the application of pure legal skills, Assistant District Attorney Leslie McFarlane now faced it. It was her job to argue against our application and something in her voice, something in her posture, something in her eyes, told me that her heart was not up to the task. Nevertheless, she attempted to cover the necessary points. She addressed the curious fact that the issue of innocence had nothing to do with this habeas corpus hearing. She said to Judge Baraka, "Mr. Harris sat up here and you've heard him, you've talked to him. Whatever his story is it is simply not relevant in this proceeding. I'd also—I'd like to point out the fact that he did not recant his story in federal court when he had the opportunity; he waited until he could get some reporters interested; it wasn't until this past summer when the TV cameras, the newspaper reporters, were there that he started telling this story."

As she debated the points of the case, she declared that, even if Michael Randell and the Millers had shaded the truth concerning a few details, "none of these rebuttal witnesses have ever recanted their eyewitness of the defendant. These people have lived with this for twelve years now. And if they had been lying for twelve years, they are doing a darn good job of it."

I agreed with that.

She rallied to the defense of Dennis White, declaring, "He did a very good job for Mr. Adams at his trial in 1977. I don't believe any of these deficiencies that Mr. Schaffer is trying to prove at this point have been proven, nor has he proven they have affected the outcome of the trial. The jury found Mr. Adams guilty . . . in spite of Mr. White's hard work and good job that he did."

We all expected that Judge Baraka would require both sides to submit written arguments and then weigh his decision for an indefinite period of time. But he was ready immediately!

He began with a disclaimer: "First of all, let me just advise everybody in here that we've been going through this for twelve years, and whatever decision I make I don't want a lot of problems—screaming, jumping up, yelling, or whatever the circumstances, crying, booing. If you're upset, go in the hallway."

He continued, "I resent the allegations that in the state of Texas and particularly Dallas, justice does not exist. It definitely does exist. . . . Systems are not the problem; it's the people. It's the people that are placed in those systems that make the difference. . . . I'll submit to you in this instance even with Mr. Adams, whether he was rightly or wrongly incarcerated, he's getting his process today, even if it takes ten or twelve years. There are some societies that not only he wouldn't be here this very day to talk about it—in summary, he would have been executed."

The judge directly addressed my mother: "And probably, Ma'am, being his mother, you may not have even known that he was charged and executed and even denied he existed."

He continued, "So when you start looking at our system, I think you ought to feel very blessed that you're in a society such as this with all the frailties of the problems that we have in the justice system. And I say this not only as a judge, but even as a black man who's recognized in many instances, our justice system has done damage to my people."

Following this preamble, he turned to the business at hand, declaring, "Making a decision here today is not hard for me, not even a little bit." He decreed that I was entitled to a new trial, based on prosecutorial suppression of evidence, perjury, and denial of the right to confront David Harris with his pending criminal charges.

Judge Baraka knew that his was not the last word. His determination that I was entitled to a new trial was merely a recommendation to the Court of Criminal Appeals, and he wanted to leave no doubt in the minds of the appellate judges what he had concluded after listening to three days of testimony. His final words were incredible, and oh so sweet:

"I would go so far as to say that if the defendant were to be retried considering all the testimony elicited and what would be presented to the jury or a court that more likely than not, the defendant would be found not guilty."

Schaffer immediately requested that the judge free me on bond, pending disposition of the matter, either as the result of a favorable ruling by the Court of Criminal Appeals, or perhaps by a pardon from the governor.

McFarlane, still doing her job, pointed out, "With all due respect to the court, your findings are simply recommendations to the Court of Criminal Appeals. They are the ones that will decide. They still have a valid conviction against this man."

Judge Baraka agreed that he did not have authority to release me on bond, although he would recommend such.

As court adjourned, McFarlane, despite her formal opposition to my case, stepped over to congratulate Mom and found herself engulfed in a bear hug. The assistant district attorney had two sons of her own—and another child on the way—and felt both empathy and respect for the mother who had stood steadfastly by her son throughout this ordeal. She asked Mom if she would be allowed to visit me again before she had to return to Columbus to await the decision by the court of criminal appeals.

No, Mom said sadly, she had already used up her allowable visiting time.

"I'll see what I can do," McFarlane said.

She left the courtroom and made her way over to the sheriff's department, where she asked to speak to whomever was in charge of visitation. As she explained the situation and asked that Mom be allowed extra visiting time, she thought: this is another move that may well cost me my job.

The press had a chance to fire a few questions at me, and some reporters tried to bait me into saying nasty things about Mulder. I was reluctant to do so, realizing that the record by itself was strong enough to condemn the former prosecutor. When asked what I wanted to say to my family, I told them, "I love you."

One reporter asked if this hearing was any different than all the others I had been through over the years. "This gives us hope," I replied. "It's not an end, but maybe it's a beginning."

That night I was back in the Dallas County jail.

32

THE TEA PARTY

SCHAFFER WROTE TO Dallas District Attorney John Vance:

There is still a reasonable solution which will prevent your administration from sporting the black eye that was so richly deserved by the former administration. I reiterate my previous request that you join with the trial judge in requesting through the Board of Pardons and Paroles that Governor Clements pardon Mr. Adams. This will moot the legal issues and make it unnecessary for the Court of Criminal Appeals or a federal court to write an opinion which, I predict, will serve as a noose around the neck of the

Dallas County District Attorney's Office for many years. More important, it would also be the right and just thing to do . . .

I ask that you speak with Leslie McFarlane and John Cruezot to obtain a more complete picture of what was developed at the evidentiary hearing. It truly had to be seen to be believed.

Leslie McFarlane finally allowed herself to view *The Thin Blue Line*, and it determined her resolve. A week after the conclusion of the evidentiary hearing, she and John Cruezot met John Vance. They explained that they were not passing judgment on my guilt or innocence, but declared that there was no question in their minds that I had not received a fair trial. To help assure that I would finally receive my proper day in court, they proposed that the district attorney's office file a response to the writ application, stating that it agreed with Baraka's findings—or at least did not disagree.

Vance at first opposed the idea, but the debate was heated. The district attorney finally agreed when McFarlane and Cruezot agreed to focus their attention on the issue of Emily Miller's testimony.

McFarlane set to work writing the response that would be submitted in Vance's name, as well as her own.

My hometown newspapers in Columbus wrote editorials favorable to my case, and these spurred members of my 1967 senior class at Grove City High School to organize a letter-writing campaign, urging the Dallas district attorney's office to drop the charges against me.

I wrote home, "I love you, Mother. I *will* be home soon!"

Near the end of January, McFarlane was ready to file her response with the Court of Criminal Appeals in Austin. It declared: "The state has no objection to the trial court's finding . . . that applicant is entitled to a new trial." She asked a secretary to type it, but not to show it to anybody else.

McFarlane signed the response personally and dropped it in the mail.

When the press learned that the Dallas district attorney's office had "joined" with the judge's recommendation, Vance summoned McFarlane to his office. He seemed to have forgotten that he had previously authorized the response, and he demanded to know how they could undo the damage. Even as they spoke, the *Dallas Times-Herald* hit the streets with an editorial commending Vance for his statesmanlike action in the interests of justice. The irony was unbelievable to McFarlane. Here was Vance, reaping praise for an action that he really opposed. Now he wanted to withdraw or amend the response.

McFarlane stood her ground, declaring that if any sort of amendment or clarification was filed, she would not be a party to it. Finally Vance relented.

As she left her boss's office, McFarlane knew that her time with the district attorney's office was limited. In one sense, that was all right. She was due for maternity leave soon, anyway, and she had no desire to continue her association with this office. But she desperately wanted to stay on until my case was cleared. If Vance fired her, he might hand over the Adams file to some law-and-order diehard who would do his best to lose me once more in the limbo of the legal machinery.

McFarlane could feel increasing hostility from those around her. Vance forbade her to talk to the press. Until now, she had enjoyed a good working relationship with her colleague Winfield Scott. Now he, too, looked daggers at her.

The wait was agonizing, but back at Eastham, I was very busy. I worked long into the night, every night, trying to answer the mailbags full of letters I received. I wanted to thank every one of these thousands of total strangers who were kind enough to write to me—some of them even sent checks to help with a legal defense fund, and I forwarded these to Mom—but it was a nearly impossible job.

Finally, I fashioned a form letter, and George Black ran off thousands of copies for me. It was a generalized thank you note and a brief update on the progress of my case. I pointed out that Judge Baraka's ruling was only a recommendation to the appellate court in Austin. "Their decision could take months or even years before it is handed down," I wrote. "Without the public support the state of Texas can and will sweep the name of Randall Dale Adams and this case under the rug." I asked each person to write to the "Free Randall Adams Campaign," c/o Paul Mowry in New York. I tried to add a brief personal comment to each of the letters.

The cost of postage ate up what little money I had in my account in the prison bank. Black brought me boxes full of envelopes and stamps.

Thanks to Schaffer's urgings, the Texas Board of Pardons and Paroles granted me a special parole review.

For the past few years, Schaffer had sent the board copies of all pertinent court documents, newspaper and magazine stories, and media tapes. Now he armed them with the latest batch of evidence declaring my innocence: a letter from Judge Baraka, recommending my release, and the official response of the district attorney's office to that ruling.

As we waited to hear the board's decision Mom wrote me, wondering if she should come back to Texas to be with me when I was released. This was a tough decision, for the first thing I would want to do is hug her. But although I was now certain that release was coming, I had no idea when it would actually occur. Furthermore, I did not want to subject her to a media circus. We could not snub the press, for it had played a major role in obtaining my freedom. We owed reporters a chance at interviews, and I felt it would be better to get it all over with in Dallas, and then move quietly off to a new life. Schaffer and Morris would be there, and they were both veterans in dealing with reporters. It would be better, I advised Mom, for me to meet her back home in Columbus. "Then the homecoming in Ohio," I wrote, "can be for us."

Schaffer wrote to me on February 23, "I hope to see you on the ground soon. I will even buy you a beer."

The following day, the board again denied me parole.

I was able to get a call out to Mom, to break the news. And I followed this up with a letter:

> If nothing else comes from this setback, it has
> forced us to readjust our sights. We knew from the

start that there was but one goal that we could accept and that was the truth in a Texas court . . . No other way will do.

Three days after the decision, Schaffer wrote to me, "Someone somewhere does not like you. If the Court of Criminal Appeals rules against us, I'm calling the FBI."

Then he penned an acid-toned letter to the Board of Pardons and Paroles:

> I could not help but notice that in September 1987, the Parole Board granted parole to Tommy Ray Kneeland, a confessed serial killer who had served less than 13 years of two life sentences and a 550 year sentence. Kneeland was separately convicted of kidnapping and murdering a housewife, a 17 year old girl and a 15 year old boy. He raped the women and cut the throats of both teenagers. Thereafter, he kidnapped and attempted to rape another female. It is inconceivable that the Board could parole Kneeland and deny parole to Randall Adams, who has served over 12 years of a life sentence for a murder that he did not commit.
>
> The conclusion that Kneeland was rehabilitated but Mr. Adams was not cannot be justified by logic or reason. You did a grave disservice to Mr. Adams and disgraced yourselves.
>
> Be assured that I will not let this rest quietly.

It was about 9:30 A.M. on March 1, 1989. I was at my desk in the maintenance department when another inmate burst through the door, yelling, "Turn on the news, turn on the news! They just overturned your case!"

Right, I thought. Five days ago, they denied me parole. Now they're going to set me free?

Within minutes, two or three other inmates brought me the same news, but I did not begin to believe it until Mr. Black scurried in and verified that the Court of Criminal Appeals had upheld Judge Baraka's ruling. The vote was unanimous, nine to zero!

Suddenly I felt an incredible, unaccountable need to be alone. I rushed outside and walked briskly around the building two or three times. Out back, alone at Eastham, I screamed, "My God, can this really be happening?!"

What do I do now? I asked myself.

And I answered, Randall, the media is on its way out here, right now. You'd better get ready.

My supervisor let me go back to my house. I jumped into a shower, shaved, and put on a fresh set of clothes.

It was not long before a boss yelled, "Hey Adams, you got a phone call."

It was Warden Waldron. "Get your ass up here," he said, "I want to talk to you a minute."

When I arrived at the warden's trailer, his message was succinct: "The newspapers and TV reporters are on their way here from Dallas. They'll be here at three o'clock. You be ready."

"I am ready, sir," I replied.

He stared into my eyes and I tried to read his expression, but I could not tell if he was happy for me, or upset that his prison was to be invaded once more. Perhaps it was both.

That afternoon, Warden Waldron turned his office over to me for a full three hours of interviews. When the last film crew left at about 6:00 P.M., he came back in and announced, "Look, we got your measurements and we got some brand new clothes being pressed for you right now. I will have one of the officers wake you up at four-thirty in the morning."

"Four-thirty? Why?"

"Because we're going to have two satellite dishes out here. You're gonna be on 'Good Morning America,' and the 'Today Show.' "

At 4:30 A.M. I was back in the warden's office. In the corner, a table was set with donuts and cookies and a fresh-brewed pot of good strong coffee. I felt giddy, like a guest at Alice's tea party. Things were getting curiouser and curiouser.

When I had finished with the early morning interviews, I stepped out of the office to find Warden Waldron sitting quietly in a corner.

His legs were propped against the wall of the trailer. Again I could not read the expression in his eyes.

He asked, in a weary voice, "Adams, are we through now?"

"Yes," I said. "Yes, we're through."

He jumped up from his chair and danced a little Texas two-step.

As soon as possible, Schaffer got me a copy of the Court of Criminal Appeal's twenty-seven-page written opinion, prepared by Justice M.P. "Rusty" Duncan III. It supported Baraka's conclusions, and reserved its most scathing denunciations for the prosecutor, Doug Mulder. I wondered how the former first assistant district attorney reacted when he read these words about himself:

> Trial courts must be able to rely upon the veracity of its officers. When deceit produces court rulings that have the effect of denying one a fair trial then the conviction should be vacated . . . It is the fundamental, constitutional purpose of this Court to insure that a convicted defendant received a fair trial. Any system of government that incorporates within its guarantees ordered liberty necessarily recognizes and appreciates the necessity of providing a process to litigate and resolve allegations of criminal conduct. In order to comply with the dictates of the Fourteenth Amendment of the Constitution, the ultimate aim of the process must be fundamental fairness. To be sure, it is not necessarily the character of the prosecutor that dictates the fairness of a trial. Rather, it is the character of the evidence that we must be concerned with. However, in the area of suppression of exculpatory evidence and the knowing use of perjured testimony a prosecutor's discretion will be necessarily involved in our analysis. In the present case, the trial court found the State was guilty of suppressing evidence favorable to the accused, deceiving

the trial court during applicant's trial, and knowingly
using perjured testimony . . .

Accordingly, applicant's conviction is set aside and
he is ordered released to the custody of the Sheriff
of Dallas County to answer the indictment in Cause
No. F-77-1286.

This was Texas, not television, and I was to spend another two
weeks in the Ham before the court's ruling became final.

District Attorney John Vance made some public noises about re-
trying me. Schaffer said he did not believe there was enough evidence to do so; he noted that, of the five witnesses whose testimony
originally convicted me, one had admitted that she was hypnotized
prior to her testimony, three had been shown to have committed
perjury, and one had virtually confessed to the murder. But, he
added, "I can't think of anything in the practice of law I would
rather do more than defend Randall Adams in a national forum. It
would be like the seventh game of the World Series, with someone
setting the ball on a batting tee with bases loaded and letting you
take the final cut."

The State Bar of Texas launched an investigation that could lead
to censure or even disbarment for Doug Mulder. He set off on a
private quest to win vindication from the court of criminal appeals.

During the fifteen-day waiting period, the losing party may file a
motion for rehearing. This is often done if the vote was close but
no one bothers to battle a unanimous decision. It is difficult enough
to get one judge to change his mind, let alone the necessary five,
but Mulder tried. Sometime during the week of March 13, he reportedly went to Austin and attempted to file affidavits with the
court. These were sworn by Emily Miller and former Detective Gus
Rose, and Mulder contended that the new documents would "change
things." It was an unusual and perhaps frantic move on his part,
but he apparently spoke with at least one of the appellate judges
and was told that the opinion could be reversed if Judge Baraka
would amend his recommendation.

Mulder then approached Baraka.

"I just told him that I couldn't consider it," Baraka later told the
Dallas Times-Herald, "that after hearing the facts, my opinion stood,

that I really wished I could do something for him, but I couldn't. . . . I told him, as he well knows, quite a few people we prosecute probably aren't guilty."

On the fourteenth and final day of the waiting period, McFarlane learned that Mulder had come to Vance with a magnanimous offer: he had a plane standing by so that a motion for a rehearing could be rushed to Austin.

McFarlane opined that such an obvious, last-ditch effort could only damage the image of the district attorney's office. This argument made sense to Vance, who by now had adopted a defensive, damage-control posture.

The relentless Mulder phoned McFarlane to report what he had earlier told to at least one judge in Austin: he was in possession of new affidavits from Emily Miller and Gus Rose. He asked her to file the motion for a rehearing.

McFarlane was dumbfounded. By now, she wondered, why would anyone believe anything that Emily Miller said?

She tried to hold her patience as she explained to Mulder that affidavits would do no good. The court of criminal appeals merely affirms or rejects a lower court's findings; it does not hear evidence.

Mulder persisted, until McFarlane said finally, flatly, "No!"

I was giddy when I was finally returned to Dallas. This day, March 20, 1989, was the date of my freedom. Now that the court decision was official, Schaffer filed a motion calling for Judge Baraka to set bond so that I could be released pending a new trial that now seemed highly improbable.

It took almost no time for Judge Baraka to indicate that he was going to release me on a personal recognizance bond.

The courtroom buzzed with excitement. I waited for someone to release my chains.

Suddenly, Winfield Scott jumped up and announced that he was filing a motion to recuse.

"What's that?" I whispered.

Schaffer replied, "We haven't made it yet, Randall, they're going to try to throw Baraka off the case."

33

THE FINAL DAY

JUDGE RON CHAPMAN called the hearing to order later
that afternoon. As the presiding judge of the first administrative
judicial region, he was required to decide whether he would hear
Scott's arguments on the motion to recuse, or whether he would
assign another judge to do so. Scott also wanted him to revoke Judge
Baraka's ruling and either refuse to set bond or set it at $100,000,
cash. Judge Chapman conceded, "It is an extraordinary remedy that
the state is seeking."

Scott's task was to prove that Judge Baraka was biased in favor
of the defense, and therefore should be removed from the case. He
offered two exhibits to prove his contention: a copy of the original
indictment against me for capital murder and a copy of the decade-

old decision of the Court of Criminal Appeals affirming my conviction.

Schaffer argued vigorously against the use of a "discredited opinion from ten years ago" that did not include any of the new evidence developed over the years, most recently during Judge Baraka's evidentiary hearing. "The relevance of that document," he said, "is nil, in my judgment."

Scott admitted that some of the issues had been discredited, but he argued that the testimony of Drs. Grigson and Holbrook, the psychiatrists, had never been attacked, and he warned Judge Chapman that if he allowed me to be released on bond, "you would be letting a man on the streets who is a killer and could easily kill again, according to Dr. Grigson and Dr. Holbrook. . . . If he failed to return to court, then we would have to . . . track him down, and it's a big country. He can go to Canada. He can go to Mexico. He doesn't have to abide by his assurances that he's going to go back to Ohio to be with his mommy."

All the old nauseating arguments were here again. Scott declared, "His occupational history is that of a drifter. . . . He was drifting through Dallas when this happened."

When Scott finished his tirade, Judge Chapman asked Schaffer, "Do you desire to reply?"

"I really do," my attorney said, "and don't quite know where to start. Maybe we're not talking about the same case." He began by pointing out that Judge Baraka was the man who had the opportunity to hear all of the evidence on both sides, presented during the three-day evidentiary hearing. Judge Baraka had considered all of Scott's arguments before, and rejected them, concluding that a new trial was in order. Furthermore, this very same district attorney's office that was now trying to throw Judge Baraka off the case had told the court of criminal appeals that it did not contest with his findings! Schaffer characterized Scott's present requests as "ludicrous."

"They're asking you," he told Judge Chapman, "to make a decision based on a false set of facts and a discredited court opinion, and to disregard the judgment of a fellow district judge who is obviously responsible, obviously attentive to the needs of the community, and obviously not going to put someone back on the streets under these circumstances if he did not feel that was what justice required."

I was not a drifter, Schaffer argued, and the fact that I wished to return to Ohio rather than stay in Dallas "just demonstrates good judgment."

And if the district attorney's office wanted to talk about the dangers of putting a killer back out onto the streets, Schaffer noted, "they weren't too concerned about the safety of society back in 1977 when they freed David Harris, and it rings a little hollow to come in today and say that since David Harris has subsequently confessed to this killing that somehow you need to keep Randall Adams locked up because he's a danger."

All in all, he summed up Scott's motion to recuse as "frivolous."

Judge Chapman asked Scott to respond to that.

"We are not filing this motion for any dilatory tactic," Scott contended. "We are ready for trial right now. We have witnesses on standby who we can call and crank up this trial this afternoon. . . ."

It was all too much for Judge Chapman to absorb during a brief hearing. He disclosed that he had already spoken with Judge Carl Anderson, the senior judge of the 54th District Court of McLennan County, who had agreed to hear more extensive arguments on the motion at a time later in the week. "I will make my courtroom available to him at any time for such a hearing," Judge Chapman said. "I'm sure Judge Baraka will do the same."

Schaffer tried to control his anger, but he made no secret of the fact that he wanted to dispose of this foolishness as quickly as possible. He had to be in a Houston court the following morning, but he agreed to hop a plane and return to Dallas for a hearing before Judge Anderson at one-thirty tomorrow afternoon.

Judge Chapman said, "All right. I'll have my coordinator determine . . . which courtroom we're going to use. . . ."

"Judge," Scott said, "if I could request that it be in your courtroom, I'd rather, as a result of Judge Baraka's attitude, I'd rather not even get near Judge Baraka. He—just to put it mildly, I think the atmosphere down there is such that I'd rather not either myself or our visiting judge have to go anywhere near Judge Baraka."

Judge Chapman mumbled, "Well, I . . ."

"That's a pretty mature attitude, isn't it?" Schaffer interjected.

"Well, that's my attitude," Scott grumbled.

Judge Chapman asked Schaffer, "Do you have any objection to appearing here tomorrow?"

"I have gun, will travel," Schaffer replied. "You tell me where to be and I'll be here, although I think we could get Mr. Scott some protection if he feels he needs . . ."

"We'll see you here at one-thirty tomorrow," Judge Chapman said. He set an interim bond at $100,000.

It was a horrible night. I had been so close to walking out of the courtroom and into freedom, and here I was back in the Dallas County jail.

A lifetime of legal lingo was stuck in my craw. I was fed up with this joke of a justice system and its motions and writs and applications and opinions—all handled with an apparent single-minded determination to pick on *me*.

Whether or not it was the right thing to do, I had kept my rage bottled up during all these years. I had followed Dennis White's advice to behave myself in the courtroom, even though at times it required a supreme effort. And what had it gotten me? Exactly twelve years and three months in custody.

Hold onto it, Randall, hold onto it, I advised myself. Give it another day, just one more day. See what Schaffer can accomplish tomorrow afternoon. They're going to let you out of here tomorrow. Or they're not.

Either way, I decided, after tomorrow, it was time to uncork the fury within my heart.

Okay, Leslie McFarlane thought, here's something else that could cost me my job. She was on the phone with Schaffer. He wanted her to testify *for our side* at the motion to recuse. They worked out an acceptable strategy. Schaffer would have her subpoenaed so that it would not be apparent that she was a willing witness.

When the subpoena was served, McFarlane notified her colleagues.

Winfield Scott commented, "You can just ignore that."

"Winfield," McFarlane declared, "I'm going to appear at court at the stated time. I've been served and I'm going to be there."

On the following day, March 21, 1989, shortly before Judge Carl Anderson convened a hearing on the motion to recuse, someone overheard a conversation between District Attorney John Vance and Assistant District Attorney Winfield Scott. Vance reportedly warned Scott not to turn this into a personal vendetta, not to launch a public attack against Judge Baraka.

When I stepped into the courtroom, I saw a woman sitting next to Steve Dunleavy of Fox Television. She had long, soft, strawberry-blond hair and a lovely smile. I knew immediately that she was Lisa Raby, the videotape editor who had supplied us copies of the Harris interview. Amidst the chaos of the moment, we did not have an opportunity to speak, but I resolved to, if and when I had the chance.

Winfield Scott was the first witness, and Schaffer drew out some surprising admissions regarding the assistant district attorney's lack of knowledge concerning the most recent developments in my case. Scott said that he had not read either the transcript of Judge Baraka's evidentiary hearing or the opinion of the Court of Criminal Appeals, concurring with Judge Baraka's findings.

Schaffer asked, "So you who announced ready for retrial yesterday haven't even read the opinion that brought this case back to the trial court?"

"That's exactly right," Scott replied. "I don't need to read it. They told me to retry it, and that's what I'm working on."

Spectators gasped as Scott lashed out at Judge Baraka, charging that it was clear "that he has an opinion about guilt or innocence. . . . We'd be a fool to try this case before Judge Baraka without a jury. . . . I think his bias goes to the point where it would affect the entire handling of the case from A to Z." He declared flatly that he believed Judge Baraka would rule unfairly against the state on matters of evidence.

"Are you telling us that Judge Baraka would not follow the law?" Schaffer asked.

"I've seen him do it before," Scott answered.

Schaffer asked if Scott had facts to back up that opinion, "or does this just exist in the figment of Winfield Scott's imagination?"

"I tried a death penalty case in his court a little over two years ago," Scott detailed, "and he would not look at the cases I attempted to show him in an effort to offer evidence in the penalty phase of that case. He would not even allow me to approach the bench with my cases. That's my . . ."

"Did you get the death penalty?" Schaffer asked.

"Yes, we did."

"So, justice has a way of working out, doesn't it?"

"Yeah," Scott conceded, "in spite of Judge Baraka it did in that case."

As far as my case was concerned, Scott charged that Judge Baraka had made unmistakable protestations of my innocence, and therefore could not be impartial while presiding over a retrial.

Schaffer pointed out that our application for a writ of habeas corpus had raised the issue of guilt or innocence and thus required the judge to comment upon it. And in spite of the fact that Judge Baraka had indicated his opinion that I was innocent, had actually denied us that point of relief because the issue had no bearing on a writ of habeas corpus. "In other words," Schaffer said, "he ruled in favor of the state on the issue you're trying to recuse him on."

"Well," Scott said, "if you call that a ruling in favor of the state, well, fine and dandy."

And what about the Court of Criminal Appeals? Schaffer wanted to know. They affirmed Judge Baraka's opinion by a unanimous vote. "Do you think Judge Rusty Duncan of the Court of Criminal Appeals is biased against the state?" Schaffer asked. Duncan was the author of the court's opinion.

"Yes," Scott answered. "I think he's as liberal as they come."

"And how about the other eight judges on the Court of Criminal Appeals that agreed with him?"

"Well, I like Mike McCormick, but that's about it for . . ."

Schaffer cut him off and struck at the heart of the matter: "So maybe the problem here is not with all the judges; maybe, sir, the problem is with you."

Leslie McFarlane took the stand and declared simply, "I found Judge Baraka to be fair to the state at the writ hearing. I have no reason to believe he would not be fair to the state at the trial."

Schaffer asked McFarlane if she believed that the district attorney's office had suppressed evidence during my initial trial.

For McFarlane, it was the point of no return. Assistant District Attorney Don Davis appeared ready to jump up and lodge an objection, but she saw Scott place a restraining hand on his arm and she knew that she was to be the scapegoat. The case had fallen apart, and they were going to blame it all on her. She was, she admitted later, "scared shitless" when she answered, "There was evidence in the district attorney's file when I received it that was not given to the defense attorney in a timely manner." She said she also agreed with Judge Baraka's contention that Emily Miller had perjured herself during my trial.

It took Judge Anderson only a short time to rule against Scott's petition and, suddenly, everything moved in a blur.

Judge Baraka was once more in control of my destiny, and within only a few minutes he officially released me on a personal recognizance bond, and the courtroom erupted.

Assistant District Attorney Leslie McFarlane hugged Mom. Her colleague John Cruezot walked over to me and asked, "Mr. Adams, would you shake hands with me?"

"Of course," I replied.

As he pumped my hand, Cruezot said, "I hope you have a beautiful life ahead of you."

34

THE REST OF MY LIFE

"THIS TIME YESTERDAY I was just coming out of the Dallas County jail," I told a group of reporters assembled in an office in the Gulf Tower in Houston. "I really don't know where the hell I have been. I am going where I am told to go. I did have a nice meal last night and a nice breakfast this morning."

Schaffer, in a jovial mood, was at my side to help field the questions. He pointed out that the transition to normal life was going to take some time. "You have to remember," he said, "the last time Randy took a ride it was on the prison bus. He has been doing his traveling in a limo today."

"I prefer the limo," I said, drawing laughs from the reporters.

Schaffer conjectured on my legal future. We still did not know whether the state would drop the charges.

"I could walk away with that," I commented. "But I would love to hear a jury say not guilty. All I have ever asked for is a fair trial."

A reporter asked if I was angry.

Euphoria had replaced my rage. "I don't think I am bitter at all," I replied. "I don't like the fact that I had those years taken away from me. But I can't replace them. These are the first two days of the rest of my life. I will not let the past years ruin what is ahead of me."

Another reporter asked a hypothetical question: if I ever had children, how would I explain this experience to them?

This brought a twinge to my stomach. I would *love* to have children, and I did not know whether it would ever happen, at this late date. After some hesitation, I answered, "I would try to explain the best way I could. I would hope they would understand. But, hell, I don't understand half of it."

"What is it you want to do?" someone asked.

I am sure I looked and sounded tired when I responded simply, "I want to go home. The only person I want to see is my mother. As far as material possessions, I have none . . . I do have my family. I guess that makes me a millionaire."

Around noon on the following day, March 23, a half dozen people gathered in the office of District Attorney John Vance. His eyes singled out Leslie McFarlane as he announced that he had a release ready for distribution to the media. This, he proclaimed, would be the extent of the comments. "No one will talk to the press," he ordered, still staring pointedly at McFarlane.

She picked up a copy of the press release and read:

> Due to recent misunderstandings and misinformation, I'd like to make it quite clear that I have no vendetta against Randall Dale Adams. His trial took place many years before I became District Attorney, and I have no personal feelings in the matter whatsoever . . . The easy route would have been to release Mr. Adams immediately. However, my obligation is not to the media or to play the part of the hero. My

responsibility in every case is to the victim, his family, Dallas County citizens, and the State of Texas. Therefore, in investigating this offense, we had to search beyond a deathrow inmate's recantation, beyond assertions contained in a documentary film produced on behalf of Mr. Adams (and which, despite its good intentions, is *no* substitute for investigation and trial according to law, before a court and with witnesses under oath), and beyond the stated conclusions of Mr. Adams' attorney (who, under our system, is hired to protect Mr. Adams' interests and not the public's interests). I believe we have made as thorough an investigation as possible, and I believe it was our obligation to make such an investigation prior to reaching this decision in this case.

Having served as a Criminal District Judge for twelve years and on the Court of Appeals for five years, I found no fault with Judge Baraka's recommendation to the Court of Criminal Appeals that the writ be granted. Had I been the presiding judge at this hearing my findings may have been the same. The recusal motion filed in this cause on Monday was in my view appropriate simply because Judge Baraka (as set out in the Motion and its attachments) had reportedly formed an opinion on the innocence of a defendant prior to the trial in the case. It was not intended to question his integrity. I consider Judge Baraka to be one of the finest judges we have. He is hard working, fair, knowledgeable, and professional. I believe there is no room in the courts for personal feelings, prejudices, vendettas or any other stumbling blocks in the way of justice.

Anyone who knows me realizes that I would *never* want to see an innocent man incarcerated. The Court of Criminal Appeals did not, however, make a ruling on the sufficiency of the evidence in this cause. It was, therefore, my obligation to make the tedious, complicated investigation of this case necessary before deciding whether to proceed with further prosecution.

This investigation into the murder of Officer Robert Wood on November 28, 1976 is now complete. I have determined that there is not sufficient credible evidence to warrant the retrial of Randall Dale Adams for the murder of Officer Wood. A motion to dismiss has therefore been filed in Criminal District Court #2 this date requesting dismissal of the indictment in cause no. F77-1286.

John Vance
Criminal District Attorney
Dallas County, Texas

Leslie McFarlane sat alone at her desk. She placed her head upon her arms and gave way to sobs of relief.

At that very moment I was staring out of the window of a Continental Airlines jet, flight 104 from Houston to Columbus. Below me I saw the outlines of the Ohio State University football stadium, north of downtown Columbus. The home of the Buckeyes, I thought. Home.

Suddenly I realized that my hands were folding and refolding a small paper napkin. My right leg bounced up and down, faster and faster. "I guess I'm a little nervous," I said to no one in particular.

Shortly after 4:00 P.M., as the wheels touched Ohio, all I could say was, "I'm home."

I scrambled off the plane as fast as I could. Finally, up ahead, I caught sight of them. There was Mom—wearing the most beautiful smile I had ever seen—surrounded by my sisters, and aunts, uncles, and cousins of every variety. I had never even met some of the younger members of the clan.

Every one of them wore a yellow ribbon.

EPILOGUE

EARLY IN APRIL, 1989, Leslie McFarlane and John Crue-
zot resigned from the Dallas district attorney's office. They declared,
separately, that it was simple coincidence that they had decided to
enter private practice at this particular time.

On April 5, the Dallas district attorney's office announced that Assistant District Attorney Winfield Scott was "terminated because of
an apparently irreconcilable policy conflict" with District Attorney
John Vance.
                              . . .

The April 1989 issue of *D Magazine* quoted Mulder: "It's a shame. But Adams isn't the first murderer to beat the system."

A reporter asked, what if he, Mulder, had been my defense attorney way back in 1977, instead of the prosecutor?

"Oh yeah," Mulder replied, "I'd have gotten him off. There's no doubt in my mind."

After reviewing the case, the state bar association found no basis for disciplinary action against Mulder.

Dennis White wrote a gracious letter to Randy Schaffer, congratulating him on his victory. Schaffer replied, "Many thanks for your kind letter. I hope that you feel vindicated as indeed you should. Doug Mulder is scum and the best part of it is that now everyone knows it."

Mom and my sisters are well, as is Ron. Several people ran private checks for us, to determine whether we could find any trace of Ray, or his fate. They found nothing. It has now been more than a decade since we last heard from him.

When anyone asks Mom about the ordeal, she is careful with her answer: "We lost all those years. They took the best part of Randy's life, of all our lives really. But God works in mysterious ways. If Randy's ordeal can somehow stop the kind of justice that Douglas Mulder controlled in Dallas County then some good will come from all of this. To date, thirteen people have had their cases reversed because of the Adams decision, so it has helped."

Some months after my release, TDC forwarded me two discharge checks, totaling $340.87.

By then, I had begun accepting invitations to speak about my experiences, often on college campuses. This was an indication that there was a great deal of interest in my story for, in truth, it could have happened to almost anyone.

Errol Morris sought the opportunity to tell my full story to the public—something he could not do in the limited forum of *The Thin*

Blue Line. He believed that the option I had signed when he came to visit me in a Dallas jail—in return for ten dollars—gave him the exclusive right to market my life story.

Randy Schaffer disputed that contention and recruited his friend Murray Fogler to represent me, without fee, in a civil action to clarify the situation. We reached a settlement whereby Morris retained the rights to *The Thin Blue Line*, and I retained the rights to my own life.

I still consider Errol to be a friend. My family considers him to be one of its members.

Lisa Raby has been a nurturing force in my post-prison life. She taught me how to walk without shackles and to think for myself. I thank her for our friendship and wish her well in life.

David Harris remains on death row at the Ellis unit.

I wish him no good luck, but neither do I wish him harm. Whether he is executed or dies of old age in a prison cell is of little consequence to me now, but I know this much: I could never be the one to twist the valve that sent lethal chemicals into his veins.